André Charlot

André Charlot

The Genius of
Intimate Musical Revue

JAMES ROSS MOORE

McFarland & Company, Inc., Publishers
Jefferson, North Carolina, and London

James Ross Moore died on May 23, 2002, not long after completing
the manuscript for this book. Its publication has been made
possible through the help of his wife, Suzon Forscey-Moore.

Unless otherwise noted, all photographs appearing
herein are through the courtesy of Joan Charlot Midwinter.

LIBRARY OF CONGRESS CATALOGUING-IN-PUBLICATION DATA

Moore James Ross.
André Charlot : the genius of intimate musical revue /
James Ross Moore.
p.   cm.
Includes bibliographical references and index.

ISBN 0-7864-1774-9 (softcover : 50# alkaline paper)

1. Charlot, André, 1882–1956.   2. Theatrical producers and
directors—France—Biography.   3. Motion picture actors and
actresses—United States—Biography.   I. Title.
PN2638.C5455M66   2005   792.02'32'092—dc22   2005000884

British Library cataloguing data are available

On the cover: Andre Charlot, New York, 1924
or 1926; Jean Patou gowns for *A to Z*, 1921

Manufactured in the United States of America

*McFarland & Company, Inc., Publishers
Box 611, Jefferson, North Carolina 28640
www.mcfarlandpub.com*

To Madeleine Gould with love

Acknowledgments

This book is being written in the shadow of the Next Big Adventure. If I disappoint anyone expecting to find his or her name here (and so many are deserving), please put it down to this distraction.

To begin at the beginning, I must thank the Castle sisters—Jessie, Judy, and Emma—who faced life's difficulties in individual ways, but shared and passed on to me an adoration of all things musical, from the silliest popular music to the works of the great composers.

When in my twenties I left the cashier's cage for college, I had the sheer good luck to find, in the valued fellowship of Gamma Delta Upsilon, Nick Beck, Ray Lloynd, and Fred Olsen, lifelong friends. I married Kay Linn, who gave me the great gift of children, my daughter Diana and my son John. I can't imagine what my life would have been like without the joy they brought me. In 28 years at Mt. San Antonio College, I acquired a work family of wonderful teaching colleagues. At the *Los Angeles Times,* Sylvie Drake and Art Seidenbaum allowed me to write about theater and books and Martin Weinberger gave me free rein at the *Claremont Courier.*

When my wife Suzon and I moved to Cambridge, England, in 1986, and my early retirement dollars were walloped by the mighty pound, we only survived with help from Patricia and Sanford Arkin, Peter and Anneliese Kirianoff, and Annette (Nettie) Lynch. More luck followed when Trevor Littlechild at BBC Radio Cambridgeshire introduced me to the listeners of his musical nostalgia program *Time Was* and so many other good people at the station.

As for the book itself, Joan Charlot Midwinter of Pacific Palisades, California, held her father's material for more than four decades, believing that a biographer would someday come along. She has been endlessly thoughtful and responsive, and I hope this is the book she has been faithfully waiting for.

Of crucial help among André Charlot's surviving relatives were his sister-in-law, Mrs. Joan (Jonny) Gladman Dixon of Bognor Regis, England; his granddaughter Mrs. Sargine (Nini) Hitchman of London and South Africa; and his niece, Mme. Odette Charlot of Barbizon, France. Paul and Simon Hitchman have also helped me excavate part of the mystery regarding their grandfather Philip.

Among the many transatlantic associates and friends of Charlot who contributed their facts and anecdotes, I particularly wish to thank Robert and Iris Nesbitt, Doris Hare, Queenie Leonard, Dennis Van Thal, and Trixie Scales. That most have died since I began working on the book and therefore never saw their contributions informing it is a source of profound regret.

As explained in the preface, my daughter Diana and my colleague and friend Aaron Sloan are jointly credited for locating Charlot's daughter, a task I had almost despaired of. Mrs. Ruth Starr of London graciously gave access to her home—once Charlot's—in St. John's Wood. Mrs. Doris Hankey of Oxford, England, helped me understand the significance of her ancestor, Arthur Weigall. Gaelle Larson of LeBourg, France, contributed expert translations. Transatlantic performer Sandra Caron, a recent incarnation of Beatrice Lillie, shed light on the relationship between Charlot and Bea. Of more general but much appreciated assistance have been Clive Barker of Coventry, England, and Miles Kreuger of Los Angeles.

The photographs and artwork which testify to Charlot's personality and genius were generously loaned by family members Joan Charlot Midwinter, Joan Gladman Dixon's son Peter Gay, and Nini and Paul Hitchman, and helpfully supplemented by Richard Mangan, administrator of the Raymond Mander and Joe Mitchenson Theatre Collection and by *Tatler* magazine.

I am grateful also to the BBC, which allowed access to radio programs in its archives, and to BBC producer Anthony Wills, who not only shepherded my 1993 radio documentary on Charlot but introduced me to actor-writer-presenter Michael Alexander, my valued friend-to-be. Of constant helpfulness—which included leading me to other contacts—has been the staff of the Theatre Museum in Covent Garden, London, in particular James Fowler, its head.

Valuable, too, was the cooperation of Special Collections at the library of the University of California, Los Angeles, the holders of the archive bequeathed to them by Philip Charlot. I am indebted to the helpful staff of the British Library, London; to its National Sound Archive; to the London offices of Samuel French Incorporated, who allowed examination of the work of Jeans, Titheradge, and other masters of the revue sketch; to the British Film Institute and to the Cambridge University Library; and to Christine Shipman, Document Supply Librarian at the University of Warwick.

And now to end at the ending. I may make some terrible omission, but among the most outstanding of the many people who have been cheering and supporting me in a difficult time with their love and affection are my wife (and editor) Suzon, my son John, my daughter Diana and her splendid daughter Madeleine, Mark and Paula Williams, Brian and Margaret Butler, Bernard Hughes, Christopher South, Michael Alexander, Nick Beck, Peter Kirianoff, Nettie Lynch, Vicky Russell, Joan Midwinter, Kerry Renshaw and Aaron Sloan. Lucky me.

Table of Contents

Preface

When we were thinking about becoming expatriates, my wife said, "Why don't you work on something about the musical theater?" Why not. In short order we found the very thing—a large and loveable critter which eventually became called the transatlantic musical. We set forth, and eventually I started to excavate.

It developed that the transatlantic musical has been around since at least the 1820s; it includes (mainly) Britons who worked in the U.S., Americans who worked in Britain, British versions of American work, American versions of British work, and influences, collaborations and downright thefts. The topic was much bigger than I imagined, I knew much less than I had given myself credit for, and the end is truly nowhere near in sight.

Researching the transatlantic musical yielded many surprises. The reputations of a few important people shrank, while the names of mystery men and women kept popping up, none more often nor more mystifyingly than André Charlot's.

I found mention of this French-English impresario over and over, particularly in relation to great transatlantic performers such as Noel Coward, Beatrice Lillie, Gertrude Lawrence and Jack Buchanan. Yet Charlot himself was never dealt with in any length. He also turned out to have a place in American theatrical history, his *Charlot's Revue* having taken New York by storm in 1924. Teased along by many side-long references, I looked long and hard for a biography, but the closest I came—and then late in the game—was a sketch in the *Dictionary of (British) National Biography*.

Actually, it raised more questions than it provided answers. But it did contain one fascinating hook. It seemed Charlot had given up his successful career some-time in the 1930s and moved to Hollywood, my birthplace and hometown. He died there, apparently forgotten, in 1956. During his last years and my first years, who knows how many times our paths had crossed? I started to track him down in earnest.

Biographers know about the blind alleys and brick walls. They also know about the startling discoveries, the serendipities. The more committed I became to learn-ing The Truth About Charlot, the more tantalizingly obscure he seemed. I began even to doubt his *Who's Who in the Theatre* entry, though these nearly always stem from material provided by the subject. It took me some time after listening to a 30-minute 1975 BBC Radio documentary to realize that the broadcast itself might hold a key to the mystery: Charlot's adopted daughter Joan was alive and well some-where in California, at least in 1975.

It turned out that she wasn't called Charlot any more, or if she was, she wasn't listed that way. More morose thrashing. One day I was looking through some clippings my daughter Diana, then a librarian at the *San Francisco Examiner*, had sent me. In a brief notation of Charlot's death, Joan's surname leapt out: Midwinter. Elation was soon followed by gloom. The item was nearly 20 years old. Was she still alive? If so, would she still be in California and where?

A longtime friend and teaching colleague was living in Santa Monica. Aaron Sloan scanned his local phonebook and there found a Mrs. Douglas Midwinter living in Pacific Palisades. Could this be Joan? It was—and what's more, she was holding onto a treasure trove of Charlot's notes, essays, contracts and photographs. A biography was now mandatory.

En route to writing my biography of Charlot, I came to several conclusions. The most important from a semi-academic point of view is that he was the genius of intimate revue, which was the longest-surviving form of musical revue and probably Britain's greatest gift to the modern theater. This kind of revue also changed the course of American revue. Many have expressed hope that revue, one of the apparent casualties of the television age, might again rise.

At least it seemed possible to re-create the form—as much as type on a page can do such a thing—for readers. And Charlot himself—simultaneously aloof and vulnerable—a man who had reached the heights of his profession, only to be thrown down among its footnotes, afforded me a very personal reason for pursuing his trail.

I think I have come to know him and, in the way I imagine to be the occupational hazard and strength of biographers, to identify with him in many ways. It made the writing, even of the challenging times, a pleasure.

One

Paris, 1882–1908

"Raring to Go"

> I remember a tall (6'2"), gentle, soft-spoken man of brilliant, enquiring mind and dry humor. His wasn't the hearty, effusive personality—his enjoyment was quiet. He was not the athletic type ... but the camera has recorded scenes of him and wife Flip on horseback, playing tennis and croquet and swimming. He was a bridge fiend which, I learned in later years, had put somewhat of a crimp in their early wedded bliss and caused my mother to vow she'd never play that game with all those awful post-mortems after every rubber. She never did.

Joan Charlot Midwinter thus opened her memoir "I Remember Papa," written after his death in 1956. André Charlot's son Philip wrote no such memoir—not a terribly unusual situation within the family of a successful man, just something that may help in understanding in a more human way the magisterial genius of 20th century musical revue and the greatest talent-spotter of his era. Charlot seems to have been blessed with "an intimate understanding" of his audience, even if his own intimate relationships may have left something to be desired. Though such a split may not qualify as a real anomaly, his life is worth pondering for other reasons. It is a tale of three cities, of monumental ups and downs, of marvelous intuitions and abysmal lapses in judgment.

> Papa was always a great animal lover and our home was populated over the years by dogs, cats, cockatoos, monkeys, marmosets, guinea pigs, fish, ferrets (these latter my brother's fiercely guarded pets). He was a member of the Royal Zoological Society. So hardly a Sunday went by that Papa and I didn't set off for the [London] zoo, carrier bag filled with vegetables, fruit, nuts and other treats. We never missed paying a call on Liza, the rhinoceros who had a passion for whole raw onions, and were often allowed "backstage" to visit special animal friends and young ones. These Sunday outings were very special, and instilled in me a love for all creatures great and small.
>
> Music was a source of joy to him... He would often sit at the piano for long stretches, sometimes playing Debussy and other of his favorite composers—sometimes just improvising. Opera he loved, and one of my most treasured memories is of the time, when I was considered old enough to appreciate it, he and my mother took me to my first *Der Rosenkavalier* at Covent Garden.
>
> He was a gourmet and, until diabetes struck, truly enjoyed fine food, but for many years, rather than take insulin, he elected to try to control it by diet, so it

Charlot and Flip on horseback in Worthing, England.

was goodbye to *profiteroles au chocolat* and a strict regimen, zealously weighed and measured by Flip. Willpower and abstinence effectively controlled his condition for a long time before he had to resort to insulin.

...[He] seemed to command affection along with respect. I don't remember ever hearing him raise his voice in anger, but he could be a stern taskmaster. He could be quite (and sometimes infuriatingly) demanding at times, but somehow one couldn't say "No!" He had an uncanny knack of inspiring devotion in those who worked with him....

During the early 1950s when Charlot was writing *People 'n Things*, an almost autobiography in the form of a series of essays, he was living in what was then the heart of Hollywood. Thus he was just as physically close to the seats of show business power as he always had been—in the heart of Paris up to 1912, in London's West End from 1912 to 1937, effectively in New York from 1924 to 1926, when Broadway seemed his for the taking. Between 1937 and 1956, Charlot lived within a block of Hollywood's Sunset Strip, lived there when it actually lived up to its reputation, but he could have been across the world so few seemed to know (or care) he was there.

In writing *People 'n Things* he may have turned in imagination to his past because, by contrast to the relentlessly sunbaked present, it was colored in such brilliant variety. But if the past did not unroll in a seamless stream all the way back to 1882, it nevertheless reappeared in images and bits of dialogue, in the lyrics of songs, the texture of stage draperies, the color of "surprise pink" (a lighting gel flattering to soubrettes of a certain age), and in the gossip and intrigues of theatrical management.

A proud man, he could have convinced himself he was writing memoirs in short bursts because at any time the work might be interrupted or perhaps permanently sidelined. Just around the corner, it seems he truly did believe, lay a real opportunity to resume life at the top. For nearly two decades he had been expecting to launch just such a comeback. Or perhaps, since he classified himself as an artist, he chose to write in vignettes for aesthetic satisfaction.

However he intended it, "Prelude to Life," the opening segment of *People 'n Things*, dealing with the years before he took up theatrical management, emphasizes his professional life and downplays his private life. It is a pattern repeated throughout the collection and in the way he actually lived his life. In this respect he anticipated David Merrick, the producer who ruled Broadway through the middle of the 20th century. Drawing a veil over what had gone before (and pretty much everything else, too), Merrick claimed that his life had begun only when he first invested in a Broadway show.

Still, it is from the pages of "Prelude to Life" that the first glimpse of Eugène André Maurice Charlot arises. He was born in the heart of the right bank of Paris in the Rue de la Michodière at 10 A.M. on July 26, 1882, a date, he informs us, that was said by an eminent astrologist to have great significance.

In 1882, the City of Light was considerably darker than it is now; electric lighting was largely unknown. The Rue de la Michodière, like most of its neighbors, was still recovering from events of the previous dozen years—the siege by the Prussians which ended in 1871, the destructive orgy of the Commune which immediately followed, and the completion of the Haussmannization of Paris.

Comparatively speaking, the street itself had suffered little from the Prussians or the Communards, but it had been somewhat rearranged by the Baron's grand design and its general six-story limit to non-commercial dwellings. It was only 1878 when Haussmann's mightiest diagonal road, the Avenue de l'Opéra, had sliced from the new Garnier Opéra (quite nearby the Charlots' street) southeastward to the Comédie Française, the Palais-Royal and the Seine, just beyond the ruins of the Tuileries Palace.

Although therefore in the heart of Haussmann's Paris, that creation both austere and beautiful, the Rue de la Michodière managed to retain a good sense of the past, including—almost at the corner of the new Avenue—the Pavillion de Hanovre, a great home erected by the Marshal of Richelieu in 1760 and possessed by many titled owners since. Nearby streets also offered the congeniality of some of Paris's best-loved restaurants. In subsequent years it became the locus of such *grands magasins* as *Au Printemps* and the *Galeries Lafayette*.

The neighborhood centered by the Rue de la Michodière remained Charlot's virtual base during his 30 years as a Parisian. His schools, his further residences and his business offices were almost all located, in one direction or another, within a half-mile walk of his birthplace, not that an impresario would necessarily prefer to walk. Charlot would display the lifelong pattern of keeping such a base from which he could roam if not the world, at least a few of the world's most interesting cities.

His father was Jules Charles Maurice, always known as Maurice. He was only 23 at the time of André's birth, yet already a cultivated, quite literary man who during his lifetime essayed many professions without achieving major success in any. On the other hand, Maurice's father Auguste was a composer who had won the first Prix de Rome in 1850 and had gone on to become director of singing at the Opéra Comique.

Grandfather Charlot's musical predilections soon seemed to be manifest in André. If Maurice found it difficult to live up to his successful father, during his own lifetime André managed both to out-achieve his father and repeat Maurice's perpetual rising and falling. Once André himself took on the role of father, a variation on this pattern would surface, particularly in regard to Philip.

André's grandmother (Auguste's wife), who lived to the age of 93, was born a Pellier, part of a family of King's equerries. Her brother Jules ran a riding school where the slender André learned horsemanship. His great-grandfather had built what André recalled as "a roomy house in about 10 acres of delightful grounds" in Sèvres, two-thirds of the way to Versailles and therefore, at the time, rather "out in the country." Many summer family holidays were spent there and it was there

André Charlot's father Maurice.

that André recalled his splendid great-grandmother taught him the French card game *grabuge*. It represented his first risk-taking. A man who subsequently took many a risk, Charlot wrote, "As you can see, I started early." The family's slightly elevated background contained even a family motto: *"Tout ou Rien"*—all or nothing—something André observed in his father at first hand. It would become the motto of his own life.

In "Prelude to Life" he professed little recall of his mother's side of the family. She was Sargine Battu, the French-born daughter of Jean-Marie Battu, a Geneva goldsmith who was eventually naturalized French. At his death, M. Battu had left Charlot's future mother "more than comfortably off." A year older than Maurice Charlot, she was counseled against marrying him—as was Maurice against marrying her—but as soon as he was 21, they married. Charlot commented, "They were both to *regret* it, and although they remained married for about 25 years [their divorce came in 1906, after which Sargine married Paul Vallée] ... I can't remember the day when they lived in complete harmony." Brother Jean was born three years after André, and their sister Jeannine six years after that.

It does not seem to have been a demonstrative family, but it does seem to have been indulgent. Certainly it indulged André, who grew into a reverie-lured soul. In later life he was characterized by some of his friends as "dreamy." Charlot's memoirs never mention a habit which must have been lifelong. Many of his friends and associates noted that whenever he was faced with a knotty problem (such as where to find a backer for a show that was tottering on the financial brink) he would simply take to his bed for days at a time. When he emerged, he had solved the problem, was as full of *bonhomie* as ever and plunged directly back into work. It seems likely that the habit was formed in childhood. Since he subsequently proved many times over that he was a human being of considerable sensitivity, perhaps taking to his bed began as a way of coping with the chill of mother-father warfare.

From "Prelude to Life," it is possible to believe that his most important maternal legacy was Emily Randall, the English maid who became the family nanny. "It is to her," he wrote, "that I owe my bilingual status. The French she spoke was painful, especially to her, and we always conversed in English." She was also largely responsible for his introduction to Great Britain. In 1896, when he was 14, his parents decided that instead of the traditional family holiday on the Channel island of Jersey, he and Jean would accompany "Emmie" on a trip to visit her sisters in Wales and London.

Charlot wrote, "I fell in love with England from the start and, curiously enough, one of the three theatres we visited in London was the Alhambra"—at the time the largest theater in Leicester Square, which was the center of English variety entertainment. Sixteen years later, he would be appointed the Alhambra's co-manager.

And there was always another family member: the dog. In 1890, Sieba, a beige Great Dane and the first in a lifelong parade of Great Danes (occasionally joined by other breeds), broke the eight-year-old's heart by being run over and killed by a tram in the Avenue de Neuilly. During the Parisian years, there was also Javotte, a white poodle, whose mind, Charlot later wrote, "became unhinged after quarantine on the island of Jersey."

The era of French history into which he was born was recovering from not only

Sargine Vallée Battu, André's mother.

war and Haussmannization; it was a very fractious time. After the humiliating end of the Franco-Prussian War and the slaughter of the Communards, the Third Republic, which at best enjoyed a barely legal grip on power, embarked upon a time-honored French tradition—instituting vast projects to redeem sacred national honor.

As well as further civic beautification and aggrandizement, these projects often displayed a darker side of *La Belle Epoque*, rampant imperialism in Africa and Asia and racist fascism as displayed in the Dreyfus affair. Yet, except when such events directly impinged upon their lives (as they certainly did once Maurice Charlot took up theatrical management), the Charlots, like most French, seem to have kept their heads down and their political preferences to themselves. It was a habit Charlot kept throughout his life, though occasionally, and whenever he thought he could get away with it, his revues would poke fun at national and local leaders in general.

In 1887, when André was five, his father suffered "a bad bout of neurasthenia" (one of the era's terms for depression) and the family made its first move westward to the countryside where they took up chicken farming. Not surprisingly, this seems to have held no fascination for André, and neither M. nor Mme. Charlot showed any gift for their new calling, so, with a large portion of Sargine's fortune lost, they gave up and moved back to Paris three years later, perhaps just in time for the family to witness the replacement of the razed Tuileries Palace by particularly lovely gardens, as well as the new tower, tallest in the world, designed by a bridge builder named Eiffel.

By 1889–90, André had already had a taste of Parisian schooling, having attended a *cours*—a primary class with lots of homework—twice a week in order to beat the national expectation of reading and writing by age six. But by 1892 the family was briefly out west again, ensconced in a rented house in Neuilly, then much more a separate village than a suburban extension of Paris. Here the eight-year-old Charlot attended with some pleasure and success ("as a day student, and that was the way I always went to school") Friars College, St. Croix de Neuilly. It was the last time he ever enjoyed schooling.

Maurice Charlot now changed direction once more, becoming sub-editor of the first illustrated newspaper in France. This meant often working till four in the morning and Neuilly, though only two miles west of what was understood to be the boundary of Paris, was too distant for such a daily routine. The first lines of the Metropolitan Railway, after all, were still seven years from completion. The family moved back to its old neighborhood and André was enrolled at the Lycée Condorcet. This was hard by the Gare St. Lazare (formally, the Gare de l'Ouest), Paris's most important railroad station and the subject of paintings by Monet, circa 1876–78. The most recent version of the Gare had been completed in 1889.

The Gare was one of the last-to-be-completed beneficiaries of Haussmann's great boulevards, so designed to move tourists from such portals. The Lycée sat essentially out front of the station in the Rue du Havre, named for the coastal terminus of the rail line. It had begun life as the Noviciat des Capucins and was the product of Brongniart, one of the leading architects of early–19th-century Paris (among his designs was the Bourse, the famed stock exchange). By the time André took up the cudgels of scholarship, the Lycée, very much in the buzzing heart of the capital, looked like the relic of semi-rural days that it really was.

Still, as he later wrote, the Condorcet had produced many a literary man and it did introduce the youth to a few schoolmates who reappeared in his later life. These included Germaine Brice, who married a future president of the Republic; Nini Hardon, who married Marshal Pétain, chief collaborator with the Germans during World War II; and Vincent Auriol, who became president of the Republic in the 1950s.

Schooling in general was not for André, who wrote, "It was the beginning of a period of nine years when every hour spent at the Lycée and every minute spent on my homework at home were sheer agony. It was not that I resented education, but from an early age, 13 or 14, the curriculum, the hours, the methods were driving me crazy."

The routine at Lycée Condorcet included 8:30 arrival, with a break at 10:30 or 11:30 for homework and lunch, another school session from 2 to 4, home for more homework and a return till dinnertime. This happened at least in theory six days a week, excluding Thursday afternoons, when André, a poor pupil, was frequently called back for more work. That happened some Sunday mornings, too.

Charlot wrote, "Gymnastics was optional on the part of Saturday afternoon; I kept clear of that. The fact that there were no games did not worry me; I already hated physical exercise." Like many people, Charlot had his own definition of "physical exercise": what he enjoyed doing and was good at. He was a more than adequate horseman and from his earliest opportunities, he was also a powerful ocean swimmer.

During this relatively boring period, he reached further conclusions—for one, that the sciences and mathematics would mean nothing to his life. But he was sure that literature, history, geography, art and music did. These were exactly the studies which were not allowed by the curriculum. So he decided (or rationalized), "I gradually decided on being an all-round dunce." This involved silently reading (with a pencil in his hand) at the back of the classroom books from his father's library while the rest of his class listened to and annotated lectures, which had to be regurgitated exactly as received once exams rolled around. Noting that he had "flunked in my yearly exams," he nevertheless consumed many of the classics in his father's library—Victor Hugo, Dumas *père et fils*, and Jules Verne.

The most important conclusion put forth in "Prelude to Life" deserves full quotation:

> In those days I was accused of being a dreamer because when I was at home, supposed to do my homework, I was either playing the piano, reading my favorite authors, or what my mother called dreaming. I called it thinking, and I could see nothing wrong with that. I did not argue the point with my mother who would never have believed that a boy of 16 could spend so much time thinking, and I formulated a line of conduct for myself, and it was this: "Don't clutter your mind and exhaust your memory accumulating facts, or you will have not time for thought. Learn to use a dictionary. Facts belong to the past, thought is concerned with the future."

The Charlot family's Parisian neighborhood was also generally the main theater district. By his early teens, and partly because of his father's occupations, André was paying close attention to theatrical trends and although he wrote that at the time he was too young to grasp its meaning, he eventually appreciated that one of the most powerful was led by André Antoine, the leader of a "little theatre" called "*Le Théâtre Libre*," in which "free" stood for free from conventions.

Antoine, along with Lucien Guitry, father of Sacha (one of André's childhood "chums" and one of the 20th century's most accomplished theater people) believed in and practiced a natural kind of acting, far removed from the "hammy" norm of the time. André was particularly charmed by one of Antoine's performances—which made the actor "infamous" for a time (he performed one entire scene with his back to the audience, because the scene's logic seemed to call for it). The influence was likely because perhaps the most notable characteristic of a show produced by André Charlot would prove to be its restraint, its subtlety. There would have to be a very good reason for any actor in a Charlot revue to go "over the top" or against the intention of author and producer.

Having essentially removed himself from academic pursuits, the now six-foot-tall André was urged by his godfather, Eugene Pouillet, a leading Parisian barrister, toward a career in law. This possibility—never much countenanced by Charlot himself—came to a crashing end when Pouillet's wife realized that Charlot's father had now switched from journalism to theatrical management. Hardly anything could be lower on the social scale. André wrote that she belonged to "the straight-laced bourgeoisie." He added that Mme. Pouillet quickly found allies and that "our circle of friends was completely reorganized."

So he escaped happily from the bar. His parents ("They were pretty good in doing everything they could to educate me") now took heed of his improvising at the piano and indulged him in a series of private lessons; since music ran in the family, perhaps they were housing a future composer. For a time he studied with Edmond Diet, a composer of light music who had been a pupil of César Franck, the heavily romantic composer who had died in 1890. Since Franck was one of young André's idols, this made apparent sense.

Though this study came to nothing, André was not yet through with the music academies. However, he had already made an unconscious choice of vocation. Maurice Charlot was managing the nearly new Athenée Theatre and André began to haunt the place. Though exasperated at the time this was clearly taking from his son's more conventionally educational pursuits, the indulgent Maurice nevertheless encouraged him to see as many shows as possible. Charlot wrote, "I became a theatre-going fiend before I was 15." Soon, already close to his mature height of 6 feet 2 inches, André was escorting his mother to first nights of opera and drama—*Bohème*, *Louise*, *L'Aiglon*.

Charlot's catalogued the riches of the Parisian stage in the mid–1890s: the performances of Sarah Bernhardt, Rejane and Lucien Guitry, the classic repertoire of the Comédie Française, as well as the revivals of operettas by Offenbach and lesser lights such as Lescoq and Planquette, the latter usually at the Opéra Comique, very much in the Charlot neighborhood.

He was also exposed to the colorful characters inhabiting the Parisian theatrical world. One such was Boni de Castellane, a habitué of as well as a contributor to the new Opéra. De Castellane's particular idiosyncrasy was to arrange for a particular group of people to occupy a particular set of seats at the Opéra. This was not, as one familiar with the era might imagine, a claque noisily boosting the show, but a clear expression of opinion. In those seats would sit only men with perfectly bald heads. Their arrangement, as perceived from upstairs, was the spelling out of a single word: "Merde."

He also occasionally took in the revues at the Théâtre des Variétés, slightly far afield from the usual territory. But his essay does not display any particular interest in or judgment on these productions.

Maurice Charlot suffered another financial disaster after two years at the Athenée. The debacle serves as a perfect example of why it is often better to be lucky than smart. Among his cast in the French version of the successful London musical comedy *The Geisha* were the English Tiller Girls, a precision (by contemporary standards) ensemble dance troupe. Not long after the show opened, an international incident between competing imperialists England and France took place in the Sudan and as a result, everything English was at least in theory to be boycotted. So the show floundered. (The next year, the powers signed a convention, but this *entente* came too late for M. Charlot.) André wrote, "Another chunk of the family fortune went down the drain, and the house at Sèvres had to be sold." Usually resilient, Maurice Charlot turned up a year later in charge of the corporation which owned the lease of the prestigious Palais-Royal Theatre at the Tuileries apex of the family's neighborhood. "This," Charlot would write, "was the turning point in my career."

Maurice Charlot's next move gave tacit approval to the inevitable: his son's future lay in the theatre. The elder Charlot appointed André as assistant reader of manuscripts at the rate of five francs per act. The young man's job was to read and analyze (in two or three pages, a task which helped him to visualize the play, a skill which became eventually all-important to him); as the three-act convention was still pretty universal that meant 15 francs per play. Looking back in the 1950s, he calculated that, with the equivalent of three dollars, a boy "could do a lot with fifteen francs in those days."

Maurice Charlot went further. He had no contract with the French equivalent of ASCAP (the American Society of Composers, Authors and Producers) and therefore could not use any copyrighted music in his shows. Despite the efforts of revolutionaries like Antoine, on the Parisian stage of the 1890s, "realism" had still not won the day and most productions were supposed to appeal to the aesthetic sensibilities. So even the most serious dramas were likely to need "incidental music" and the best of this music perhaps prefigured the accompaniments to silent film and the scoring for sound films. (Incidental music to European stage plays was still in existence into the 1920s.) The elder Charlot solved his problem by employing Charlot the younger, who recalled:

> So, when he needed some unimportant music played off stage on a piano, I was "commissioned" to write it and paid three francs royalty per performance. When the show was a success it yielded me 100 francs a month; that wasn't hay, and I didn't have to play the piano!

It was while he was doing these jobs that he was admitted on a probationary status to the harmony class of Xavier Leroux at the Paris Conservatoire of Music. There he was introduced to standard notions of harmony and inculcated with prejudices such as avoiding "consecutive fifths." This led Charlot the student to scorn— as was the fashion—the disturbing work of the impressionist Claude Debussy, a composer perfectly at home with consecutive fifths. Regardless of this brainwashing, when it came time to apply for full-time status in the Conservatoire, Charlot said no: "I had the sense to realize that I had no real composing talent, that I would not be the cross between Beethoven and Chopin which had once been my ambition."

With the benefit of fifty years' hindsight he continued, "I loved the good things of this world ... [but] composing did not buy them ... [and] I would never be capable of the necessary abnegation." As part of this declaration of independence, André was soon declaring Debussy his "musical God." When he became manager at the Alhambra, he finally met the deity and negotiated with him.

André's adolescence (prolonged when set aside the standards of most of the 20th century but perfectly standard for its time) was drawing to a close. He writes of having suddenly developed a desire to learn German, of his mother's procuring a German teacher, and of further rebellions against study. In the summer of 1900, André went to live with a German family in Hamburg, en route visiting museums in Belgium and Cologne. He failed to learn very much German but improved the French of the son of the family, and, he added, learned to swear in Spanish. On the journey home, he saved money by purchasing a third-class ticket and managed a tour of Holland before arriving in Paris "with only a couple of francs left in my pocket."

André Charlot as a young man (courtesy Joan Charlot Midwinter).

He stayed on working for his father at the Palais-Royal from 1899 to 1902, and there is no indication that this was an onerous task for him. Unmarried children of any age were expected to remain at home and it was no different with Charlot. Always discreet about his private life, the tall and increasingly handsome young man with the deep-set eyes beneath strikingly dark and large eyebrows would reveal a great deal about his profession but left no clues to possible romances during this time in his life.

At the end of 1901, Victor Demonte, one of Maurice Charlot's backers, offered André the post of Secrétaire Général of the large Chatelet

Theatre, very much on the eastern edge of the Charlot neighborhood, where Demonte was "sub-rosa manager." The effective end of "Prelude to Life" finds Charlot assessing this big break:

> The job did not faze me. It consisted of press relations and all round assistance to the management, and I knew everyone in Paris connected with the Press and the Theatre. The salary was the usual one for beginners, only too glad to get a chance—NIL. But I knew I would learn a lot working with Alexandre Fontanes [the "real" manager] who knew all the tricks of the trade in staging and management. We are in January, 1902. I am 19. I have a desk of my own, in a room of my own—no more Professors to confuse me—at last I'm able to work and raring to go!

"Prelude to Life" does not afford many insights into his private life—it is more an expanded *résumé* or *curriculum vitae* (with digressions) than anything else—but it comes closer than any other single element in *People 'n Things*. He was determined to keep the arenas of his life discrete, determined that the only "life" that should matter to the outsider is his life in the theater. The man beneath the myriad nature of his work, the intensely private soul within the larger and larger public figure? His response might have been a Gallic shrug.

Between 1902 and 1905, his Secrétaire Généralship at the Chatelet meant that he was really an assistant manager and press representative. He took particular pride in being assigned to search out talent, particularly in London. Twice he successfully brought back troupes of the Tiller Girls, possibly to his father's rueful sighs. While at the Chatelet he was associated with two of Jules Verne's best-known works for the theater, *Michel Strogoff* and *Around the World in 80 Days*. On the occasion of the 1000th performance of *Carmen* in 1904, it was his happy task to contact the composers Saint-Saëns, Humperdinck and Puccini, as well as others, for their reactions to the popular opera, thus widening his contacts and probably his sense of his place in the world.

Following his father's pattern, he also took up theatrical journalism, serving at first as columnist and editor for *Le Petit Bleu*. He continued to write for this magazine until 1908, even though he got such assignments as being sent to England to report on the Henley Rowing Regatta, about which he knew absolutely nothing.

In 1908 he moved to similar jobs at *Le Soleil* and *Le Monde Illustré*, a weekly also distinguished by the caricatures contributed by two of his good personal friends, Rip (Georges Thenon) and Sacha Guitry. He also regularly contributed to the theatrical monthly *L'Art du Théâtre*. One aspect of these years gave him particular pride. Believing strongly that most play reviewers knew little but did great damage, he was proud "that I never did agree to write a notice of a play…. To write about the theatre in a constructive manner was part of my life, and I enjoyed it, but the very idea of criticizing the work and efforts of others was somehow repellent to me—I simply could not do it." He came to regard critics as egomaniacs, deluded by their belief that they were "entitled to judge." This attitude, unsurprisingly, continued throughout his lifetime.

In 1905, managing the Chatelet's touring season, he took *Around the World in*

80 Days on a successful engagement to Brussels. Between 1905 and 1907 he was back at the Palais-Royal as assistant manager. There he was involved in more than 15 productions, including *Une Revue au Palais-Royal* (1905). This may have been his first close-up experience of revue.

In writing of the theater of his Parisian youth, Charlot virtually ignored revues. One possible reason is that revues, being "light" entertainment, were simply not to be given equal ranking alongside the "serious" business of the theater. How could a revue match up to a production featuring Sarah Bernhardt? Throughout his life he was at pains to point out that he was an impresario for all seasons: comedy, drama, melodrama, pantomime, musical comedy, revue. So in these growing years, he pretty much accepted revue as he found it, often as a seasonal diversion from the yearly round of theater. When he got his big chance in 1912 at the Alhambra, he brought with him the kind of revue he was familiar with. It was much later, when he was the acknowledged master of the genre, that he found it necessary to describe and define exactly what this kind of revue entailed.

According to his retrospective study of the form, the kind of revue which he began to work with once he was his own man and "raring to go" was of very recent evolution. It was the particular refinement of a form which had been gathering in significance since the 1840s when the name itself assumed regular usage. Those were the years when the Folies Trevise was built; 1869 saw the completion of the Folies Bergère, a large pleasure palace within the family neighborhood's boundaries. Starting in 1885, one of the attractions of the Folies Bergère was its yearly revue.

In general, revue (in France its meaning was more or less permanently mingled with that of "follies"—which started out as open-air public places where citizens danced, drank and watched small-scale entertainments) emerged as an offshoot of variety. It eventually went through a somewhat "literary" period in which small plays were of major importance and gradually found its audience with a particularly trendy version of variety. In some way or another, however, any revue had to "review" the events of the year (or season) just ended, and therefore seem as up to the minute and knowing as possible.

By the time Charlot was ready and willing to participate, revue had gradually assumed a single tradition which could readily be divided into two subdivisions. An evening of revue indeed included an obligatory "tour" of a year or season—sometimes this was accomplished by touring a particular city or country—and there were two indispensable tour "guides." These were the *compère*, all-knowing and eager to impart knowledge and implication, and the *commère*, ostensibly the person to be guided but quite a knowing "audience" on her own. They sometimes assumed other characters as the evening's tour moved along, but their overall presence provided the framework for what in a 1934 essay Charlot called this "medley of spectacle, topicalities, sketches, songs, etc. with a full cast, consistent in size with the theatre where it is being produced, and no attempt at a plot of any kind."

As for the subdivisions, some of which developed even while Charlot remained an aspiring underling working his way up through the Parisian theater world, he described them circa 1911:

There were two outstanding revue writers in Paris—Flers and Rip. They were equal in importance, but their style of work was as contrasted as day and night. Flers' revues were of the spectacular sort—very much of the Ziegfeld Follies type. They had an appeal to the eye, but very little to the brain. They were always staged in the large music-halls of the days, and Flers was the king of this type of revue for years.

Rip was a few years younger than I; his reputation was well established, but quite recent, and he was one of my closest pals. His revues were always staged in small theatres, where his caustic wit had made him the idol of the boulevards and the fear of those who had the slightest chance to be ridiculed.

Of a Ziegfeld Follies type indeed. It was from the shows he saw during the first decade of the 20th century at the Folies Bergère that Florenz Ziegfeld, under the spell of his French lover Anna Held, and indeed at her urging, derived the idea for his own Follies, the ostentatious super-variety extravaganzas which ruled the American musical stage starting in 1907.

Regardless of his relative downplaying of the importance of revue, it was during this second stint at the Palais-Royal that Charlot began to work in the form. In "Jobs and Productions" he even labeled, in retrospect, a couple of its shows as "intimate revue."

Between 1907 and 1908 Charlot enjoyed his first managership at the Pierre Lafitte Publications' cosy and highly intellectual *Théâtre Femina*. Lafitte published a number of magazines, including *Femina*, which was even well known in the U.S. He held sway in a luxurious building and, as Charlot later wrote, "made use of his glamorous surroundings to attract the old, but already forlorn French aristocracy."

The magazine traded on snobbishness: "The lower classes enjoyed reading the names of titled ladies ... daily contact with Lafitte forced me to realize that he was genuinely impressed by crowns and coronets." Lafitte explained to Charlot that he wished to run a theater—"for isolated performances, and used to organize some shows, produced to publicize his magazines." The unorthodox approach appealed to Charlot.

Building his theater, Lafitte had the stalls (orchestra) hinged on the back wall, with a mechanism making it possible to lift the front portion of the floor to the level of the stage. In theory, the theater could become a large ballroom in less than a half hour. It didn't work quite that well—two hours was more like it. There were also restrictions which caused great difficulty—all scenery had to be built of iron and asbestos. And the dressing rooms were high above the stage, reached by a narrow winding staircase.

For the Théâtre Femina, Charlot invented a dramatic and music school for amateurs—playing upon the egos of the "would-be upper crust." Le Conservatoire des Amateurs was labeled a teaching organization and Charlot engaged "the most celebrated members of the theatrical profession, the greatest musicians" and the students paid royally. (Throughout his life, the man who hated school repeatedly played the role of schoolmaster.) He also organized concerts of "very modern music," Les Concerts d'Avant Garde, private performances of new works by Debussy, Dukas, Ravel, and others, conducted by his friend Pierre Monteux, later a renowned conductor of major symphony orchestras in America.

One of the highlights of the Femina seasons was a "gala jubilee performance" in honor of and featuring Sarah Bernhardt, whom André had idolized since first seeing her onstage in 1897. The gala included poetry by leading poets recited by Paris's most renowned performers, a musical interlude arranged by the youthful Reynaldo Hahn (later famed as a composer and interpreter of Mozart) and a one-act play about the wife of Henri IV starring Bernhardt, who was then 64 and very ill. Charlot made sure that she had a specially heated "gold tent" for a dressing room, the house was liberally sprayed with her favorite perfume, and her dressing table held a pumpkin-sized posy of Parma violets.

Alas, when the play was almost due, Bernhardt announced that she would be unable to walk down the one step into the set. She said she could not perform. But if André could remove the step…. The stage crew was assembled and even agreed, though terrified, to use a plank of wood (forbidden!) to fill the gap. Charlot later wrote, "I would have challenged the whole fire brigade and the President of the Republic." They were a few minutes late in getting onstage, but the play went off well and André retained forever an admiration for Bernhardt, this "trooper" who now needed, alas, because of financial necessity to keep performing. Did it cross his young and optimistic mind that he might one day be in a similar position?

The season at the effete Femina seemed an unlikely preparation for his next job as business manager for the brawling Folies Bergère itself. There his life would take more than one definitive turn.

· TWO ·

Paris and London, 1908–1912
"Brimming with Confidence"

During the season of 1908–09, as the business manager of the Folies Bergère, 26-year-old Charlot watched Flers, master of spectacular revue, at work on the latest edition of its yearly revue. This one presented a youthful Maurice Chevalier, who went on to become one of his century's most popular international entertainers, and included in its chorus the 15-year-old future star Yvonne Printemps. As "business manager" André also operated in one of the most enjoyable and personally advantageous areas of his era's musical theater—first as a talent scout and eventually as an agent. Because he was bilingual and familiar with London, Charlot was particularly in demand for acquiring English talent.

In the globalized 21st century, it's almost unremarkable for shows and performers from one national tradition to find success in other lands—musicals like *Cats* and *Les Misérables* ring cash registers merrily thousands of miles from "home," attended by enthusiastic audiences who have no idea of the tradition from which these shows have sprung. And despite the best protectionist efforts of theatrical unions, one nation's stars readily find ways of transforming into stars of equivalent magnitude abroad.

This is nothing new. By the time Charlot joined the chase, this regular transatlantic ransacking of Broadway by the West End, of Paris by Broadway, of the West End by everyone else, had been in operation for at least a century. In the waning years of the 19th century the American producer Charles Frohman, who had as a youth been treasurer for a minstrel troupe which found great acclaim in Britain, made a specialty out of importing British musical comedies, performers, composers and lyricists. Even then, Frohman was simply following tradition on a larger scale. The practice had been going on ever since the years closely following the War of 1812. Indeed, it was only in those years when it became marginally possible to distinguish American musical theater from its British parent at all.

When Frohman decided to expand his operations further in 1897 by purchasing a theater in London, there was grumbling on both sides of the ocean. But it made good business sense and turned out to be an historical event since Frohman soon scored great London successes with American musicals beginning with *The Belle of New York* (1897). Such American musical comedies could not have existed

18

except for the invasion of Broadway, earlier in the 1890s, by something new—London musical comedy. These shows, popularly known as the Gaiety musicals, were quickly picked up by Broadway.

The business of raiding each other's theaters led not only to such notable successes but also to fraud of a relatively harmless variety. The "famous American juggler" billed in London might never have been heard from outside a few hick towns in the States, while "the darling of the [Music] Halls" brought to Broadway by American vaudeville impresarios might have been hiding a provenance similarly flawed. Barnum was not the only one with a good eye for what the traffic would bear.

Throughout national upheavals, the transatlantic musical theater continued to thrive and by the time Charlot and his contemporaries came on the scene, the regular Atlantic crossings of the elegant vessels of the Cunard fleet—the *Berengaria*, the *Carpathia*, and most particularly the *Aquitania*—served as virtual second homes for producers, directors, talent scouts and agents. These luxury craft were also the hoped-for destinations of many a composer, lyricist, set designer and performer.

The transatlantic musical is the background against which the next several epochs of Charlot's life was played and the source of his greatest success. He procured (and appreciated) talent, usually of the English variety, and his talent-sourcing was to bring him a wife who would be a partner for forty-seven years.

Charlot's father-in-law, Thomas Gladman, Sr.

Florence Emily Gladman was one of twelve children born to Thomas Gladman, a printer, and his wife Eliza Matilde, who was always known as Tillie. This soubriquet was an unusually logical shorthand in a family given to arbitrarily labeling its members. Florence, for instance, was never Flossie but always Flip and there seems no explanation. Thomas Gladman, descended from a "hearty yeoman," was so described in the early 19th century by the essayist Charles Lamb, whose mother's sister married that yeoman.

Thomas Gladman originally came from Hertfordshire, one of the "home counties" circling London, but by the time he started his family, he was living in Islington, now one of the more aspiring parts of north London. Gladman had no theatrical background, although he was, according to his youngest daughter Joan (Jonny), "a very frequent visitor to the music halls and could give a very good account of the songs and acts of all the famous ones." One of Islington's most famous venues is its venerable pub the Angel, and perhaps Thomas Gladman sang along there.

Whatever the impetus, the Gladman family seems in general to have been quite stagestruck. A number of Gladmans entered the theatre, first of all the eldest, brown-eyed Kit, and the second eldest, blue-eyed Flip. They attended M. Paul Valentine's theatrical academy in north London and when they emerged decided to call themselves the Gladwin Sisters because the name sounded more elegant to them. They formed a double act strongly emphasizing dance and toured Britain with some success, enough for Parisian scouts to take an interest.

When the Gladwins performed in the City of Light (they had not been recruited by Charlot), one of their features was an Apache act. Flip wore a tatty black dress and a cap. The climax of the act was Flip's doffing the cap to let loose a remarkably long cascade of blonde hair, bringing the audience to its feet.

There are conflicting accounts of how thoroughly the sisters were chaperoned by Tillie in 1908–09 when they met André Charlot. Some in the family believed that the dashing young Frenchman had really been in love with Kit and turned to Flip in retaliation for being rebuffed. On the other hand, he was said to wear a cornflower in his lapel to match Flip's blue eyes. Whatever the truth, André and Flip were to stay together for the rest of his life, the relationship bearing up under

Florence "Flip" Gladman in Paris, c. 1908–09.

some turbulence. The Gladmans readily welcomed Charlot into the expansive warmth of a family which must have represented to him all that was lacking in the cold domestic life of his parents.

How they cosseted him! When Charlot entered their lives, or vice versa, the Gladmans were living in a large house in Bognor, West Sussex, on England's southern coast (Bognor had not yet become Bognor Regis as a result of King George V's regular visits, which ended at his death in 1935). The Gladmans and Charlots virtually merged and would live together for a time during the First World War when bombs partially destroyed André and Flip's London home.

During his single season at the Folies Bergère and before his launch into matrimony and parenthood, Charlot, still under 30, further complicated his busy professional life by taking a job with the Sherek and Braff talent agency. Though Braff's main office was in Paris, Charlot was reg-

The young Mrs. Charlot, date unknown.

ularly sent to London, where he specialized in scouting the variety houses. In this capacity he also visited Germany, Holland, and Belgium. Another great leap forward followed. In 1909 Charlot accepted Sherek and Braff's offer of opening an office in New York and in October sailed with Flip from Cherbourg on the *Kaiser Wilhelm der Grosse,* arriving in Hoboken, New Jersey, on the 13th.

In one of his later essays, Charlot somewhat pompously referred to his time with Sherek and Braff as an action deliberately taken, "wishing to study the international agent business." He and Flip found the going in New York very difficult indeed on the "regal pay of $30 weekly." The inefficiency of Sherek and Braff in getting even this amount, not to mention "petty cash" payments to the young couple, made things even worse, and though Charlot made many contacts and signed a number of *artistes* (including a now long forgotten comedy act called the Two Bobs and the perennial "red hot mama," singer Sophie Tucker, who thereafter played occasional roles in Charlot's life), after six months he was fed up. He closed the office in April 1910 and returned to London aboard the *New York*.

Charlot subsequently left the firm's London office and decided to try Paris once more. He and Flip took a cottage in the Ville d'Avray, Seine-et-Oise (a suburban *arrondissement*, for once well outside the Charlot neighborhood), and two days later on July 1, 1910, their son Phillippe André Jean Charlot was born. In the official records, Charlot was listed as an English father, living in London, although he did not actually become an English subject for another seven years.

Shortly thereafter, and with his mother's financial backing, Charlot went into the Paris agency business for himself, establishing offices at 29 Rue d'Argenteuil, well within the southeastern margin of the "Charlot neighborhood" and quite near most of the era's major theaters. He quickly signed up a group of rising stars, including the singing actress Irene Bordoni (herself a future transatlantic star—Cole Porter wrote one of his shows for her), the rangy actor Raimu (eventually a major international film star) and the comic Harry Baur.

In 1911 came another break. The entrepreneur Cornuche appointed Charlot the manager of his two semi-outdoor summer theaters, Ambassadeurs and Alcazar. Perhaps in gratitude, Charlot was to honor Cornuche as a genius—the man who in 1890 had "created" perhaps the most famous Parisian restaurant of its day, Maxim's (given artistic immortality by *The Merry Widow*, its era's most popular musical comedy), in league with his chef friend Chauveau, and later "re-created" Deauville, at the time that most elegant of cross–Channel watering holes. Cornuche was, according to Charlot, "a triumph of self-made man.... He had the polish and distinction of an ambassador, a most charming man, welcome in all the spheres of the Parisian world." In short, he was a model to be followed.

The Alcazar had quite a fascinating pedigree, having survived for many decades and outgrown its status as a *café-chantant*, a place where one could go to hear the latest music and often some of the newest comics—in short, one of the versions of cabaret. Brimming with confidence and undoubtedly seeing himself as a self-made man, Charlot assured Cornuche and everyone else he could manage all these jobs concurrently, despite the fact that "[the two theaters] were the two most popular spots in Paris from May to September."

The Cornuche connection, as well as Charlot's long friendship with the revue writer Rip, soon got him into an interesting tangle. Rip, the light-footed satirist, had humiliated Flers, the spectacularist, in a recent revue sketch and was subsequently vanquished in a duel by the expert swordsman Flers. Now Cornuche told Charlot to commission Rip to write the next Ambassadeurs revue. Flers was already set to do the Alcazar show, whose opening was planned for almost the identical date. And Flers was the person who had recommended Charlot to Cornuche!

Word reached the proud Flers quickly, and when next they passed in the street, Flers turned his back upon Charlot. In response to the insult, he got several friends, including Rene Blum, the brother of future prime minister Leon Blum, together to confront Flers and challenge him to a duel. Finally the two teams of "seconds" conferred and the duel was called off, which was probably a good thing for Charlot's well-being. Interestingly, the "insult" continued to gnaw at Charlot. Years later, he managed to compensate for it, without ever forgetting it.

While working for Cornuche, André also organized a concert tour for the soubrette Yvette Guilbert, and, as both agent and part-manager, participated in *La Revue sans Gêne*, a revue partly by Rip, starring the actress Rejane in her own theater and co-starring the English musical comedy performer George Grossmith, Jr.

Meeting Grossmith was one of the keys to André's future. Grossmith was the son of the original, legendary star of the Gilbert and Sullivan operettas. The elder Grossmith had introduced all the tongue-twisting "patter songs" so beloved of lyricists and performers on both sides of the Atlantic. Together with his brother Weedon, the prolific elder "GG" wrote a novel called *The Diary of a Nobody*, in the process creating an archetypal Englishman, Charles Pooter, the rising but terribly insecure middle-class Londoner. (Both father and son were in their primes known as "GG," though for the moment the younger was still "Junior.")

The younger Grossmith was also already a man of some influence in London theatrical circles and went on to a career of considerable transatlantic fame, including later years in American film. He was an historically late example of "actor-manager," a breed which flourished during an era in which the products of a given theater would clearly reflect (and often star) its manager, who was more likely to be lessee than owner.

When Charlot met him, Grossmith could already have been seen as a great innovator in London theater. He paved the way for a distinctive English version of revue and can be called one of its founding fathers. As we shall soon see, by 1909 Grossmith had already been staging short "revues" as one segment of variety bills at the leading London houses. After the engagement with Rejane, Charlot booked Grossmith into Deauville, and the two became firm professional friends.

If meeting Grossmith was of major importance in these years leading to 1912, so was Charlot's connection to two outstanding theatrical personalities, Loie Fuller and Gaby Deslys. Fuller was an American who had already pursued a colorfully varied career in the performing arts before her first trip abroad in 1889. A free spirit who was said never to have lost a friend or paid a debt, Fuller came to London as a "skirt dancer," performing a contemporary specialty within musical comedies and variety shows in which she maneuvered within a series of voluminous skirts, creating momentary patterns highly pleasing to the aesthetic senses. She did not originate this genre. Some of the earliest fragmentary motion picture sequences focus upon the swirling patterns created by various skirt dancers.

Between 1891 and 1892 in the United States, however, Fuller's dancing became highly original, showing an unprecedented understanding of the new possibilities of stage lighting afforded by electricity. Her "serpentine dance" was performed in a fluttering, transparent, voluminous skirt of Chinese silk (she later wrote that one day she had shaken a piece of silk and seen "a thousand movements unknown to that moment ... a movement vocabulary") and lit by red, blue and yellow lights

Loie Fuller (courtesy of Mander & Mitchenson Theatre Collection).

which she had carefully positioned. She brought this dance to England and then, in late 1892 (when Charlot was only 10 and not yet stagestruck), to the Folies Bergère.

Fuller, whose physical attributes (a pudgy torso, a pug face, the muscular arms of a charwoman) were not ideal for a dancer, was an immediate sensation during the *Fin de Siècle,* these dying years of a weary century. Dancing three originals, "Violet," "Butterfly" and "White," Fuller was transformed into a fairy onstage. She captured the imagination of Parisians—intellectuals, scientists, artists and ordinary folk alike. The symbolist poet Stéphane Mallarmé called her performance "an artistic intoxication and an industrial achievement ... [she] blends with the rapidly changing colors which vary their limelit phantasmagori of twilight and grotto ... the dizziness of soul [is] made visible by an artifice." In 1893 the artist Henri Toulouse-Lautrec made fifty "spatter" lithographs of Fuller, varying the colors to illustrate her lighting range. Soon there were Fuller sculptures, hats, ribbons, shoes and petticoats. Fuller took personal credit for transforming the Folies Bergère, long a favored venue for assignations, into a destination suitable for family outings.

Fuller settled in Paris, and although she never learned to speak French, her achievements from then on eventually brought her membership in the French Academy of Sciences and the French Astronomical Society. She had learned about the properties of light from the astronomer Camille Flammarion and how to create dazzling—if deadly—effects from chemists Pierre and Marie Curie, discoverers of radium and therefore the forerunners of the nuclear age. The honors were for the constant flow of inventions emerging from her mind and laboratory. These included "underlighting," allowing her to dance on a completely darkened stage atop a pane of glass lit invisibly from below, thus creating the illusion that she was suspended in space; a series of onstage mirrors which formed an octagonal room, creating an illusion of many figures whirling in all directions; and various secret formulas for magic lantern slides, colored glasses and gelatins.

By the mid–1890s, Fuller was performing dances in which 500 yards of gossamer thin silk nearly 100 yards around the hem were thrown higher than 20 feet aloft, so that she was constantly awhirl. At the 1900 Paris Exhibition dedicated to the new uses of electric light (an event eagerly attended by the 18-year-old Charlot) the facade of the Loie Fuller Theatre featured an "immense veil of pleated plaster caught in mid-flight." Between 1892 and 1908 she choreographed more than 130 dances. She went on to create dances for new works by Debussy. She eventually created "optic plays" in black and white that evoked witches and dreams.

In the heady years surrounding the turn of the 20th century, Fuller and other avant-garde practitioners of the new technologies inspired belief and creativity in many other creative people and in many forms. The choreographer Ruth St. Denis attributed her own use of stage lighting and draperies to having seen Fuller in Paris. Others did not confess their debts. The generous Fuller also sponsored Isadora Duncan's first European dance tour in 1902.

Although he was by then thoroughly aware of Fuller's work, Charlot made his first direct contact with this genius of lighting when he interviewed her in 1908 for *Le Monde Illustré*. He later remembered her in part as follows:

> I don't think I have ever met a more intelligent woman.... Her brain was phenomenal, her range of knowledge almost frightening.... Her Paris house was the haunt of all the brilliant people—and was not infrequently habitated by the bailiffs, to her total unconcern.... Often their visit was due to sheer forgetfulness on her part. Unaware of her bank balance she would order the most elaborate electrical equipment to test a theory.... The predicament did not worry her in the least, but she eventually paid up, not grudgingly but with that indifference which showed a genuine disregard for mere pelf.... She had also two very human qualities which made her lovable—apart from her simple sincerity—a wonderful love for her mother and a genial warmth in her friendliness, which made bounce and side utterly foreign to her.

From the beginning of his revue-producing career, André Charlot would be noted for his sophisticated, highly aesthetic use of stage lighting It would be hard to imagine Charlot's expertise—certainly his willingness to experiment—without Fuller's example. As a youth, Charlot had no background in theatrical lighting except what he saw on the stage from the stalls, and as far as we know, he never "ran the lights" once he became part of the backstage team. Intimate revues were shoestring operations, so nowhere was illusion more clearly called for.

The kind of theatrical illusion that would characterize Charlot's revues stemmed directly from the magic that Loie Fuller had shown him. It was true from the earliest days of his London management that the atmosphere and ambience in a Charlot theater was more beautiful, less showy than those housing his competitors' products. The influence of Loie Fuller's costume and lighting innovations stayed with Charlot throughout his career, and he passed it on to further generations of theatrical "magicians," notably Robert Nesbitt, who revived the British spectacular revue beginning in 1940—and who brought spectacular (but not nude) revue to Las Vegas after World War II.

Before leaving Paris, Charlot worked with both Fuller and Duncan, another (more flamboyant) "free spirit" who helped transform modern dance. Charlot concluded that while Fuller was "an artist of the first rank without effort," Duncan, with whom he in his agency period worked on a series of concerts, "was an artist of high rank with considerable effort." He went further: In an uncharacteristic departure, he wrote that Duncan was "a cow"—not, in English parlance, what any woman of reputation or intelligence would care to be called.

A reprise of Charlot's words about Fuller is revealing. He showed himself particularly interested in the *artistry* of anyone claiming to be an artist. In later years, whenever it fell to anyone to describe the impact of one of his intimate revues, the words "artistry" and "taste" invariably were employed. And Charlot, the dreamer, was particularly impressed by Fuller's artistry "without effort."

Fuller's was one kind of influence on Charlot. That of Gaby Deslys, the reigning *femme fatale* of her era, was a very different sort. Though apparently without intending to do so, Deslys became indirectly instrumental in Charlot's appointment in 1912 as the co-manager of the Alhambra. Hers is also another tale of the transatlantic musical theater.

Born Gabrielle Caire in Marseilles in 1881, Deslys lived only until 1920, though she packed a great deal of life into those 39 years. By 1902 she was appearing in the chorus of Parisian revues. Even before her own days of stardom, she was attracted by the half-world inhabited by some of the easier ladies of the Folies Bergère and the jewel-laden lives they led. She became well known about town and by 1904 was called Gaby Deslys, noted for her physical charms and pleasant renditions of satirical songs. In 1905 she played *commère* in a revue at Paris's Olympia.

In 1906, on the recommendation of George Grossmith, she made her first trip to London, appearing in the burlesque *Aladdin* and stunning the audience in a bathing dress that appeared to be slashed to the waist. Her London reputation was immediately secured. She even became one of an increasing number of celebrities to endorse commercial products—in this instance, Pears Soap. She secured a contract with the Alhambra, and soon under English tutelage became an accomplished if not gifted dancer.

For the next two years Deslys divided her time between Paris and London, where her image as a saucy and daring woman who wore terribly revealing clothes took particular hold. In 1909, after a brief season in Berlin, it was rumored that the German crown prince Wilhelm had fallen for her and that his father, Kaiser Wilhelm, had bought her off with the three largest black pearls in the world. This romantic linkage was followed by suggestions of many more, one of which, to the youthful King Manuel of Portugal, was apparently true enough. In 1910 she was summoned by Manuel to perform in Lisbon, where newspapers soon were able to report that she now held the most priceless jewels in the royal collection.

Gaby Deslys (courtesy of Mader & Mitchenson Theatre Collection).

International communications being relatively leisurely in 1910, little if any of this was known in London when Deslys returned for further triumphs at the Alhambra. Up to this point, she had negotiated with the Alhambra's manager, Alfred Moul, but through him she eventually met the peripatetic Charlot, who in 1911 became Moul's Paris talent representative. Moul's decision to make Charlot his Paris representative apparently stemmed from the 1909–10 reports André had sent back to Sherek and Braff about New York performers. Moul found Charlot's way of writing and thinking amusing and fresh.

In October 1910, while Deslys was playing an engagement in Vienna, a revolution occurred in Portugal. Though the young king escaped, his alleged liaison with Deslys now became front-page news all over Europe, and some papers blamed her for the revolution. Deslys finally confessed to a friendship.

For her next Alhambra appearance, Deslys, who had threatened to break her contract because of more lucrative offers from the U.S., included the first of several "bedroom sketches." The negotiations for this event, which included a bed costing £1,000 ($5,000 in the American money of the era), were mainly carried on by Charlot. Letters between Charlot and Moul show that Charlot was opposed to such expenditures, though Moul understood that Deslys's presence on his stage would be worth much more than that.

In the light of later maneuverings between Charlot and Moul over Deslys, it can be seen that Charlot's attitude toward what he saw as performers' major concern—money—would carry over into his own dealings once he was in charge of a theater. It would also go without saying that he would never deny any luxury to himself or his family. Perhaps, too, Moul's final and fatal (once he lost Deslys, the next thing to go was his job) balking at Deslys's next set of demands may have been influenced by Charlot's regular admonitions.

When the Portuguese ex-king took up residence in England, the connection between him and Deslys remained shrouded in as much mystery as she could arrange. That was the situation in the spring of 1911, when she went to America to appear in shows for Jake and Lee Shubert, the era's most ruthless theatrical monopolists.

Her notoriety had preceded her and she was an instant celebrity, "the most famous professional beauty in the world." She took with her to New York the entire show from the Alhambra and, in addition to a $4,000-weekly contract, the promise of an original operetta to be called *Vera Violetta*. In that show, where she was mercilessly upstaged by the young Al Jolson, she met Harry Pilcer, a dancer who became her partner and paramour. Pilcer wrote for her "The Gaby Glide," a song-and-dance which was quickly an international success.

After *Vera Violetta*, Deslys returned to Europe and a series of sensational engagements, but not, in London, to the Alhambra. Another large variety house, the Palace, had stepped in—providing bedroom scenes, erotic dances with Pilcer and all the rest that a London audience expected. The Alhambra's best drawing card was no more. All the blame stuck to Moul.

Moul's days were numbered and Charlot's were close at hand. By the time 1912 was in full swing, a series of major changes in London musical theater were under way, among them changes to the variety houses in Leicester Square.

This pleasure quarter, close by Soho of evil reputation, had long been one of two hubs of London theater and variety. Leicester Square vied with the Strand, that long thoroughfare which arose from the newspaper offices of Fleet Street and flowed straight to the more stately and public precincts of Trafalgar Square. But this rivalry had of late been sidelined. During the years that brought the 19th century to a close the West End of London was opened up by the cutting through of two major arteries, Charing Cross and Shaftesbury Roads (now the heart of the theater district), and the further development of the London Underground (subway). Between 1888 and 1918 a great boom in theater-building—particularly featuring smaller houses averaging about a thousand seats apiece—transformed the entertainment expectations of London.

A number of additional factors had conspired to change the role of the theaters in Leicester Square. The extremely large music halls (some seating as many as 5,000) which, alongside the network of local halls, had provided working-class Londoners with entertainment and social contact, had been gradually demolished and a definite pecking order established among what remained. Among the halls, the "locals," so often adjuncts to pubs, could no longer expect to lure top-of-the-line talent. These gravitated to the venues within Leicester Square.

In the Square itself could be found at opposite corners the Hippodrome, built in 1900 with a 1,340-seat capacity, and the Alhambra. More or less directly opposite the Alhambra was the Empire, like the Alhambra a venue of the old style, seating almost 3,000, while on the side closest to the Hippodrome was the great impresario George Edwardes's Daly's Theatre. Daly's was a much smaller house where Edwardes showed the musical comedies and operettas that had, along with the Gaiety in the Strand, established the style and reputation of English musical comedy—and of English-language musical comedy.

Excepting Daly's (itself originally a venture of the transatlantic musical theater, having been built as part of his empire by the American entrepreneur Augustin Daly) these ranked—with the nearby Palace (built in 1891 with 1,450 seats) as the top-of-the-line variety houses in London. And as the top-ranked houses, they had reputations to defend and hefty salaries to meet.

The typical fare at the Alhambra, originally built in 1854 but rebuilt after an 1882 fire, included a regular presentation of "ballet," by which should be understood rather stately, pageant-like productions which can be seen as the precursors of the more revealing numbers in Ziegfeld's Follies (beginning in 1907) and the productions of Ziegfeld's less tasteful competitors—one of whom, Earl Carroll, was destined for a major impact on André Charlot's life and career.

The Alhambra, like the Folies Bergère (whose building was actually designed to imitate the Alhambra's own exotic and oriental lines), carried with it the reputation of a house of assignation. Similar opprobrium clung to the Empire, where pink body tights gave the illusion of nudity to the dancing girls. After various clean-up campaigns in the 1890s, both houses opted for audience appeal which was less controversial. After 1900, the Empire began to vary its variety bills with something new urged upon it by the trans–Channel, transatlantic Grossmith—something he called "revue."

As the momentous year of 1912 began, London theater had probably never been more competitive or varied. The opportunities for a raring-to-go young man like André Charlot seemed endless. But just how would he—should he—shape his future?

THREE

London, 1912–1914
"Let's Put on a French Revue"

A degree of social unrest and a relatively high level of nervous energy may be said to have characterized the period in Britain preceding 1912, particularly in London. Even though the power of the British Empire remained in theory at its height, the death of the free-and-easy Edward VII in 1910—and therefore the fading of the golden haze now known as the Edwardian Era—had changed the outlook for many Britons. A general popular dissatisfaction had led in 1911 to a parliamentary act superficially calming the waters by removing some of the influence of hereditary peers in the House of Lords. The class structure of Britain was not completely secure. The year 1912 itself brought significant strikes among miners, dockers and transport workers.

Abroad, though it did not impinge directly upon the man in the street, the long-simmering war in the Balkans seemed further from solution than ever before, causing a typical gridlock in government thinking. Though hardly anyone in Britain noticed, a man named Lenin was exerting greater and greater influence in Russia as the editor of *Pravda*.

The large Leicester Square variety houses were experiencing particularly hard times and most of their entrepreneurs were casting about for a solution, something new to lure the customers. A general "reconstruction" of the physical Alhambra had not really improved its fortunes, which remained pegged to the rather arthritic ballet. A solution—revue—was en route, via the transatlantic musical theater, though no one could quite see it coming at the time. As a genuine player in this theater, André Charlot was regularly on the prowl for something new. So were Albert deCourville and Charles Blake Cochran.

Despite a French surname, deCourville was a Londoner with wide acquaintance and big dreams. He had been a journalist and a friend of the international set, including the yachtsman and tea entrepreneur Sir Thomas Lipton as well as Edgar Wallace, the writer of thrilling tales of derring-do well known throughout the empire. He had presented variety shows at medium-sized London venues. At the Hippodrome for Edward Moss, deCourville had lured the contemporary composers Ruggiero Leoncavallo and Pietro Mascagni to conduct cut-down versions of their operas *I Pagliacci* and *Cavalleria Rusticana*, thus setting in motion the belief that these short operas should always henceforth form a double bill.

The Alhambra Theatre in Leicester Square, London (courtesy of Mander & Mitchenson Theatre Collection).

In 1907, deCourville had seen Ziegfeld's first *Follies* first-hand. Its showiness, its pace, made a great impression. By 1912, at age 30 (he was Charlot's exact contemporary), deCourville was regularly shuttling between London and New York. He judged that the time was right for bringing to Moss the idea of a "big, spectacular musical show" like Ziegfeld's.

Charles Blake Cochran was ten years older than Charlot and deCourville, and by 1912 he possessed a great deal of transatlantic theatrical experience. This had begun when he was 18 and made his first visit to the U.S. in the profound belief that he would "earn his living on the stage." He met Ziegfeld in 1893, when the latter was still promoting the strong man Eugene Sandow, and after a seven-year stay returned to London. In 1899 he took up management and agency very much along Ziegfeld's own lines, including the promotion of escape artist Harry Houdini, cowboys, midgets, rollerskaters, boxers and wrestlers.

Cochran was nothing if not an eclectic showman. A regular importer of French talent during the following decade, he first encountered Charlot in Paris during his agency years, finding the Frenchman's bilingualism of great help in negotiating contracts. By 1912 Cochran was presenting a religious spectacle inspired by the German master of illusionist theater, Max Reinhardt, at London's vast Olympia exhibition hall. In terms of sheer magnitude, *The Miracle* proved a success but in box office terms it marked the beginning of one of Cochran's career downturns. (Out of the downturn eventually came Cochran's "invention" of intimate revue. Later on, he would be Britain's best-known theatrical producer.) So in general terms, 1912 found Cochran "resting."

Variety is properly seen as one of revue's origins, but another antecedent was musical comedy and by 1912 the best days of English musical comedy were already in the past. Its simple original stories (which typically traced their ancestry to Cinderella), so often based on "real people" (for example, aristocratic-male-seeking shopgirls), were fading from fashion and "fashion" was of great importance, since these productions, usually graced by simple but hummable melodies, had been placing upon the stage what the trendy young person was—or would be—wearing.

The real inventor of "musical comedy" was George Edwardes. "Guv" ("Guv'nor" or "the boss"—Charlot would eventually acquire this title himself) had reigned supreme for more than twenty years from his bases of Daly's and the Gaiety. But by 1912, he was not in good health, and worse, his librettists, lyricists, composers and performers were getting old. With older forms such as burlesque and burletta truly dead and variety and musical comedy in trouble, the time was right for something new.

In 1911 Charlot, still juggling several jobs, made another trip to New York, this time in his capacity as talent representative for the Alhambra. He particularly wanted the glamorous Shirley Kellogg, who was then singing the up-and-coming composer Louis Hirsch's "The Wedding Glide" in a successful Winter Garden show. (If this and such numbers as "The Gaby Glide" sound like copies, essentially they were. These were the palmy days of a dancing craze somewhat inaccurately known as "the ragtime craze," and no show could consider itself complete without such songs.)

In New York Charlot ran across deCourville. While awaiting an appointment with Kellogg, Charlot visited some cabaret shows and signed up several performers who became hits in subsequent Alhambra productions. DeCourville and Charlot got along well enough; Charlot recalled a trip to Atlantic City where they were wheeled in rolling chairs along the famous Boardwalk. But Kellogg never kept her appointment. DeCourville had played a remarkably persuasive card. He married Kellogg, who spent the next decade as the star of the large-scale shows deCourville mounted at the Hippodrome.

Back at the Alhambra, Charlot's fortunes came to be settled largely by a man named Schwelm, later identified by Charlot as the theater's power behind the throne. Schwelm was a partner in a major City (the "square mile" center of British finance) stockbrokering firm. The firm held the Alhambra's debentures and Schwelm had thoroughly lost confidence in Moul, whose vision seemed firmly stuck in the past. Schwelm had already tumbled to the fact that the new thing was revue, as Grossmith's small "turns" at the Empire were already proving. Under pressure earlier in 1912, Moul had in fact staged a "revue"—Grossmith's *A Guide to Paris*—but Schwelm believed his heart was not really in it. To stop the hemorrhaging of Alhambra money, a real revue producer was needed.

The behind-the-scenes negotiations which brought André Charlot to nominal control of the Alhambra do not seem to have been documented, but Charlot believed, no doubt correctly, that Grossmith, who was already serving in an advisory capacity to the Alhambra board, had been his chief recommender and backer. The board decided for Charlot, though weighing the young man's relative lack of top-flight experience as well as his "foreignness," it stipulated a co-managing director who would have to be English. When the names of Cochran and deCourville were put to Charlot, he demurred—they were too well known and would have too much influence. And he was particularly sore about deCourville's recent "theft" of Kellogg.

Cochran, whose journalistic connections marked him in Charlot's eyes as a particular threat to elbow him out at the first opportunity, was also unappealing. Given the choice, Charlot opted for Montague Leveaux, a recent Cambridge University graduate who had been serving as press agent for the Empire. Charlot already liked Leveaux's work and

Montague Leveaux (left) and Charlot at the Alhambra Theatre.

was willing to let him handle the business end—as long as the creative/artistic management of the Alhambra was his. Later, when Charlot deemed that Leveaux was guilty of growing a "big head" over their success which entitled him to "meddle" in production, he persuaded the board to give him complete charge.

All this maneuvering aside, Charlot's acquaintance with international talent, and specifically the possibility that he might regain the services of Deslys, must finally have played a part in his appointment. Deslys remained the surest drawing card in London and even their edgy business acquaintance would have been a plus. Charlot's personal connection with the *femme fatale* was older than his professional connection. They had met around the turn of the century when André was still working for his father, who was a friend of a man who had taken Deslys as his *protégé* (Charlot's term); once he took control at the Alhambra, these connections finally paid off.

Charlot wasted no time. He turned over the operation of his Paris talent agency—averring that it had always been beneath him—to his brother Jean, who proceeded to make it a success. The "promotion" to London did not particularly awe the Paris press, which reported that Jean was taking the London job while André stayed at home.

So, without any record of responsibility in running a major theater, let alone in creating major revues, André Charlot came to London in the summer of 1912 charged with the responsibility of reviving the fortunes of one of its flagship theaters, if not the musical theater itself. He stayed for 25 years, in the process becoming British by nationalization. He and his small family took up residence in the Hyde Park Mansions, a block of flats not far from Marble Arch and therefore the shopping heart of London, quite near Gordon Selfridge's mammoth American-style department store. They stayed in that flat for nearly four years, moving on to a larger home during World War I, when Charlot's intimate revues were the talk of London. There at the Hyde Park Mansions Charlot's canine menagerie made its London debuts. The animals included a black Great Dane called Queenie as well as a little black mongrel.

Regardless of any strings that may have been attached to his early days at the Alhambra, it is hard not to imagine André Charlot stepping with great gusto into the role of impresario. Though he might be self-effacing in private, he carried with him throughout his London years an air of the magisterial, an absolute ruler of his realm whose judgments carried the weight of finality. With his family at hand, and thus comforted—when he wished to be—by domesticity, Charlot went to work with Grossmith on *The New Alhambra Revue.*

Regardless of the promise which now caused the houses of Leicester Square to scramble for it, revue as a major attraction was still quite a new idea for most Londoners. When the term "revue" itself became well enough known, the producers of some successful 19th-century shows retroactively reclassified them as "revue." One of these was *Under the Clock* (1893), whose creator was (Sir) Seymour Hicks.

It was really a particularly witty burletta and burlettas themselves were generally heterogeneous productions designed to outwit the licensing laws by getting as much dialogue as possible into a variety show. The sporadic importations of French revues since 1905 had served mainly a novelty-seeking audience. What most theater-conscious Londoners knew of revue was mainly through Grossmith's experimentations. Under the theater licensing laws of the era, such a "revue" was only one necessarily brisk "turn" on an evening's bill. The first of these was only seventh-billed and had to compete with monkeys, dogs, tumblers, instrumentalists, a "fairy ballet" and the newest threat to stage shows, the biograph (motion picture) machine.

Grossmith's mini-revues often adopted the traditional "tourist" motif—the first one circling one of London's newly trendy areas. They sometimes profited from interpolations by up-and-coming composers such as the American Jerome Kern (in this era Kern wrote so often for London shows that it was rumored that Frohman signed him because he thought he was English), although generally they relied upon familiar melodies, to which had been substituted topical lyrics.

By 1912 these mini-revues had become the major attraction of the Empire bill. One of these, *Everybody's Doing It* (1912), while unashamedly ripping off the songs of Irving Berlin, included a parody of Gaby Deslys. In May of 1912 Grossmith transferred his operation to the Alhambra, where *A Guide to Paris*, it was hoped, would stem the continuing decline in the ancient house's fortunes. As we have seen, it didn't, but it was an interesting failure. The revue, beginning at a main Parisian railway station, was a fairly careful imitation of the kind of show Grossmith had known in Paris and an apt prelude to "real" "French" revue—the kind Charlot adapted for London.

The earliest Charlot shows at the Alhambra were not really known as Charlot shows. Grossmith, author or co-author, represented what London knew about revue. He was also a well-known performer on the musical stage. He had learned his trade in a theatrical era when the star performer (sometimes, as we have seen, also the theater's impresario) was all. He would have perfected a "character"—perhaps a wise hayseed—which audiences expected and demanded to see. In musical comedy, the necessities of plot were regularly bent or sometimes entirely set aside in favor of the star's "persona."

Grossmith's "sketches" embodied such a tradition. Many London revues following Grossmith's were written by variety stalwarts like Harry Grattan, himself a player in some of the shows. A performer with a well-defined character himself, Grattan tended to create situations in which a variety star could simply repeat his usual familiar gags and stunts, perhaps accommodating far enough to wear a costume somewhat in keeping with the show's "story" line. So this "necessity" ruled when Charlot began to create revue in London. One of Charlot's gifts was realizing, during World War I, that this kind of writing was no longer enough. Grattan, who made history by writing the earliest intimate revue, nevertheless became an occasional member of Charlot's stage "company."

In taking on his Alhambra responsibilities, Charlot was also entering the somewhat arcane world of English theatrical law. Ever since the days of Restoration in the late 17th century, "theaters" and English governmental authorities had been engaged in a particular kind of struggle. The core was simple—who would be allowed to present what and, secondarily, who would make the decision. By 1912 this war was more than two centuries old and characterized by the "theaters" gradually finding ways around the existing laws, by the authorities finally enforcing and tightening these laws, and so on, generation after generation. Originally intended to "purify" legitimate drama by limiting its performance to "experts," the "patent theater law" actually helped create musical theater.

NERMAN

George Grossmith looking toothy in *Princess Charming*.

A shy encounter between Hermione Baddeley and George Grossmith in *The Five O'Clock Girl*.

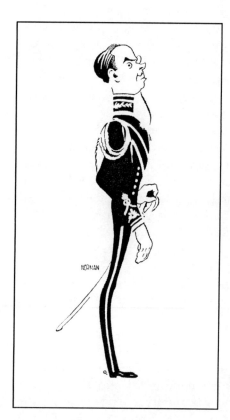

"GG" in *The Cabaret Girl*.

The currently crucial interpretation of the "law" which Charlot would operate under at the Alhambra was the division between "music hall" and "theater." The Alhambra was a variety house—a music hall—and therefore not permitted to do what the theaters did. This division particularly focused upon the "sketch"—or playlet. Theaters could do them, but music halls— at least in theory—couldn't.

Once in power, Charlot joined Grossmith and other "variety" managers in lobbying to modify this law. Further, since shows in "variety" houses were clearly variety shows, they should offer a certain number of "turns"—and a revue of any size counted as only one "turn." Since the shows that Charlot planned were much longer than Grossmith's earlier experiments, this meant a very long evening of entertainment. And although Charlot soon managed to demote the opening "turns" on an Alhambra bill to the status of curtain-raisers, while using the motion-picture sequence as a closing house-clearer, he was still stuck with these requirements. Eventually, however, he was able to change things.

Before the opening of Charlot's first show there occurred one of those events which helped to determine which way the dice of fortune would fall. The late and soggy summer of 1912 had brought an infestation of flies to London. During these days, Charlot proved himself quite an astute predictor of what might catch the fickle, novelty-seeking potential audience's attention. The slogan "Kill that Fly!" was on billboards everywhere. The title of the revue was changed very late in the game to *Kill That Fly!*, a theme song was written, and the show opened on October 12.

Kill That Fly! employed many performers who had been part of Grossmith's troupe, as well as an original musical score by Melville Gideon, an American composer-crooner who may be classed among Charlot's earliest "discoveries." Gideon came to Charlot under amusing circumstances: he arrived in the Alhambra offices while Guv and Leveaux were revising their program and announced, "I open here next Monday."

It developed that Gideon had a cable, purportedly from both Charlot and Leveaux, offering £80 weekly. Gideon insisted that this must have been the skullduggery of a New York agent to whom he had paid £20 in fees. Charlot and Leveaux, somewhat charmed, then invited Gideon and his partner Mabel Bunyes to audition. They liked what they saw and heard, and they liked Gideon's general, self-aggrandizing push. Thus began a career both illustrious and ultimately sad. Another of the original cast of this revue, who thus gained a foothold in show business, was a youth named Edmund Goulding, who would return the favor 30 years later in Hollywood, where he had become a major film director.

Although nowhere near the scale of the largest Parisian revues, it was felt that *Kill That Fly!* had to uphold the Alhambra tradition for lavishness. So it was played against lavish scenery suggesting the most elegant parts of London and Paris and such exotic locales as Honolulu. Among Charlot and Grossmith's borrowing from the French were the "plot's" peregrinations, which were guided through 24 separate scenes by a *compère* (in this incarnation, a journalist) and *commère*.

Kill That Fly! proved rich in topicality: there were satirical jibes at the fripperies of hat-making, at the newly trendy "science" of eugenics and (without much of a logical connection) at the corruption, not to mention linguistic strangeness, of New York policemen. The show's many in-jokes were directed at the producers Frohman and Edwardes. This imported one of the characteristics of Parisian revue— the ingrown world of the theater. It was also an instance of what was currently permitted on the British stage. While it would be perfectly all right to lampoon Edwardes and Frohman, even to the point of using their real names, no "public figure" such as a member of parliament or of the government, and certainly none of the royalty, could be so caricatured, though there were plenty of acceptable methods of coming close.

Edwardes was shown to be more focused upon his love of horse racing than upon his shows, so much so as to hire the wrong people to write his shows because he misunderstands their names. Wordplay and a love of malapropisms were longstanding staples of the English stage and they became indispensable to revue.

Montague Leveaux, Flip and Charlot in fancy dress, date unknown.

Frohman's "crass" American products are parodied in a playlet called "The Pink Belle of the Cabbage Patch: or, If You Can't Get Wise, Get Rich," which ends in impersonations of Frohman's usual American musical comedy stars, Edna May and Bert Williams.

The curiosity of *Kill That Fly!* helped carry it into a second version, which opened January 16, 1913, and boasted some fairly spectacular visual effects, including an ingenious "starting machine" for a lengthy sequence set on "Ascot Heath" (designed by Heath Robinson, a British precursor of the fantastic "inventions" of

American cartoonist Rube Goldberg—and an indication of how quickly Charlot had understood the popular and trendy enthusiasms of London) and featuring a dancing chorus of girl jockeys. One of the sharper moments of this sequence was the observation that at this race course, theater people were specifically barred from entering the royal enclosure, since they were seen as good only for fund-raising. The London periodical *The Sketch* simply called *Kill That Fly!* "the best thing of the sort that we have seen yet in London."

Late in October 1912, the Charlot-Grossmith show received a further accolade—and, within the theatrical world, acknowledgment—when the last edition of Harry Pelissier's *Follies* opened in London. For several years, the portly, ingenious Pelissier had run this enlarged version of "concert party"—a show wherein a small troupe clad as Pierrots sang, danced, and did monologues and satirical sketches. Within this edition was found *D ... That Flea,* "a burlesque of a revue." The audience joins in singing, "Our music's rot/It's got no plot/But it pleases us somehow/So don't be shy/Come on and try/To kill that fly!" (These lyrics are about as accomplished as those of the real title song.)

It's particularly significant to remember what kind of revue Charlot chose to bring to London in light of what happened December 23, 1912, when deCourville opened *Hullo, Ragtime!* at the Hippodrome. He called this largely incoherent variety show a revue. In their several jaunts to Broadway, deCourville and Charlot showed markedly different reactions to Ziegfeld's Follies, even in its relatively austere 1907–08 beginnings. Whatever the Ziegfeld shows were, they weren't coherent. It wasn't long before deCourville was calling himself "the English Ziegfeld." By 1912 Ziegfeld's shows were becoming the toast of Broadway, but his annual variation on "glorifying the American girl" proved the closest approach he ever made to coherence.

In *Hullo, Ragtime!* (its popularity ensured by riding the coattails of the newest rage) there were sketches of a sort, and in one of them, "The Alhambra Brothers," Charlot and Leveaux, were portrayed as two peripatetics jammed into the same overcoat, arms linked and legs tied together. They were billed as "The two headed impresario, the greatest novelty in Leicester Square."

In this sense, Charlot had tentatively "arrived" as a presence in London musical theater. What was also true was that, despite its real achievement, skillfully adapting a truly French revue for an English audience, *Kill That Fly!* did not prove as popular as *Hullo, Ragtime!* The bandwagon for pseudo-ragtime music had been rolling since Irving Berlin's appearance in London in 1910. DeCourville's show was replete with newly familiar rags, while all the original music was supplied by the youthful Louis Hirsch. Capitalizing as much upon this trend as they could after having been beaten to the punch, Charlot and Grossmith hired Hirsch himself to appear, performing his own songs, for two weeks in *Kill That Fly!* (The interpolation also shows how very like a variety show Charlot's early efforts could seem.)

By early 1913 Charlot was already acquiring additional publicity and approval for the Alhambra by allowing the National Sunday League to stage there its Sunday Evenings for the People, the first "a grand orchestral concert with the Meistersingers Orchestra."

In his early days at the Alhambra, Charlot had to deal with something familiar enough to a Parisian—a claque, a part of the audience who applauded artists who felt they were not likely to get applause otherwise and were willing to pay for the boost. The Alhambra claque's leader managed to get a goodly, raucous group together by handing out free passes. Charlot, who had never enjoyed quite such control in his Parisian days, managed to get rid of the claque at the cost of being threatened with shooting and the dubious "plus" of being licensed to carry a gun himself.

The year 1913 brought significant changes to Charlot's Alhambra rule. There was somewhat less of Grossmith, who as transatlantic performer, author and producer was always into something new. His interest in revue gradually declined and by the end of the decade he had become a leading importer of American musical comedy.

Charlot's second Alhambra revue, opening May 9, 1913 (he abandoned the French convention of one revue a year), was considerably more "French" than the first. *Eight Pence a Mile: The New Stop Press Revue*, named for the now reduced amount of money ordinarily charged by London taxi drivers for a tour of the capital, was indeed a fanciful tour of London. As author, Grossmith was joined by Fred Thompson, later to carve out a career as a transatlantic librettist (one of his most notable shows was 1930s *Girl Crazy* with George and Ira Gershwin). The show's fourteen scenes, including flashbacks and flash-forwards in time, were sometimes enhanced by fanciful cross–Channel leaps to Normandy. They also showed clearly the lingering Alhambra tradition, since a "pastel ballet" and tributes to "Omar Khayyam" and "The Orient" found their ways onto the bill.

At least during his London years, Charlot never did cut his ties with his homeland, regularly visiting family and friends and particularly keeping up his professional connections. One of the ways in which *Eight Pence a Mile*, sticking to the *compère-commère* formula, was particularly French was its impresario's importation of Parisian friends and experts. The show had a highly exotic look due to the designer Paul Poiret.

Poiret had then only a year's experience in French revue, having been hired to work with the Russian artist-designer Erte in 1912. (Erte went on to become one of the dominant set designers for American revue, particularly the Ziegfeldesque variety, during the 1920s.) Poiret's costumes, headdresses and jewelry for the Charlot show tended to underline his claim to have been an Eastern prince in a previous incarnation. (Poiret once gave a Parisian ball in which three hundred guests in costumes designed, made and paid for by their host joined slaves black and white, male and female, their outfits shimmering with thousands of pearls and surveyed by Mme. Poiret in a golden cage high above.)

With these continental infusions Charlot's second revue could boast of an elegance previously unseen on London stages. Of equal significance to the success of *Eight Pence a Mile*, but of greater significance to Charlot's future, were the contributions of Phyllis Monkman, a willowy dancer, and the all-purpose veteran entertainer Robert Hale (the father of a subsequent generation of British musical stars, Sonny and Binnie). Monkman may in fact be regarded as the first component of what in short order became a regular Charlot company. The creation of such a company,

Eight Pence a Mile at the Alhambra, **1913** (courtesy of Mander & Mitchenson Theatre Collection).

Poiret's men's costumes for the Persian Ballet.

well versed in the ways of revue, was one of Charlot's most important contributions to defining what eventually was known as English revue. Monkman starred in one of the Poiret oriental numbers, "The Flowers of Allah," as a suitably provocative shackled prisoner.

Eight Pence a Mile also featured Charlot's earliest experimentation with the kind of stage lighting he had witnessed in Loie Fuller's presentations. In "Black and White" only the dancers' (white) hats, gloves and boots were visible. (It was the 1920s before London theater house lights were regularly dimmed for performance and therefore Charlot's departures were all the more innovative.)

Charlot's third Alhambra revue, *Keep Smiling*, was even bigger. More of Charlot's friends, the set designers Ronsin, Marc Henri and Laverdet, joined Poiret. The French connection was notable even in the house program, a near copy of the format used in Parisian theaters. It actually included advertisements for a number of Parisian theaters, including the Folies Bergère.

Keep Smiling introduced another member of the Charlot "repertory company" in the person of Lee White, an itinerant American singer with a throaty voice who brought a knowing comic edge to some of the exotic proceedings simply by showing up garbed as a harem queen. There were shipboard scenes, an Assyrian ballet to the music of contemporary composers Borodin, Glazunov and Ravel, and a Turkish/Persian number in which a partial riposte to ragtime, the "Tango-tease," was

Paul Poiret's costumes for the Persian Ballet, *Eight Pence a Mile,* **1913.**

incongruously placed. The finale of *Keep Smiling*, a show which went through two editions, was called "Troubadours and Follies," filling the vast Alhambra stage atop a massive staircase. This time the reviewer for *The Sketch* gasped, "for brilliance and kaleidoscopic effect … it has never been equaled." Charlot's early English revues were anything but intimate.

During the run of this revue, Leveaux bowed out, leaving Charlot in complete charge. It was not long, however, before Cochran joined the team as "publicity director," though there were probably two reasons for his brief tenure. If the Alhambra's backers wanted to keep an eye on Charlot, who better than Cochran? It also represented a gesture of goodwill on Charlot's part to a competitor who had briefly fallen on hard times. (In later years, a genuine rivalry between these impresarios developed, and in similar circumstances, Cochran did not come to Charlot's aid.) During the run of *Keep Smiling* Charlot kept his European credentials alive by exporting two ballets from *Eight Pence a Mile* to Berlin's Winter Garden.

Although, largely because of the sheer size of the Alhambra, none of these three shows could match the financial success of deCourville's original paean to ragtime or its follow-up in December of 1913, *Hullo, Tango!,* they had, with some style, at least restored the ancient venue to its traditional status. In pursuit of ballets suitable to the Alhambra, Charlot was willing to go a long way. In so doing, he was able to meet one of the gods of his early life, Claude Debussy. When Charlot learned that a friend whom he had imported to costume a Theodore Kosloff dance was also a friend of Debussy's, he determined to seek an original ballet from Debussy. Negotiations followed and Charlot was able to convince his co-directors that this "new-fangled" composer would be worth a £1,000 ($5,000) fee for the writing of an original "Chinese" ballet.

Unfortunately, Debussy fell ill—it turned out that he had only five years to live—but he agreed to have his symphonic poem *Printemps* cut down in size, though it would still be the lengthiest part of the next Alhambra show. Convinced that Debussy was the only person to perform this surgery, Charlot traveled once more to Paris, where he found himself "looked through" quite impersonally by the great man, who nevertheless did the work quickly and dispassionately, and then Charlot was gone. *Printemps* was the most original music on the stage of any London house that year and thereafter Charlot was able to employ other works of the modernist master, though the "Chinese" ballet was never written.

In May 1914, Charlot produced another ambitious show, *Not Likely* (in its second edition this became *Everything New? Not Likely*). Hale, White and Monkman were joined as stars by the sultry Argentinian-American Teddie Gerard, the French designs were in place, there were original songs by Gideon and the American Harry Tierney (later the author of *Irene*) and in July for two weeks, the new American comic-singing sensation Eddie Cantor, then on honeymoon in London. But it was the show's second edition that introduced a woman who proved professionally and personally irreplaceable to Charlot—Beatrice Lillie, who went on to become generally known as "the funniest woman in the world" for at least the next forty years.

Lillie was a Canadian who had formed a singing trio back home with her mother and sister Muriel. Despite occasional moderate success, the group, specializing in sentiment, was not a star attraction and Lillie set out on her own, eventually obtaining some solo singing engagements in medium-ranked London music halls. It was during this neither-here-nor-there period that she decided to audition for a Charlot revue. Her decision coincided with Charlot's confinement to the London Fever Hospital with scarlet fever. (For an apparently robust man, Charlot accumulated throughout his lifetime an impressive number of illnesses.) She sang for the regular stage director in the production team who then called Charlot at "the only room in the hospital which was graced with a telephone" to describe the audition with a "skinny shrimp who appeared full of possibilities."

Charlot okayed a "short commitment" to Lillie for *Not Likely* and upon emerging from the hospital set up a fresh audition at which Lillie was supported by her sister, recently arrived from Canada, at the piano and her mother Lucy standing by with additional vocal aid. Charlot called the trio's appearance "a perfect daguerreotype."

Charlot sat side by side in the stalls with his stage director, watched and listened. Lillie began to sing her ballads—all of them sentimental and all sung perfectly straight. Charlot recalled:

> ...from the very beginning I found it difficult to control my laughter. It was not that she sang badly or out of tune, but the material she was using was so

obviously the antithesis of what was meant for her ... I am afraid I prolonged the audition beyond the limit of Bea's endurance. She did not know what to make of ... the blank expression I was forcing on my face. It was not sadism on my part, but I was too amused to ask her to stop.

Charlot was wrong in one respect: such sincerely maudlin songs were and remained one course of the feast of comedy Lillie was destined to place before her audiences. They fitted perfectly alongside her characterizations of impeccably highfalutin society ladies who might suddenly rollerskate around the stage. And for her part, Lillie realized almost immediately that Charlot had correctly sized her up: she was a natural-born clown. In "Portrait of a Super-Clown" Charlot wrote:

> I remember she had one gesture which was so extraordinarily effective that everybody tried to imitate her. None succeeded although it was, or looked, so very simple. It was only the raising of her right hand, but it was done in such a provocative way that the very movement seemed to live by itself. People roared with laughter, and oh, how hard have her imitators tried to get that gesture!

Of all the "discoveries" which helped make Charlot famous, it was Lillie who would remain longest in his employ and affection. When the Charlots moved in early 1916 to a large house in St. John's Wood, London—probably their happiest home—it was on a road just around the corner from where the Lillie trio made their home. Bea was at the Charlot house almost daily and became a virtual part of the Charlot family, always present at their Sunday tennis, dinner and games routine. Bea referred to her discoverer as "Dada." Charlot played avuncular and semi-fatherly roles with what seemed like consummate ease, though in reality he often proved himself an aloof parent. In later years, when Charlot's star had set, Lillie was the one ex-star who would repeatedly come to his assistance, both professionally and financially.

In *Not Likely* Lillie made her debut as "The Doll" in a rather lavish sequence called "From a Christmas Tree." She also appeared as one of the Eight Marvellous Hoofers, a pretty direct parody of a second-rate act (like deCourville's Ragtime American Octet?), who were palmed off as "direct from their American triumphs. It is positively the greatest dancing act in the world, bar none. All the songs in this act are fully protected by copyright." The number gave Lillie her first chance to show off the comic possibilities inherent in dancing *almost* correctly. She was eventually added to another sketch as "the paper boy," which presented her first opportunity to show how attractive she could be when dressed as a youthful male.

The theater critics who had not already recognized Charlot's expertise in revue were impressed by *Not Likely* and its sequel. In the 1915 *Stage Yearbook* it was called the best of the previous year's London musical shows, but in the characteristic approach of that publication, it was also predicted that the craze for revue had just about run its course. This turned out to have been one of its more demented predictions, since by the end of 1914 everything was in place for the most important developments revue had yet seen.

Influential, of course, was the outbreak of war in August 1914. As the war itself developed and wore on (as with most wars, this one was expected to last only a few months), the need for brisk, light entertainment increased. Today it remains to a degree almost unbelievable that British soldiers who had been in the trenches in the morning could be attending a West End show the same evening, but such was literally the case. But what kind of show? Musical comedy had lost its freshness and that all-important feeling of being "up-to-date." While variety performers retained their popularity, the special connection they enjoyed with their audiences had changed. The first 1912 Royal Command Variety Performance had conferred "respectability" on these performers and with few exceptions—the mistress of double meaning Marie Lloyd being one—they had gone upmarket and a particular class-based kind of oneness with an audience had vanished.

Within revue itself, the most significant development came not long after the outbreak of war, when Cochran, returning from his employ with Charlot armed with a shoestring, staged *Odds and Ends*, which theater historians have called the first intimate revue. It opened in the small (500-seat) Ambassadors Theater in London on October 16, 1914. The lobbying of authority by Charlot, Grossmith and other managers had gained some changes in the licensing laws allowing such "theaters"— as opposed to "music halls"—to stage revues. Charlot himself probably did not realize how quickly the change would revolutionize British musical theater.

For *Odds and Ends* Cochran imported some of his favorite French music-hall performers—in particular the glamorous Alice Delysia and the comic Max Dearly— and hired Harry Grattan to write a "book" based upon the recent real-life exploits of a troupe of English dancing girls who were in Germany at the outbreak of war and had a very complicated time getting home.

What Grattan did was to employ the device of a darkened, bare stage occupied only by the stage doorkeeper of a deserted theater in a seaside town. As the door-keeper chatted with the audience, the stage gradually filled with paraphernalia brought in by porters, and finally by a troupe of refugee actors, including English dancing girls. None of them seemed to know what country they were in or why they were there, but eventually it was concluded that since they *were* players, and this *was* a theater, they would put on a show and, since "we have some English dancers, let's put on a French revue."

What followed was Grattan's artful imitation of improvisation, including timely discussions of champion boxers, illustrations of the essential friendliness between French and English people and a boudoir scene burlesquing "Delysian undress"— or was that Deslysian? Grattan's particular gift, which he was to repeat many times over the next few years, was to make audiences momentarily believe that they are simply overhearing, simply and accidentally present at a real-life moment in the lives of the members of the cast. The effect is to make the audience feel itself to be a part of the show, and that turned out to be one of the main charms of intimate revue.

Odds and Ends, despite a slow first week (critics did not know what to make of this "unstructured" event), picked up momentum and eventually proved one of the biggest financial successes in Cochran's career. Its sequel was equally successful and by mid–1915 there was a scramble to get on the revue bandwagon. Charlot, still coping with a 3,000-seat "nut" to crack at the Alhambra, can hardly have failed to notice.

FOUR

London, 1914–1919

Perfecting Intimate Revue

Within the British theatrical world, musical subdivision, a realization paralleling the general society's was dawning: the war would not end soon. Consider the progression in feeling and understanding, ending on a dying fall, that is represented by the successive titles applied to that grinding conflict—the Great War, the War to End All Wars, World War I, the 1914–1918 War.

Charlot quickly hatched a policy which he felt suitable to wartime. (It's interesting that he *had* a policy. No one expected a showman like Cochran or a spectacularist like deCourville to have one.) And when he saw that the public mood had outrun the policy, he changed it. Perhaps his "dreaming" was, after all, thinking.

As 1914 became 1915, the "lesson" of Cochran's *Odds and Ends* had not yet been learned by the producers of revue. But the most obvious fact was how many shows across Britain were willing to call themselves revues. Not that they had very much in common (except, as it seemed, an obligatory parody of Gaby Deslys) nor that they very much resembled what Cochran, deCourville or Charlot were doing. Lacking any revue tradition, a successful revue was anything so labeled that an audience turned up for. Despite this, by the end of 1915, at least the intimate revue was assuming a definitive shape and the shape was given by Charlot. By 1920 this shape would dominate English revue in general and in 1924 its influence would begin to spread abroad.

It's interesting to realize that in Britain these wartime years brought about the distinctive intimate revue; in America, so says the theatrical historian Gerald Bordman, they were the years when "the modern musical" was born. Perhaps, in subsequent years, English musical comedy simply copied America's, while American revue simply copied England's—that is, Charlot's.

The triumph of intimate revue was not readily predictable at the beginning of 1915. Charlot could not attempt anything like Cochran's shoestring shows while needing to fill the Alhambra, so for a time he went even larger. With Lillie and other members of his growing theatrical family now in hand, he created more and more varied entertainments. There were two more Alhambra shows—*5064 Gerrard* in March and *Now's the Time* in October. The title of *Gerrard* was the telephone number of the Alhambra's backstage. A press release claimed that it was the winning entry from a competition engaged in by 8,000 participants. Whatever the truth of that, it was a great, sprawling show which, according to one reviewer, would have been best appreciated onstage in a merry-go-round.

An excellent show which has sometimes, if puzzlingly, been called Charlot's real debut on the London scene (perhaps the fading of Grossmith's influence was responsible), *5064 Gerrard* marked the successful culmination of Charlot's quest— luring back Deslys. Like the rest of London, he had had to wait for her to play out her American adventure. Finally securing her services was not particularly straight-forward, either, since the redoubtable Deslys had booked herself for her own revue, *Rosy Rapture*. The show was written for her by one of her latest admirers, (Sir) James Barrie. American followers of theater may be surprised to know that the dour-appearing creator of *Peter Pan* had already shown himself in London as a writer of witty short plays (though Barrie's enchantment by Deslys might surprise them even more!).

One of the original features of *Gerrard* was an "impersonation" of Deslys as Miss Rosy Rapture by Robert Hale, one which Deslys herself, visiting one evening, found accurate enough to send her into convulsive laughter. But *Rosy Rapture* closed quite quickly. Fearing that her audience-drawing invincibility, now punctured, would deflate entirely unless quickly repaired, Deslys was happy to accept Charlot's offer to join his show.

Charlot wrote with surprising fondness of the experience. He had been worried about the impact the hiring of Deslys would have on Monkman, whom he believed he had built into a great star. Deslys and Harry Pilcer were given a "wonderful dance" which he believed might surely shake Monkman's confidence. But when Deslys arrived for her first rehearsal—ordinarily clothed with her hair in paper curlers—the first thing she did was to take Charlot aside and tell him to place her number at the end of the first act, so that she did not have to follow Monkman, who could *really* dance. She added, "I would look a bloody fool if I had to follow her." Charlot understood. He agreed and, at least in one respect, changed his opinion of the temperamental Miss Deslys. *5064 Gerrard* proved the most successful of Charlot's Alhambra productions.

One wonders in retrospect whether, even considering the box-office fillip provided by her presence, the salary Charlot had to pay a drawing card like Deslys was a factor when the opportunity arose to go smaller. Ever liberal with his own and his family's pleasures, he remained parsimonious with his staff and "stars." (Once he opted for smaller shows, he kept them "starless" as long as he could get away with it. In one memoir he grumbled that he had eventually to raise Monkman's salary from six pounds a week to a hundred—in American terms from $30 to $500—in times when money went a long way.) Despite this, his "discoveries" generally stayed with Charlot beyond reasonable expectations. Finally, however, a contemporary remark displayed its truth: "Charlot discovers stars, but Cochran makes them into constellations."

Lillie was a key component of *Gerrard*, singing Berlin's "I Want to Go Back to Michigan." Dressed as a farm boy, she sent audiences into gales of glee. (Later, she wrote that the humor must have come from anyone wanting to go to a place with such a silly name.) *Compère* and *commère* tour London once more, this time in search of wartime contrabands; they are fleeced by a sham antique dealer, witness an exotic vestal virgin ballet and visit Murray's Club, the nightclub-of-the-moment, where they are entertained by a "beauty chorus." One of this chorus, demonstrating all the trendy dances, is Lillie as "Miss Foxtrot." There is a bevy of militarily clad girls called the Alhambra Scouts, a mammoth spectacle called "The Pearl Necklace," in which a chorus all in white, except for a couple all in black, are looped about the stage to create a necklace effect, and a finale in which blonde-bewigged Pierrots gradually fill the entire vast stage. Were there really a hundred of them?

Charlot was an extremely good public-relations man. He continued the Alhambra's community-service outreach and showed a nodding acquaintance with the course of the war with a "Russia Day" on November 15, 1915, featuring many stars from the contemporary musical stage, including Grossmith and Lillie, as well as a balalaika orchestra and Russian dancers.

During the war, many of the London theaters, including Charlot's, were commandeered during the afternoons—not for anything clandestine, but for sewing parties which produced garments for refugee children. Jonny Gladman recalled her mother attending these and being congratulated for the skill with which she produced "liberty bodices" made of scarlet cotton lined with white flannel. They were "guaranteed to ward off the cold and any chest complaints." Jonny added, "We thought they were little horrors."

In *Now's the Time* White and Lillie were featured, the latter in male evening clothes looking strikingly like Chaplin's little tramp (impersonations of Chaplin were now as *de rigeur* as those of Deslys had been) as a combined *compère-commère*. The show survived an opening night punctuated by the first zeppelin bombing raids upon London, giving the song "Where Did That One Go?" additional meaning. Another member of Charlot's regulars was added in the person of a stagestruck Egyptologist named Arthur Weigall, who gave Monkman a Cleopatra ballet, complete with Sphinx. Weigall went on to become a true member of the family, marrying Muriel Lillie. Soon Weigall and Muriel were writing songs for Charlot shows.

These were excitingly troubled times for his professional life. By mid-1915 the ownership of the Alhambra had changed—it became part of the reshuffling and consolidation of theater holdings which characterized the West End's wartime. Perhaps partly from necessity but surely from an awareness of which way the winds were blowing, Charlot now decided to try something different, something small, and not at the Alhambra. For the moment he retained a managerial role for other productions there. The highly successful musical comedy (in fact, it had many of revue's strong points) *The Bing Boys Are Here* opened there in April 1916 and spent most of its long run under his management. (This was originally a Grossmith show but Grossmith, like many others in his profession, had found a congenial way to spend wartime in military service.)

It was November 1915 when Charlot entered the field of intimate revue. *Samples* opened at the Playhouse, a 679-seat house off the Strand, whose new lessee was Frank Curzon, a man generally committed to a policy of straight popular drama but apparently willing to take at least one gamble on something new. *Samples* (actually

Some More Samples of Odds and Ends) in every way confessed its indebtedness to its Cochran-Grattan progenitor. Imitation was ever the sincerest form of show business. But what is important for this account of Charlot's professional life is what he proceeded to do with the form—and what Cochran did not.

Cochran, ever the restless showman, did not linger long in "intimacy." Two intimate revues was plenty for "CB" and he was soon making new revues which seemed as large as their theaters would allow (the Ambassadors could never hold him). Eventually he dropped revue completely, as we shall see effectively leaving the genre to Charlot. He returned to it after the war when he saw how profitable Charlot had made it.

Perhaps Charlot's venture into intimate revue was purely experimental. But once he was there, he made the form his own. His progression from *Samples* through *Buzz-Buzz* (which opened just after the Armistice in 1918 and went on to be Charlot's longest-running show and the longest-running revue in British history) was largely one of refinement and astute attention to a demanding, impatient audience.

This progress owes a great deal to the wartime climate, not least in some easily overlooked facts. Among the entire youthful British generation decimated by the war were many lesser entertainers who had been unable to use connections to secure easy berths. In the large-scale revue, there were not vast (American-style) female choruses, but in fact mixed choruses. The outbreak and prolongation of war vastly reduced the supply of "chorus boys" for British shows.

When intimate revue emerged as a dominant form, it retained the chorus, but of a size commensurate with the small-scale theaters where they worked. These choruses were almost exclusively female and it was Charlot who realized that a chorus of approximately eight young women, chosen for their ability to sing as well as to dance, and to have enough intelligence to partake in sketches, was the way to the future. (In fact he founded his own chorus-training school.) It should also not be overlooked that in the crazy-quilt days of that war, soldiers arriving from the front for an evening of revue and other pleasures (they could arrive and leave whenever they wished) would also in an intimate revue enjoy a close-up look at pretty girls.

The Charlot policy referred to earlier was simplicity itself—there would, he decreed, be *no mention* of the war in any of his shows. During the final Alhambra shows the policy worked very well, especially by contrast to the various lugubrious patriotic interpolations characterizing other offerings of the London stage in general. Going to a Charlot show meant truly escaping.

But the reality of the war quickly spawned a "realistic" humor which was certainly noticeable in the shows which were put on near the battlefront itself. The policy would have to be overhauled in light of its audience's hard-won sophistication. In fact it was Grattan, the author of *Samples*, who can be credited with the first sallies along these lines.

Samples is built, if at all, around the plight of one Eustace Slackitt in finding his role in wartime. At the moment, "slacking," letting someone else shoulder your combat responsibilities (everyone was supposed to volunteer), was a hot topic. In creating Slackitt, Grattan also managed to rid revue of the *compère-commère* tradition. Slackitt (Melville Gideon) appeared in most of the evening's segments, pro-

ST JOHN'S WOOD

FAUCONNET

Fauconnet's drawing of "Removal" to 11a Cavendish Road, 1916.

viding a nominal thread of meaning for those choosy enough to look for one. And if he was not present, he *might* become present, so a few of what otherwise would have seemed unrelated "turns" could even be justified. *Samples*, hedging its bets, also declared it would harbor "no patriotic numbers!" But there was quite a note of wartime realism and urgency in songs like "Will You Be My Sweetheart for Tonight?" which stated clearly that "only for tonight" was the contemporary norm for romance.

The beginning of Charlot's career in intimate revue coincided almost exactly with an important change in his non-professional life. Was he betting on overwhelming success in his new ventures? The Charlot clan moved from the Marble Arch flat into a much larger world.

The house where they moved in early 1916 was in St. John's Wood, not far from Regents Park, whose recently refurbished zoo would become a regular family attraction. It was therefore well removed from the West End, suitable for Charlot's gentleman persona. Then as now, the St. John's Wood area would have been described in English terminology as a "leafy suburb"—that is, possessing enough room among the houses for trees to grow and prosper. The new Charlot residence, which had been built in 1846 and for a time was a girls' school, was located toward the bottom end of Cavendish Road, off the main Wellington Road thoroughfare. At the very bottom of Cavendish Road stood the home of English cricket, Lord's. A thoroughly desirable "establishment" residence, indeed.

When the Charlots decided upon the house, it was called number 13, but Charlot would have none of that. For the years of their residence, the house was 11a Cavendish Road. The French designer Fauconnet, a friend of Charlot's since childhood, and one of the artists who had helped him revolutionize the look of West End theater, provided a comical announcement of the Charlots' surely chaotic moving day.

11a Cavendish Road, which resumed its original number once the Charlots departed in the middle 1920s, was and is a rangy and very solid-feeling two-story house (with basement) set back from the street and possessing a lengthy back garden, all lawn and flower beds, at whose rear stood a mulberry tree. At the time, there

The house in St. John's Wood.

was a conservatory to the left of entry, which eventually filled with playing children, as well as dogs, including Paddy, an English sheepdog under the misapprehension that he was a lap dog, and Boogie, an overlarge black poodle. Paddy wound up dividing his time between the Charlots and the Actors' Orphanage.

The rooms at 11a were ample in size and high-ceilinged and there was a basement kitchen, from which would emerge the after-midnight suppers of scrambled eggs and bacon traditionally accompanying a Charlot opening night. On such an occasion a cook, housemaid and butler were highly present. The Charlot *ménage* must also have been enhanced by a nanny—it was what Charlot knew and it was what an impresario should have.

Zeppelin bombs, like the majority of bombs, did not fall with great discrimination and several hit leafy St. John's Wood. In 1917 one went through the roof of 11a Cavendish

Road, rendering the house uninhabitable. For the balance of the war and a while afterward the Charlot entourage decamped—including Tiny, another in the procession of Great Danes—to Bognor, where they took up residence with the Gladmans.

Before the exodus to Bognor, and before 1916 was out, Charlot, who often would be characterized by his reluctance to embrace new technologies, saw the merit in gramophone records and awarded—for £100—the exclusive right to record the revue *This and That*. Too bad it wasn't a better show. (In 1917 he granted similar rights to Columbia to record the musical comedy *Flora*, which was also not one of his best ventures.) It was also 1916 when Charlot indulged himself in an experiment—a double bill of *Pierrot's Christmas* (a wordless play) and *Poached Eggs and Pearls*, a two-act comedy. A mixture of a fantasy and a "novelty," the bill was critically well received but actually a money-loser. As one who trusted the audience above all other critics, Charlot was convinced of his necessary future direction—more and more intimate revues.

His progress (from *Samples* to *Buzz-Buzz*) toward a definitive form of intimate revue is also a record of the discovery of performers perfectly suited to the demands of revue, with its lightning-like shifts. But from the standpoint of theatrical history, of even greater importance was his understanding and nurturing of a new generation of authors. These changed the nature of the theatrical sketch.

After Lillie, Charlot's discovery of performing talent must be headlined by Gertrude Lawrence, who became her generation's most renowned stage actress on both sides of the Atlantic. In fact she was a discovery of one of Charlot's American discoveries—or perhaps two. It was one evening in Swindon, Wiltshire, quite definitely an out-of-town venue, when Lee White and her singing-dancing partner Clay Smith (they would eventually marry) were on a busman's holiday at the small local theater when they spotted Lawrence. They recommended her to Charlot, she auditioned for him, and soon she was in one of his revues, where, as almost everywhere else she worked, she almost immediately caused joy and consternation, simply because she was determined to go her own way. Charlot wound up firing her repeatedly and always took her back. "She was just a crazy kid," he wrote.

It is more difficult to say that Charlot "discovered" Jack Buchanan, who ultimately became the epitome of British sophistication on the musical stage and in film, rivaling the man who became known (particularly by himself) as the Master, Noel Coward.

Buchanan eventually escaped into his own entrepreneurial performing career, but only after his New York sensation with *Charlot's London Revue* there in 1924. By more than one account, Coward had been simply turned down after an audition for Charlot, who eventually bought songs from him. (In his own good time, the disciplinarian Charlot deemed that the youth had served his penance and hired him to write a revue, though only in collaboration with a more seasoned author-lyricist.)

As for discovering writers, Charlot was lucky to be in the right place at the right time. During the runup to war, a theatrical movement had begun throughout Great Britain which eventually ended revue's connection to its music-hall past. It is best called a local repertory movement and its main stated ambition was to bring to the attention of a wide audience (ideally a nationwide audience) the new developments in serious theater occurring throughout Europe and the United States. Thus confronted, young authors began to think differently.

Commercial success always being desirable for the struggling author, the newly trendy form of musical revue might prove a likely market. What this eventually meant was that revue sketches became an art form of their own, with beginnings, middles and ends—just like real plays—only compacted to the greatest degree (few ran beyond six minutes) and packing the greatest possible punch at their denouement. Musical revue thus generated and benefited from a couple of generations of sketch-writing specialists gifted with wide horizons.

Partly because of his French background, Charlot was already particularly partial to authors. The French Society of Authors, Composers and Publishers had since 1851 given authors absolute control over the production of their works—no play could open without a contract with the Society, no work could be performed unless the author was a member, a Society representative collected royalties every evening, no manager could run more than one theater, no author could take over a theater to run his own play, all casting was subject to the author's approval, if an author wanted to direct his play, no one could overrule him, and no manager could buy a play outright. Few if any of these restrictions applied in Britain—or in America—at the time, but Charlot's orientation was certainly toward the author. He added to these French notions another strong conviction: no actor *could* have a conception of a part separate from the author's.

One of the new authors—one very quickly snapped up by Charlot—was Ronald Jeans, who proved so durable and practiced in the field of playwriting that he eventually wrote a book on the subject. At the age of 24 in 1911, Jeans had been one of the founders of a regional repertory company in Liverpool. For them he wrote plays short and long and inevitably, beginning in 1915, revues that featured parodies of Gaby Deslys. Sooner or later these skills went on brief display when the rep visited London, where one reviewer noted that with Jeans, "humorous, genial satire is the salient of real revue" and Cochran (always the talent scout, whether actively engaged or not) called Jeans a writer of *real* revue, adding, "Revue should give the atmosphere of an impromptu entertainment, just as a cartoon of a great black and white artist appears to have been dashed off in a few moments." Cochran eventually signed Jeans to a contract, but it was Charlot who struck first.

When *Tabs* (1918) went into its second edition, it was Jeans whose work replaced much of the original, which had been written by Grattan. The changeover caused Charlot a good deal of grief. In May 1918 he had been taken to a military camp near London to see a revue staged by "Camp Shows." Its music was written by Ivor Novello with book and lyrics by "a newcomer, Ronald Jeans." Charlot was "tremendously impressed" by Jeans's wit and style and decided immediately that Jeans and Novello would be involved in his next revue.

Grattan had written *Tabs* and fully expected to write its second version. When Charlot asked the veteran author to collaborate with Jeans, Grattan was offended (Charlot commented unnecessarily that he had a tremendous ego), but he finally agreed to some additional scenes. Grattan carried through with his bargain, but not very graciously. Finally, Grattan asked Charlot to withdraw all his material from the second version "and left us in a huff." But Charlot believed that Jeans's contributions had already completely overshadowed Grattan's. A comment by the reviewer of the *Weekly Dispatch* must have twisted the knife: "Rarely has been seen so improved a revue."

A resume of one of Jeans's sketches may suggest why. For one thing, its mood was much more in line with rueful late-wartime feeling than the cheerful antics left over from the variety stage. In Jeans's "The Bystander," a series of one-on-one conversations centers upon a rose—a gift which passes between wife and husband to a typist, to her admirer, and finally to the wife again. Clearly Jeans knew his Arthur Schnitzler (*La Ronde*) but it did not matter whether his audience knew that or not. Jeans and the tribe of sketch writers who followed him further changed the nature of revue, which would now showcase quick, knowing wit.

The age of Grattan and revue as an offshoot of music hall was over whether anyone knew it. Still, Grattan's departure distressed Charlot. Looking backward from the 1950s he wrote, "I was very fond of Harry.... Unfortunately his (well-paid) success had gone to his head.... We did not speak for years."

Highlighting Charlot's progress from *Samples* to *Buzz-Buzz* does not mean dealing with every show. It is, however, worthwhile mentioning that during these years intimate revue found suitable London homes. The size of these homes contributed to revues' success. The theater-building boom which began in the 1880s had created a host of houses with capacities below 1,000.

Most congenial to Charlot during the years when he was remaking intimate revue was the Vaudeville in the Strand, run by John Maria Gatti and his brother Rocco. The Gattis descended from Italian-Swiss immigrants who from 1847 began making London's best coffee and ice cream, later branching out into music halls, theaters and very advanced restaurants. They even set up an electrical firm when it became necessary to keep their nearby holdings properly supplied. During wartime, the Gattis withstood the considerable pressure of theatrical chains from both sides of the ocean and went their own way with Charlot as their chief benefactor. Exactly how congenial the relationship can be surmised in this outburst from a theater critic in 1922:

> What merry, bright little pieces they continue to give at the Vaudeville! Walk into the Vaudeville, and you are certain to be amused. It is absolutely frivolous entertainment, destitute of vulgarity ... a hotch-potch of clever nonsense. The Vaudeville has done for years what the Co-Optimists have done for months.

The Co-Optimists, a rather inspired glorified concert party along the lines of Pelissier, had become a major hit during 1921—and worse, it had taken, at least momentarily, Phyllis Monkman, courtesy of one of the Co's, Laddie Cliff, who had married her. The Gattis remained great professional friends and benefactors. A dozen years later, in an hour of drastic need, Charlot turned to the Gattis once more and they responded.

The smaller theaters also afforded Charlot the opportunity to "expand the business," always a fond goal of his, and by the mid-war years he was essentially operating two revue companies, which meant that there was almost always a new Charlot revue or a new version of a revue on tap for the theatergoer-leavetaker. Feeling himself on the crest of a wave which showed no signs of a backlash, in 1917 Charlot committed himself to a 14-year lease on the Prince of Wales Theater just off Leicester Square in the direction of the regal Haymarket.

The burgeoning popularity of intimate revue also made it possible, despite the shrinkage of the male talent pool, to secure more-than-adequate replacements for any male principals who went into military service. This was the case in 1917 with Jack Hulbert, a comic and dancer with a huge chin who had been partnering Monkman since early 1916. When Hulbert's comfortable sequence of postings to training camps around London finally ran out and he had to head eastward to entertain other troops, Charlot was able to bring Buchanan in (i.e., discover him)—but not without a little panic.

The Scotsman Buchanan had actually been spotted in a road company of the moderately successful musical comedy *Tonight's the Night* by Monkman's sister Dorothy. She persuaded Phyllis to come along and see him. The verdict? "He looked wonderful, he had charm, he could dance, he could do everything." When Hulbert was called up, Charlot discovered to his horror that the previously assigned understudy really could do none of these things. Dorothy went in search, finding Buchanan in a scene characteristic of the roles he would play, lunching at the Trocadero with one of Charlot's chorus girls.

The entertainer Douglas Byng later used part of his autobiography to describe the effect created by the dancing team of Phyllis Monkman and Buchanan:

> They both looked as though they had been out all night and they probably had. But in any case it was a lazy sort of tap dance they did together which was very nostalgic. It wasn't the usual "full of zip and pep" type of dancing. It was almost languid and it was very attractive. In its way it was quite sensational because they even had a finale which wasn't a finale. It was a sort of "the party's over now" number. That was most unusual then because I don't think anybody else had ever tried this before.

Although one would never have characterized a Charlot revue as "languid," the Buchanan-Monkman dances clearly harmonized quite well with shows created by a man who appreciated "genius without effort" or at least its likeness. This particular revue, *Bubbly*, had its literary side, too, including a sequence of four short playlets using the same plot—including one in the style of O. Henry, another called "Muck" which spoofed rugged naturalism, an Oscar Wilde parody and a "confession." Buchanan handled them all. During the run, a young woman named Marjorie Robertson was in her own words "one of the vast numbers of hopefuls queuing for one of his famous revues." Later known as one of her country's most beloved performers, Dame Anna Neagle made the grade at 32 shillings (less than a pound and a half) for her first half-week. But, she rationalized, they had steak and chips to eat during rehearsals. When later Cochran realized the value of a Charlot-style chorus, he of course poached Robertson/Neagle.

It was during the run of *Bubbly* that Charlot was able to settle the score with his old mentor and adversary Flers. A French entrepreneur named Volterra, who was a program seller at the Olympia Music Hall in Paris when Charlot met him in 1900, came to London with a proposal: he was preparing a revue for the Casino de Paris and wanted to borrow Monkman and Buchanan. (It seems remarkable that, being such a prize, Paris was able to continue life pretty much as normal during most of the war and ordinary travel between Britain and France continued.)

As the two worked out the details, Charlot was reminded that Flers was the overall director of revue at the Casino. The subsequent contract specified that Flers could not interfere with Charlot's staging of the Buchanan-Monkman segments nor could he even speak to Charlot or either of the two performers. Eventually a brief armistice was arranged during rehearsals, during which Flers and Charlot straightened out some difficulties with the production—but without reconciling. In fact, recalled Charlot with some glee, they often turned against Volterra! Finally, Flers could not stand it any longer and withdrew from his connection to Volterra—which, it turned out, was exactly what Volterra wanted in the first place.

The period between *Samples* and *Buzz-Buzz* is also interesting for the insights provided by Charlot's account books. (These, it should be said, are among the most closely guarded business documents in Britain, a land where "commercial secrets" are deemed inaccessible.) As we have seen, Charlot paid as little as possible to his employees while living his personal life to the edge of his income and beyond. In 1916, for example, he signed Rebla, a juggler whom he gradually built into a good comic performer, for a minimum of eight weeks at £25 weekly—quite a goodly sum. At the same time he signed chorus performers for a year (!) at £2½ pounds per week. Another 1917 revue, *Cheep*, made excellent use of the austerity of the age by opening with the same number which had closed *Some* and included such lines as "We had to cut down our dresses. The censor can't have it both ways."

A young man named Noel Coward later wrote of seeing this show and realizing that Lillie was a comic genius. The show was also notable because Lawrence was given her first chance at doing a revue's lead numbers. Lillie had set up the situation by arranging at the last moment to be "sick," although she was spotted—by Charlot himself—at a performance of *Chu Chin Chow*, a musical version of "Ali Baba and the Forty Thieves" that proved the most popular musical comedy of wartime. But her Dada could never stay angry at Bea.

Cheep divided its profits among Smith, White, Grattan (the printed copy of the libretto is stamped "Property of H. Grattan") and Charlot. Notably, White and Smith were soon "on their own" and as we have seen, Grattan, who had rated equal billing with Charlot on a provincial tour of *Some*, was not long for this employment.

Elsewhere the account books show that in April 1917 Charlot engaged himself as manager of ACH, Ltd., a company which proceeded to sell £20,000 in shares in itself. The incorporation was accompanied by a loan of £4,000 from Mr. K. Heistein of Lancaster Gate. Later in 1917 Charlot secured a two-year option on two French plays, *La Reine S'Amuse* and *Son Petit Frère*. It was also 1917 when Charlot, still operating wherever he could, booked a Gaby Deslys (with Harry Pilcer) show into Manchester for a week. He was promised "65 percent of the gross." In 1918 Charlot managed to extract £3,000 from B.J. Redman to finance the production of

Tabs at the Vaudeville and in the same year an H.D. McIntosh had secured—till 1920—the Australian and New Zealand rights to all of Charlot's London productions. By this time Charlot was operating out of an office at 6 Arundel Street just off Fleet Street. His stationery showed quite an attractive logo, a capital A inside a larger capital C, which nearly formed a circle.

Exactly how much Charlot was intending to expand the business can be surmised from a glance at the plans for a planned tour of "the revue which opened at the Prince of Wales 13 September 1918." In the end there was no such revue but *Buzz-Buzz*, which opened at the Vaudeville in December, made history. In this almost-tour, however, there were 44 separate venues and subsequent Charlot tours followed its pattern.

It was in 1918 that Bea Lillie got Charlot to agree to listen to a friend of hers one afternoon just before rehearsal. According to the friend (Noel Coward) Charlot "informed her afterwards that he would not have his valuable time wasted on trivial young composers who played the piano badly and sang worse, and that never in any circumstances was she to do such a thing again." Naturally, Charlot remembered it differently. Or rather, he insisted he didn't remember it at all. According to Charlot, Coward, "an awkward, lanky youth of 18," came to the Comedy Theatre and offered him a song:

> Doris Joel, daughter of the millionaire Sally Joel, brought Coward to see me. I had probably seen Coward before, but had no reason to remember him. He had been on the stage from the age of ten, with no more, but no less success than a boy of his years could expect, and he came to me as an actor who wanted to be a writer. This is what he had written:
>
>> Peter Pan has had to do the latest dance;
>> Wendy too thought she would like to take a chance;
>> Captain Hook was really most disgusted;
>> Smee and Starky seemed to look quite flustered,
>> And pretty little Tinker Bell
>> Said to Peter Pan,
>> "Clap your hands if you believe in fairies,
>> And come and dance as well"
>
> Whereupon Coward sat down at the piano.... I must say that even then he knew how to put a song over.
>
> I bought "The Story of Peter Pan" on the spot, for a sum which I have forgotten, and put it into my revue Tails Up in June 18.... If the words were not the first of Noel Coward's work to be sung or spoken on any stage, I know of none earlier.

Both versions sound plausible, not least because each description makes its author look good.

Between the end of 1915 and the middle of 1918, while Grattan gave way to Jeans (and John Hastings Turner, Dion Titheradge, Arthur Wimperis and other younger, more astringent authors), the "feel" of intimate revue gradually changed. It had actually achieved a basic form before *Buzz-Buzz*. But the tale of that revue is worth the telling, not least for the way it shows—and it certainly must have seemed so to Charlot, shuttling between London and Bognor—that the luck was all running his way.

The show had been on the drawing boards as *Coupons* in reference to the ever more ubiquitous rationings of later wartime—the unthinkable, rationing bread, was actually scheduled for 1919. Its sketches and songs were generally designed to carry this motif through the evening. But late in the game Charlot discovered that a "provincial producer" had already taken that name and was threatening legal action or at least a financial deal. What to do? By this time, of course, Charlot, an excellent publicity man, saw that creating a little more mystery about the show's name would probably be a good thing.

Then the war ended, quite suddenly, with the show set to open in just a few weeks' time. *Buzz-Buzz* profited immensely from the timing and another stroke of Charlot luck or astuteness. As opening day neared, Charlot had posters out front of the Vaudeville painted to call it ---- ----. Conjecture raged. A fairly large portion of press and public settled on *Jazz Jazz* as the surprise (he had seen to that, too). It was the first new show to open after the Armistice and audiences flocked to it. Eventually it ran for more than 600 performances, the best record of all his shows. As a concrete example of what English intimate revue was like at the end of the war, here is a tour of *Buzz-Buzz*.

An opening in which the cast of twelve sang about the onerous task of "waiting for the star" was followed by the arrival of a famous explorer (the star, Nelson Keys, hardly a Charlot regular—Charlot was already livid over his proclivity to keep all the clothing specially ordered for him to wear in a show and even to order more!—but quite a draw) at "St Victorialoo Station" and the gradual introduction of the other principals, including Lawrence as a lady taxi driver.

Within the opening sequence was "Who Killed Missis Grundy?" a Jeans lyric alluding—quite carefully—to changes in morals during wartime, as well as a laddish song-of-a-type, "There Are So Many Girls Around Me," which evoked the old days of musical comedy. In fact this opening sequence, notable for its concise rendering of such types, can be read as a hail-and-farewell to olden days and a preface to the new.

A comic sketch, "The Merchant of Venison," displayed the motif of rationing coupons as well as demanding from its viewers a fair bit of Shakespearean knowledge. (It was also timely since London had just experienced a Shakespeare season.) A song, "I've Been Waiting for Someone Like You," brought Gertie back with the current Charlot heartthrob Walter Williams. Its denouement packed the revue "punch," when lovey-doveyism gives way to fact: "I've been waiting for someone richer than you." No coupons here. A "Christmas 1918" sketch does get back to the theme of wartime deprivation as the elders simply cannot stop themselves from taking over the children's toys. Another song-and-dance, a romp against a slightly spooky backdrop, is followed by "Coupons for Kisses," a slightly saucy sketch featuring a song and terrible puns having to do with coupons. At the first act finale, all is revealed—"Everything Is Buzz-Buzz Now" enlists the entire company in a number crafted around "buzz," a slang term currently "hot" and very flexible—one might even call it a "buzz word." When audiences filed into the street at intermission, they found *Buzz-Buzz* freshly painted on the theater posters.

Charlot's sense of timing was acute. The first act took exactly one hour and eight minutes. The second act opened with Lawrence in a fully-staged "Winnie the Window-Cleaner," another slightly "blue" evocation of slipping moral standards as seen from the outside. Then came another Jeans sketch, "Home at Last," in which newlyweds take 11 minutes to try to cope with wartime-caused shortages in their new home. Perhaps these two will not be able to overcome the lack of coal for heating? The song "Live and Let Live" suggests with a good deal of sharpness that a generosity of spirit, while often a cover for selfishness, might actually benefit other people. Lawrence returned in a spoof of current "exotic" song and story in "I Left My Heart in Maori-Land" and Keys followed with "If I Went into Parliament." A sketch and lyric by Wimperis, "Miss Sunshine and Mister Rain," subliminally evoked "Coupons for Kisses," being pretty obviously staged within the same sparse setting—in fact a creation of Weigall, whose head and heart now seemed a long way removed from Egypt. It also provided something "cute" within the general astringency—the yearnings between the familiar figures on a tiny barometer, the likes of which could be found in many a contemporary home.

The interpolated American hit "K-k-k-katy" allowed the audience to learn and sing along. The lengthy closing sequence (29 minutes) managed some wartime references but nothing really about coupons, unless the doings of hoarders (one is suspected of hiding in a closet—"Well then, it's the very place for sealed hoarders") are allowed into that category. In his autobiography, Keys later wrote that during this complicated number, at a moment when he was under threat, his children, seated in a theater box, shouted down, "Don't you shoot our Daddy!" Charlot was all for giving them a season ticket so they could do it every night. A raucous "Corpse-Reviver Rag," lampooning a cocktail craze as well as the pretty well worn ragtime craze, brought down the curtain. *Buzz-Buzz* had run to 10:25, leaving its audiences plenty of time for more postwar celebration.

Buzz-Buzz also succeeded with the critics: "Who shall say that revue is not intellectual?" *(The Times)* "Brains has gone to the sticking together of this revue from whatever angle one regards it" (*The Sportsman*).

But how had all this happened? The show lacked virtually all of Charlot's "regulars" (it would be another year before Gertie blossomed into a star). No Bea, no

June modeling the very essence of her appealing sweetness.

Lee White, no Jack Buchanan. *The Sketch* had in fact puzzled before the opening, "For the first time in the recollection of any playgoer, a piece has been produced in London without a name on the programme." Just a show that was the 1918–19 epitome of intimate revue. Charlot's *Buzz-Buzz* success increased throughout the run. In early 1920 an M. Edward Bandran was granted "Indian and Far Eastern rights" to *Buzz-Buzz*. This meant that it might be seen from Greece to the Dutch East Indies.

The run of *Buzz-Buzz* was further distinguished by yet another Charlot "discovery":

> Armed with a letter from his old friend Harry Abrahams, who was my uncle, I met Charlot [wrote June—then June Tripp—in her autobiography The Glass Ladder] in his comfortable, book-lined room, dark yet cozy, with deep armchairs and a baby grand. Charlot rose behind his desk, held out his hand.... [He was] tall, broad-shouldered, with a dome-like forehead, and an awe-inspiring way of looking at you down his handsome, high-bridged nose. He had considerable charm and a slight French accent. With fingertips together, he said, "I completed casting this morning. My only suggestion is that you come into my chorus."

June, who became one of the "feathery-dancing" stars of her era with a kewpie voice to match, found the suggestion not at all "lowering"—the Charlot girls already were known for their talent and personality and usually got a line or two of dialogue. And after all, Charlot was always on the lookout for future stars. Although June's mother was not pleased (nor with the £4 weekly salary, since as a precocious teenager she was already making £35), June accepted.

Lawrence, Buchanan, Teddie Gerrard, Douglas Furber and Maisie Gay confronting (or pleading before) "the Gov," probably inspired by Charlot's legendary reluctance to pay competitive salaries.

June gave an insider's view of working with Charlot. Rehearsals were like "a cocktail party without the cocktails"—small groups forming and dissolving as greetings were exchanged, hands shaken, cheeks kissed, cigars offered and lighted. Gertrude Lawrence clued her in: she was "Lawrie" and Charlot "Guv'nor" or "Guv." The girls who had been with Charlot longest had the best places at the communal dressing table, close to a coal fire in winter and open windows in the summer. June got to understudy Lawrence's "Winnie" number—with not much success. Charlot tossed her a sheet of music and asked her "to arrange a dance for the new Cairo number." But she had to choose her costume from the existing stock—"part of a clever scheme for avoiding swollen heads." June's career lifted off with her Charlot

Charlot (left) and Maurice Chevalier "boxing" at Bognor Regis.

experience. At the end of the run of *Buzz-Buzz* June was making £10 weekly. She told Charlot that when she worked for him again, he would have to pay £100. And she banged the door shut. Charlot mused, "And she means it and one day I WILL pay her £100." Fifteen years later, he did.

During the family's "exile" in Bognor, Charlot appears to have created an aura of nearly constant celebration. He invited his professional family down for holidays and weekends, meanwhile pressing his inside–London connections for the best of everything, including, undoubtedly, many a crate of black market food. Charlot-in-Bognor lingered long in the memory of Jonny, who seventy years later could recall the fun of hiding with Philip and seeing Lillie pursued and kissed by a local admirer in the summer Bognor twilight, the bluff camaraderie of Charlot and an old friend called Maurice Chevalier staging impromptu boxing matches in the garden and of long, long ocean swims by her magisterial brother-in-law, swims so prolonged that the young ones feared he would never return.

In Leeds in June 1918, a daughter was born to the third eldest Gladman girl and fourth child Maud (called Mip by all the family) and Jimmy Hennessy, a dashing, hard-drinking man. There were difficulties from the beginning. Mip had had rheumatic fever when she was 14, and not long after the birth, mother and baby Joan returned to Bognor, where Mip's health worsened. Jonny became the infant's virtual full-time caregiver. Two years later, Joan would become the adopted daughter of André and Flip and acquire Philip as a big brother.

FIVE

1919–1923

Transatlantic Days

The years between *Buzz-Buzz* and the Charlot invasion of New York in 1924 are in professional terms a record of "expanding the business." There doesn't seem much that Charlot believed he could not tackle in those days. However, a retrospective glance at this era reveals yearnings and weaknesses that would eventually bring him woe.

In 1916 he had been supplied by Ziegfeld with a short film called "The Amazing Rehearsal." As part of *5064 Gerrard* it was not particularly successful since the American performers were generally unfamiliar to a British audience, and in any event in those days of British revue, film was used mainly as a clearer-outer—it finished the music-hall bill, just following the revue.

Despite the reputation he gained by his innovations in revue, in many ways Charlot was deeply conservative both personally and professionally and certainly one who perceived everywhere great threats to the business of the theater. One of these threats, of course, was film, and yet in 1917 he and Weigall entered into a tentative partnership to produce "AC Films"—André Charlot Film Productions under the direction of Arthur Weigall, with offices at Garbrand Hall, Ewell, Surrey.

One of the ambitious Weigall scenarios, "The Spirit of Adventure," was purchased by Charlot for an advance of £100 and a promise of rather generous royalties. As manager, Charlot proceeded to engage Bannister Merwin, a man of some experience, to produce the film (in line with contemporary British stage practice and terminology, "produce" really meant "direct," while "manage" really meant "produce"). The film was scheduled to begin shooting at the outset of September 1917, starring Monkman, by then a proven box-office attraction. Contractually, Charlot made sure that Monkman's stage duties (at the moment, *Bubbly*) would take precedence over the film. In October, Charlot agreed to increase Merwin's production budget. But this project came to nothing.

Early in 1918 Charlot hired Lieutenant A. Simmons of Liverpool for two years as "expert advisor." As an overriding presence, Simmons would be responsible for making just about all the decisions regarding film properties and production, with the exception of "star *artiste*." As was typical of Charlot, however, money was in short supply and in fact was dependent upon AC's ability to charm backers. One such, the same Mr. Heistein previously mentioned, seems to have been involved in André Charlot Film Productions and finally did not have, or at any rate, did not put up, the required funds. No films emerged and the studio finally folded up, showing losses from which at least Weigall was apparently able to escape. The association between Weigall and Charlot endured, though Charlot never got around to producing a play of Weigall's called ironically enough *The Opportunity*.

Charlot's admiration for cinema lingered and a small portion of his stage work actually did find its way onto film. For a time a documentary series called "Around the Town" was a regular part of cinema programs in Britain, alongside other regular features providing brief footage of current theatrical offerings.

Number 114 of the series includes a Charlot sketch called "Quantity Street" (Quality Street was and is a brand of English chocolates, particularly popular during holidays). In the excerpt committed to (silent, of course) film, Bea Lillie is an apparently *grande dame* who responds to the antics of a one-man band by slapping her knees and otherwise behaving raucously. All in all, nine players are onstage, representing all sorts of "quality" street person, but one by one they are put off by Bea's coarseness and leave the stage. Finally, a title tells us, when she puns "A horse may be driven but a pencil must be lead" they return to the stage and try to drag her away, kicking and screaming. Yet she insists on finishing!

"A Few Glimpses of the Revue 'Puss Puss'" (1921) includes Bert Coote in a parody of the popular detective Bulldog Drummond. Dressed in a long coat, he struggles with a dummy. In another sequence, Lee White and Clay Smith dance with eight "penguins."

Charlot's private life during these years was a mixture of tumult and of considerably greater contentedness. Not long after the war's conclusion, the Charlots were able to reoccupy 11a Cavendish Road and when Mip died in 1920, leaving baby Joan informally in Jonny's care, her wish that her daughter live with the Charlots as their own was honored without hesitation. So Joan, at first accompanied by Jonny, moved in to complete the family.

Though a joyful event for the Charlots, Joan's father was opposed to the arrangement and attempted to remove her, at least once by force. She was formally adopted in 1922 and Hennessey was not to be heard of again. Perhaps it was the sheer public image and reputation of Charlot at his most magisterial; he was clearly a successful man possessed of resources.

For several years, the family's life at Cavendish Road appears to have been idyllic. The arrival of the small girl seems to have allowed Charlot to locate and act out feelings that were truly paternal, not merely paternalistic. Jonny's relationship with Joan, combining the functions of aunt, elder sister and surrogate mother, has survived all their other close relationships. A generally benign relationship between Joan and Philip, her senior by eight years, evolved. Though his manner was sometimes aloof, he read her bedtime stories and, as the years passed, was willing to help her with her schoolwork. Whether Philip was repeating an earlier good fortune of his own or had decided to give to Joan what he had never received is unclear. Joan's arrival probably meant a great deal to Philip, whose childhood had already left him with damaged vision because of a siege of whooping cough.

The general joyfulness of Cavendish Road traveled with the Charlots when they visited the Gladmans, particularly at holiday times. As much of the far-flung family as possible, including the French branch, would gather together. It would never be really Christmas until André and Flip and the entire entourage, which might include the inevitable Great Dane and the occasional badly behaved monkey, arrived by chauffeur-driven car. Even when he worked within walking distance of his home, Charlot went by special motor.

To the Christmas celebrations Charlot always brought armsful of surprises, games and books like *Peter Pan*. He always presided, of course, over the gift-givings. It was he who was in charge of the "table fireworks" which somehow he managed without setting anything else aflame. The "well-pickled" Christmas pudding—made by Tillie and containing hidden silver charms—could be ignited only by Charlot. He frequently sent Flip to the gathering ahead of time; beautifully dressed and wearing a fresh orchid, she was the picture of elegance getting off the train. (Charlot was never seen out of formal attire except when swimming in the sea.)

When Christmas was held at Cavendish Road, the celebrations were similar.

Joan "Jonny" Gladman as a teenager (courtesy of Peter R. Gay).

Sunday visits to the zoo in Regents Park were occasions where Charlot managed to charm the keepers into special viewing privileges for his guests of all ages. The usual Charlot animals were all there at St. John's Wood, supplemented by a cockatoo called Cocky with a vocabulary limited to "A piece of apple pie!" Charlot awarded Cocky to the Gladmans, who eventually gave him back to the zoo.

During these years, the menagerie was increased by a rabbit given to Philip by Tillie. The rabbit became fiercer as time went on and bit the legs of the players at back garden tennis. The family often played mah jong, the craze of the era and a rarity for Charlot, who generally preferred intense games of bridge with other fanatics.

Professionally, the years succeeding *Buzz-Buzz* were for Charlot a case of onward and upward, pure and simple. He was able to manage his new leasehold on the Prince of Wales Theatre successfully, occasionally subleasing it to Grossmith and his partner Edward Laurillard, as well as allowing other impresarios such as (Sir) Alfred Butt to produce work there. Among

Charlot's own Prince of Wales ventures was *Dede* (1922), a musical comedy adapted by Jeans from a French original. He was still developing Gertude Lawrence's talent and this was her first venture outside the realm of revue.

Charlot was soon staging shows in as many as five theaters at a time. In 1919, he flung his enterprises far afield, staging a tour of *Bubbly* in South Africa. Of course he did not accompany the company. In one of his "legitimate" plays at the Prince of Wales he managed the London debut of an actor named Ronald Colman. A triumph followed by tragedy was Charlot's engagement of Will Marion Cook's Southern Syncopated Orchestra (featuring a brilliant young clarinetist called Sidney Bechet) at the Philharmonic in early 1919; most of the company was later lost at sea whilst en route to another engagement.

The musical theater branch of the British entertainment world indeed could be interpreted as having fallen at Charlot's feet. By the end of the war the *only* revues were intimate revues *à la Charlot*. DeCourville had gone into eclipse in the later war years when his ostentatious shows could be supported neither economically nor morally. (As has been previously hinted, Charlot's shows, meantime, gleefully exploited the joys of perpetual shortage, which meant a reliance upon perpetual invention.) DeCourville did stage a brief and opulent post-war comeback with a revue which brought the Original Dixieland Jazz Band from the States—for one performance, that is. DeCourville's star gave an "it's either them or me" ultimatum and the jazzmen were gone. But only just around the corner, where they took up residence in a night club for many months.

The influence of the Original Dixieland Jazz Band is accurately labeled as the beginning of Britain's enthusiasm for jazz and therefore the source of what soon was a golden age of British dance bands. The message was not lost on deCourville, who shortly gave up on spectacular revue, started his own night club, and hired the best dance bands. It should be noted that from the beginning this "golden age" was not meant for the everyday Briton—that was not the British way. It was for people entitled and equipped to afford the best clubs and hotels. But it was only a few years before radio (the new British Broadcasting Company or BBC) changed all that. The surging success of the bands owed everything to the nightly airings from posh places, and the bands got better and better with the influx of American sidemen and the development of native talent. Many of the leaders of the new hotel and club bands were American, including the Massachusetts man Carroll Gibbons, well ensconced at the glittering Savoy Hotel (one of Charlot's career-long favorites) by the middle of the decade. It is difficult to get a line on what Charlot may have thought of all this dancing—he was no dancer himself—but about radio he held very strong opinions indeed.

Though eschewing revue, C.B. Cochran had had one of the era's biggest theatrical hits—a stage version of a popular cartoonist's views of the war called *The Better 'Ole* (as in, "if you can find a better [fox]hole, go to it"). After the end of the war and a sojourn promoting boxing and wrestling, he returned to revue. His new stars were sequels to the recently deceased Deslys, the Dolly Sisters, Rosie and Jenny. The Dollys even claimed some of Deslys's admirers, including the amorous department-store magnate Gordon Selfridge, Jr. But for the moment Cochran had given the field away. He further cooperated in Charlot's ascendancy by slipping into bank-ruptcy in 1924; it would be two years after that before Cochran understood how to make first-class revues again. He managed that in the simplest way: just hire Char-lot's people.

Of greater current importance to Charlot circa 1920–22 was the renewal of British-American musical theater, which had reasonably enough languished during the later years of the war and its early aftermath. But at the outset of the Twenties, as America lifted off on the "biggest spree in history," Britain was in every way becalmed. Call it pre–Depression, call it pre–Slump. The general mood was malaise and it lasted.

At this time, the British–American musical theater ran only in a single direc-tion. By 1922 American popular composers were writing original musical come-dies—and in one case (George Gershwin) a revue score—for London. Kern, working now with British–Americans Guy Bolton and P.G. Wodehouse, who had helped him create America's mold-breaking wartime "Princess theater musicals," was turn-ing out a show a year for Grossmith, now happily riding this latest transatlantic wave. When Gershwin arrived to find himself already famous for "Swanee" (he said, "I thought they thought I was Kern or somebody"), he found not only deCourville but Grossmith's team ready to sign him up. Cole Porter was already contributing songs to Cochran revues and by the end of the decade was writing whole original shows for the West End.

But who was there to carry the British message to Broadway? Charlot's earlier visits to New York had left him with a strong desire for success there. Though he was able to hide this dream from the London theatrical world pretty effectively, that did not stop him in the early postwar years from trying to line up the producers, the theater and the company for an invasion of Broadway. The first signs came in 1919, when he talked a backer, Raymond Pollak, into advancing £2,250—at the then-current rate of exchange a good $10,000—£250 for the cost of travel and £2,000 on deposit in a New York bank, for a jaunt to New York to line up talent for London and make soundings for just such an invasion.

Charlot sailed from Liverpool on February 1 on the *Carmania*, making sure to carry one of two cases of champagne with him. This was not a response, Charlot wrote, to the looming Prohibition amendment in the States, but because "we have always found champagne to be a pleasant antidote to the bad temper of the sea." As further insurance, Charlot had the second case placed aboard the *Adriatic*, then in New York, which was the ship he intended to return on: "New York is a lone-some spot when one is poor, the one spot of the world where success counts for every-thing."

The trip produced variable results. A number of performers signed up for Char-lot's forthcoming London revue *Bran Pie* (a major hit at the Prince of Wales), but subsequently broke their contracts, including one of its principals, Florence Lewis. But *Bran Pie* (the title refers to a British version of "grab bag" in which the good-ies are hidden in a tub of bran), largely built around Lillie, proved a worthy suc-cessor to *Buzz-Buzz*, even surviving the departure of Lillie in December 1919 to become Lady Robert Peel. Peel was a baronet with occasional financial difficulties who eventually agreed to become one of Charlot's theater managers. White and Smith returned to the Charlot fold to shore up the second version, but stayed only five of their promised ten weeks, whereupon Monkman and Buchanan returned and order was restored. A third version featured Jack Hulbert and Odette Myrtil, as well as the juggler Rebla.

Charlot described *Bran Pie*, somewhat mysteriously, as "the type of revue I had had in mind for a long time, and I had been tremendously keen to produce, ever since the Alhambra days. I also decided to try a new system, that of having entirely new versions of a show." (He carried this system through with great success two years later.) *Bran Pie* also survived for a time the serious illness of Charlot, who proceeded from a thrombosis caused by an operation for appendicitis to double pneumonia.

The 1919 trip to New York had, however, produced other results. Charlot acquired from the legendary George M. Cohan material which was used in *Bran Pie* and from other sources several additional sketches by various authors intended for use in later offerings. A number of these were actually produced in the U.K. provinces. He acquired the rights to present *Three Wise Fools* in Britain (shortly presented at the Comedy) from another legendary personage, John L. Golden, one of the original White Rats, the actors' organization which had successfully challenged the big syndicates' monopolization of American theater.

Most interesting of the 1919 deals, but perhaps most disappointing to Charlot, were two abortive partnerships. One was with Charles B. Maddock, whom he had met during his New York foray of 1909–10. Maddock was manager and partner for B.A. Rolph's enterprises. Maddock and Charlot envisioned a New York version of *Charlot's Revue* built around Monkman and Buchanan, as well as a New York production of the straight play *The Officer's Mess*, already a success in London and on tour, starring Ralph Lynn, one of Charlot's regulars. The other, originally prompted by Lee Shubert's attempts to steal the Maddock deal, was with Shubert himself. Two separate corporations—Charmad for revue and Charbert for *The Officer's Mess*— were formed, though all three were partners in both.

Once back in London, Charlot proceeded to sign up Monkman (an exclusive "first refusal" contract for five years), Buchanan and others for the New York revue, and at salaries which must have caused his frugal heart many a flutter—£1,000 weekly for Monkman, plus steamship fare, and "not more than £500" for Buchanan. (Buchanan eventually agreed to a "five-year refusal" deal and £500 weekly, providing he got equal billing with Monkman.) However, various subsequent occurrences, particularly the historic Actors' Strike in New York, caused Maddock and Shubert to back off, and although Charlot sent his accountant to New York late in the year to revive the deal, Maddock and Shubert refused and the plans were abandoned.

The connection between Charlot and Grossmith continued; in 1920 Charlot commissioned an English version of *La Reine S'Amuse* so "GG" could have a go. It was at least an artistic success. On the personal front, Charlot's frequent returns to France during these years included a lengthy stay in Nice with Flip and Philip. On the trip, Charlot paid an obligatory visit to the casino in Monte Carlo, though he did not record its outcome. By 1922 Charlot was regularly staging the annual Theatrical Garden Party for the benefit of the Actors' Orphanage Fund. In the gardens of the Royal Hospital, Chelsea, the casts of Charlot companies such as *Bubbly* and *Rats* entertained most regally.

Early in 1922 Jessie Matthews became a part of Charlot's professional life. Three decades later, when he was preparing to write *People 'n Things*, Charlot recalled the event:

> Vivid in my mind is Jessie Matthews as I saw her first, among a crowd of candidates for the chorus of one of my revues. It had been a morning of hard work. Girl after girl had stepped forward, sung and said her little pieces, answered a few questions, and stepped back again. Out of hundreds who had applied for places in the chorus, only about a dozen remained. And suddenly one of them walked out of line to the front of the stage, leaned over, and said to me "What do you mean by keeping us waiting all this time? I want my lunch." I gasped. That I should be so addressed in my own theatre by a mere child, not yet 15, was beyond belief. Her eyes flashed and she stamped her little feet. "What a little spitfire," I said to myself, "What personality." By all the rules I ought to have ordered her out of the theatre. Instead I was knocked speechless by admiration of her colossal nerve. All the other girls were staring at her in horror. "What is your name?" I asked. "Jessie Matthews," she replied. "Very well, Miss Matthews," I said, "you may go and have your lunch." As she started off, I called after her, "And you may come back." Everybody must have wondered why I said that—everybody but my chorus mistress, Carrie Graham. She knew that I had already decided to give Jessie Matthews a job, so impressed had I been by her. From the moment I clapped eyes on her, I was sure that she was destined to make a big name. Her very petulance was an attractive part of her personality.

So Charlot put her in the chorus and for a while put up with the very same kind of unorthodox behavior that had caused him to fire Lawrence repeatedly. She amused Charlot; he added, "She could bring me to the brink of rage, and instantly turn the frown into a smile ... I could see how far Jessie Matthews was going."

Matthews chafed in the chorus for a while and, when the opportunity arose, decamped to Cochran, doing a number or two in his imported version of Irving Berlin's *Music Box Revue* (1923) before re-entering Charlot's troupe in a complex manner thoroughly typical of her character.

Charlot's devotion to "expanding the business" resulted in a fascinating sidewards step in 1922 when *The Midnight Follies* opened at the Hotel Metropole in Whitehall near the Houses of Parliament. (Charlot and his friend and co-producer Paul Murray had "warmed up" for this venture with a 1921 revue called *Pot Luck*, which was subtitled "A cabaret show in two acts.") *The Midnight Follies* was London's first foray into the field of full-fledged cabaret in hotels or restaurants (the few floor shows which had been presented were in private clubs) undertaken in alliance with Grossmith, Murray, A.E. Malone and Francis Towle, who was the managing director of the Hotel Metropole and its satellite hotels throughout the U.K. Everything along these general lines had previously been limited to six "turns" by ruling of the London City Council, which at the moment was the licensing authority.

In the early months of its existence, and while Towle put what he thought were the finishing touches on his negotiations with the LCC, the *Midnight Follies* offered exactly this six-turn format. But after the show proved such a success in Towle's hotel in seaside Brighton, the time seemed right to open in London. On December 5, a cast of twelve headed by Gertie, Tex McLeod (a storyteller in the Will Rogers vein) and Carl Hyson (who had arranged the dances and ensembles for *Pot Luck* and was the husband and longtime dancing partner of expatriate American Dorothy Dickson, now the most glamorous of West End musical leading ladies) opened a full-fledged show at the Metropole.

The show went on every evening "Sundays excepted" for £2, "including supper" and offering an evening of dancing which began at 9:30 and the "follies" from 11:10 onwards. It was a lavish show in the Charlot sense of the word, with costumes by Poiret and decor by Marc Henri and Laverdet. The music by Christine Mitland and Jack Howard and lyrics by Donovan Parsons were serviceable. An idea of the show's appeal can be gleaned from some of the numbers, such as "Midnight Folly," in which the characters include The Cocktail, The Small Follies, The Goddess of Wine, The Spirit of Melody, Ballet, My Lady Nicotine, The Bouquet and The Party Spirit (Gertie). Lawrence was the obvious star with several numbers, including the puzzling solo "Pom-Pom Ti-looah-ay," "Gipsy Night in June" (as the gipsy) and "A Tale of Many Colors," in which she came on, following Pink, Orange, Blue, Lavender, Yellow, Green, Purple and Red, as the best of them all, Gold.

A later scholar on cabaret evoked the scene:

> Cabaret first invited notice from dramatic critics when Charlot presented the Midnight Follies at the Hotel Metropole.... To sit at tables while watching a show, to eat and drink while chorus girls "highkicked" seemed abandoned, or daring at least.

Charlot happily raided his stock company to support the principals, and during its brief existence the *Follies* presented singing actress Margaret Bannerman, comic singers Norah Blaney and Gwen Farrar, all-purpose performer Odette Myrtil, Lynn and Buchanan himself. Alas, the show represented one of the rare setbacks in this ascendant segment of Charlot's life. As he later wrote,

> Unfortunately, Towle had been too hasty in taking things for granted, and his untimely opening before the permit had been officially granted caused a fracas with the LCC. Towle lost the battle, and on January 1, 1923 the Metropole was forced to go back to the six-turn routine. I retired from the organization on February 4, 1923 and it was not until some time later that Towle and the "non-club" restaurants finally got permission to operate like the clubs.

When the Midnight Follies resumed, *sans* Charlot, they also resumed their success, running till 1927 and continuing to draw a sophisticated clientele ("Women *en masse* wore velvet").

By 1922, Charlot's name and graphic image were indeed ubiquitous in the theater world. He allegedly penned one of the serial "Stage Stories" (number 56) that appeared in West End programs. It purported to be the report of a "press representative" who had interviewed Charlot and Murray in their offices at the Prince of Wales. (By then, Charlot was seriously considering moving his entire family to the

Prince of Wales building. Despite his successes, he was still overspending on himself and his family and having trouble making the household sums add up.)

In the story Charlot was kidded about looking more like "the accountant of a prosperous city concern" than a producer. He was willing to be interviewed, but he had only ten minutes before "an important luncheon appointment." They were shortly joined by Murray, a "spruce-looking gent with an Irish accent with a slight trace of American." Murray begins to tell a "funny [apparently slightly racy] story" about a New York hotel adventure, while Charlot is interrupted by a telephone call—nearly all the tables for tonight's *Follies* are taken—did he want his? Then Ronald Jeans and Dion Titheradge arrive with new ideas for the revue *Snap!* A further interruption: Grossmith. Then "The Co-Optimists want to know...." The reporter flees: his conclusion is that "Managers DO work." (The central notion of this article was largely echoed seventeen years later when Charlot, by then trying for a comeback in California, wrote a radio script centered on himself in a Hollywood hotel being interrupted by many of his former stars.)

Einar Nerman took particular delight in caricaturing Charlot in his stylish sketches in the weekly *Tatler*. Often in a particularly lovely orange, black and white, he was able to catch Charlot's pompadour, jutting eyebrows, pleasantly plump shape and trademark pipe or cigar.

It was 1922 when Charlot indulged himself in an onstage dig at some of his least favorite people—critics. It came in the form of a Ronald Jeans sketch for *Snap!* The sketch had four sections, and before the first, a board in center stage was unveiled: THE SKETCH WAS PRODUCED LIKE THIS. After four pages of dialogue, the curtains closed; next came a board reading IN DEFERENCE TO THE CRITICS OF THE MORNING PAPERS CERTAIN CUTS AND ALTERATIONS WERE MADE. The following sketch was nearly the same, with alterations in character and atmosphere: now it was two and a half pages long. Another curtain, another board: THE CRITICS OF THE EVENING PAPERS HAD SUGGESTED OTHER CHANGES. Same sketch, different characterization and atmosphere: one page of dialogue. Curtain and last board: AFTER THE CRITICISM OF THE SUNDAY PAPERS SOME FINAL TRIMMINGS TOOK PLACE. The curtains opened, disclosing the set. The doorbell rang. The curtains closed again. Black out. Charlot records that the critics in the audience joined everyone else in laughter.

Between 1922 and 1924 Charlot stepped up his development of Gertrude Lawrence's talent and popularity. After another ostracism, he rehired her (and Flip was instrumental, saying that only one actress in London could do it) when Bea became ill just before the opening of *A to Z* (1922) and had to miss a great deal of the run. In the third version of the show, Charlot saw that Gertie could not go on being expected to be a Lillie clone and encouraged the emergence of her own brand of charm. He subsequently built an entire revue *(Rats!)* around her.

Charlot's revues became more sophisticated and knowing. The two best intimate shows of their era were 1922's *A to Z* and *London Calling* (1923), the productions which in fact (with some bits from *Rats!*) would form the basis for the New York *Charlot's London Revue*.

An exotic and highly decorative Nerman sketch from "Rats" with Lawrence, Alfred Lester and Rex O'Malley.

Jean Patou gowns for *A to Z*, 1921.

A to Z (at the Prince of Wales), its alphabet-derived title stemming from its 26 component parts (the intermission helpfully counted as one), can be thought of as the show which made Buchanan a true Charlot star, the "anchorman" who held it all together. In sketches and musical numbers he was able to project a remarkable ability to seem simultaneously goofy in the truest of "sillyass English" senses (being not only Scottish, but almost pathologically shy, he had to work at that) and the smoothest, most understated of dancing romancers. A better example of the successful revue performer could not be imagined.

Poor Buchanan had to suffer from Charlot's sometimes bizarre sense of humor. On one occasion Philip, then a prankish 12-year-old, sitting in a stage box with his friend Bert Coote, Jr., pelted Buchanan with chocolate creams during his big number "And Her Mother Came Too"—and Charlot laughed.

Despite all this and occasional other practical jokes, Buchanan turned down an offer from Cochran for five times what Charlot was paying. Why not? Charlot had flattered him: "I know you can write your own ticket for next season but you will stay with me, won't you, my boy?" Buchanan's biographer noted that though the salary was ridiculous, it was true that Charlot also gave Buchanan his early chances to produce and direct.

A to Z also boasted the earliest incisive sketches by Titheradge, an Australian who had acted in the Liverpool Repertory and on both sides of the Atlantic, but whose West End writing experience had been minimal. He eventually wrote or collaborated on five Charlot revues, often in tandem with Jeans. These were the best Charlot revues of all, the platform for the legendary conquest of Broadway. *A to Z* also boasted Novello's best revue score, in fact his best musical writing until the improbable series of musical melanges which gave his career a definitive twist in 1935.

A to Z was Charlot's most expensive "intimate" revue to date, largely thanks to its major backer, Lord Ned Lathom. They had met in 1921 and Lathom, an ardent amateur theatrico with wildly fluctuating taste (one of the all-time London theatrical disasters, a 1926 show called *White Birds*, sank under his banner), had told him of his desire to be involved in staging a revue.

Meeting at Lathom's country house near Liverpool, Charlot and Lathom decided that the revue would be written by Novello, Jeans and Titheradge. As the revue's preparation proceeded apace, Charlot learned that Lathom "wanted everything on an impossibly magnificent scale." The gowns, the first London effort of Jean Patou, another of Charlot's importations, cost £10 apiece, a staggering figure for the time. Charlot tried—or swore that he tried—to put the brakes on Lathom's spending, but to little avail. As it turned out, *A to Z* was a major artistic success, running 52 weeks. Although it never recouped its investment (Lathom lost £15,000), his lordship said it had been worth it—he had got twice that value in the fun he had. In fact, the show could have run longer and Lathom might have recouped all his investment, but Charlot had, alas, sublet the theater and so the show came off, in a grim foreshadowing of a debacle which, four years later, set his career reeling out of control.

As if to prove that *A to Z*, which he said marked a high point in his life, could be bettered, in December 1922 Lathom invited Charlot to Davos, Switzerland, where Noel Coward was also his guest at the Hotel Belvedere. (In a later memoir, Coward revised the emphasis, claiming that Lathom had "commanded" Charlot's presence.) The idea was to show Charlot what a genius Coward had become.

The young Noel Coward (right), with Henry Kendall (left) and Douglas Byng.

In the hotel's ballroom late one evening, Coward played and sang "Parisian Pierrot" and other songs for the first time in public. This was pleasing to Charlot, who tried never to put a song in any show unless he had heard it performed by its composer. He later wrote that Coward had "persuaded me of his greatness." He was not quite so effusive about Coward's sketches—which he did not allow the author to read to him. Reading them over in his room, he quite liked the "telephone sketch" (this was later "Early Mourning," a tour de force performed by Gertrude Lawrence) but thought the rest "stank to high heaven."

What happened the day after Coward's "audition" is recalled quite differently by its major players. Charlot claimed that he had told Coward he wanted to use some of his material but added a suggestion that Noel do what Cohan did—write, produce, and star in a whole show of his own. Here, wrote Charlot later, "Coward revealed his lack of confidence—no use arguing, he must have some help." So, according to Charlot, it was Coward's idea to collaborate.

Coward eventually contradicted this interpretation. He recalled that Charlot was "expansive and benign" and that "a series of cigar laden conferences" followed. He worked on the sketches in the morning and submitted them to Lathom and Charlot in the afternoons. Within a few days the whole show was roughly laid out. Thus was born *London Calling* (its title the daily coming-on-air announcement on the BBC). Coward also recalled that Charlot had taken him aside, breaking the news that he would be unable to pay more than £15 weekly to such an inexperienced author—but not to worry, Coward would surely make money on the royalties.

The Davos expedition produced other highlights. At lugeing the next day, no one thought to inform Charlot that the snow was so hard that in a bowl at the bottom of a steep dip there was a sheer sheet of ice. Roaring down at 40 mph, Charlot braked, only to find himself skidding. He stopped braking just in time and up the side of the bank he tore "at a frightening rate," missing the top only by inches. Regaining control, he made it to the end of the run, where Coward, Lathom, the premier actress Gladys Cooper and the rest of Lathom's collection of celebrities were convulsed in laughter the imperious Charlot could not quite appreciate.

(Some years later, when Lathom went broke and Charlot was attacked for causing his downfall by theatrical writer Hannen Swaffer, Lathom wrote Charlot a letter exonerating him completely. He had £30,000 yearly to live on, he said, and in addition to the £15,000 gleefully spent on *A to Z*, he said he had dropped only a couple of thousand on *London Calling*.)

In 1923, according to Charlot's version, Coward still felt unable to do a show on his own and so they agreed to call in Ronald Jeans. Writing in the 1950s, Charlot noted that *London Calling* would have been Coward's first one-man revue if he had followed Charlot's advice. After *London Calling* and the versions of *Charlot's Revue* that used some of its material, Coward took Charlot's advice—but only in shows staged by Cochran. Charlot wrote, "I must admit he had acquired some needed expertise, working with Jeans and myself."

In future years Coward always talked of *London Calling* as *his* show, rarely if at all mentioning Jeans. Coward appeared in *London Calling* performing his own material. (Charlot recalled "having to ask Noel to get out of the cast because the men in

the audience could not stand his
effeminate mannerisms. I bet he has
not recorded that episode in his
memoirs"—memoirs which, published in the 1930s, seem to have
hurt Charlot deeply.) But in some
admiration Coward recalled a
chaotic dress rehearsal of *London
Calling* in which the only person
who seemed completely peaceful
and at ease was Charlot, who sat in
the stalls with Ned and his friends
and seldom raised his voice.

Coward was pleased that he
had talked Charlot up to £40 weekly
with an option to leave the show
after six months. Coward did not
accompany the Charlot troupe during its 1923–24 conquest of New
York. He charitably said that
Buchanan there performed his satirical number "Sentiment" much better than he had ever done. *London
Calling* also showed Charlot at his
most tenacious—when the comedian
W.H. Berry refused to appear in the
third version because he contended
their contract was "only verbal,"
Charlot went to the Actors Association solicitors and eventually
received £1,000 in damages from
Berry without having to press legal
proceedings.

Noel Coward in *Brighter London.*

This revue made theatrical his-
tory. *London Calling* marked the first collaboration between Coward and Lawrence,
a prefiguring of one of the musical theater's most renowned partnerships. The flighty
Lawrence was flawless when inhabiting any of Coward's sketches, and when the pair
performed together, they displayed an ironic coolness that in its turn created a style
which would dominate the transatlantic stage for at least two decades.

Not quite everything that Charlot touched during these years turned to gold.
In July 1923 he had been asked by Claude Graham-White and Ethel Levey (the
expatriate American ex-wife of Cohan's who had helped deCourville's shows so
much) to dine with actress Marie Dressler, whom Charlot admired and whose Hollywood fame still lay in the future, and the world-class socialite Elsa Maxwell, who
was still writing for the theater.

The idea was to discuss doing a London show for Dressler. Graham-White agreed to organize the finances and Charlot proceeded to sign Maxwell and Dressler for 7½% of the gross apiece. He went on to sign up Jeans and Titheradge to help out Maxwell in writing words and music. However, when word of the enterprise got around the small world of theatrical London, there was an uproar. Dressler and her husband running a show in Britain years earlier had stranded a company unpaid out in the provinces.

The Actors Association became quite interested. Charlot could not find it worthwhile to fight Dressler's battle, but the parties were apparently near a settlement when Dressler, who feared opening-night reprisals, decided to back out. The show was cancelled and, after leaving England, Dressler sent a check to the association.

Regardless of this setback, by mid–1923, armed mainly with his glittering reputation, Charlot was ready to make the long-anticipated foray to Broadway. The actual deal was struck with Archie and Edgar Selwyn, during another Charlot pilgrimage to New York once more financed by Pollak. Charlot had met Archie Selwyn during the London run of *Rats!* and this fortnight's "look around" the Big Apple included a good deal of entertainment paid for by Selwyn.

Charlot mounted a full-scale publicity campaign leading to *Charlot's London Revue*, working with Walter Wanger, at the time a young man briefly in exile from Broadway. One of Wanger's (dubious?) achievements while in London was the conversion of the Royal Opera House in Covent Garden to a cinema. (Fortunately, the conversion did not last long.) One of the campaign's more benign events was a competition for the "loveliest barmaid in Britain," who would become a member of the Charlot company traveling to New York. All this was rigged in advance, of course. The "loveliest barmaid" was Bobbie Storey, whose natural habitat was Rules restaurant, a long-established hostelry much famed for its preparation of native English game. Rules, still a part of London theatrical life, was a particular favorite of Charlot's, being virtually across the street from the back door of the Vaudeville Theatre and his office there.

One of Maisie Gay's many matronly but madcap personas.

Charlot's London Revue gradually was assembled, largely from the sketches and songs from *A to Z* and *London Calling*, but also from Jeans's work in *Rats!* The cast was also mostly drawn from these shows. Charlot wisely chose to go with his own products, even though this meant leaving behind one of the most outstanding assets of *London Calling*, the wife of his stage manager O.D. Harris, Maisie Gay, who was none too pleased at being bumped.

The bumper was Lillie, who was by now entirely too great an asset to be alienated—after all, Lady Peel was already being wooed by other impresarios on both sides of the Atlantic and they were prepared to pay her more money. (She later wrote, "They spread the jam thicker there.") Lawrence not only retained the material from *London Calling* but acquired from its originator, Teddie Gerard, a Philip Braham song called "Limehouse Blues." With material provided by Jeans, Titheradge and Coward, *Charlot's London Revue* would rely upon its youngest, brightest and freshest people.

On December 19, 1923, the new company—Lady Peel accompanied by Robert and Buchanan accompanied by a veritable entourage of his regular chums—embarked on the last and highly publicized stage of its Gotham odyssey aboard Cunard's *Aquitania*. One of Charlot's key decisions had been to take Jessie Matthews along as part of the chorus.

Off to New York: (left to right) Gertrude Lawrence, Charlot, Bea Lillie and Jack Buchanan, 1923.

On December 22 the troupe did not miss the opportunity of staging, with appropriate coverage by wire on both sides of the ocean, the first ever revue staged in the mid–Atlantic. The finale was "America" which, since they used the same tune, seamlessly became "God Save the King." The proceeds went to aid the British and American Seamen's Institute.

The show was heavy on sketches and relatively light on music, perhaps because Charlot and Braham, his musical director, were unfamiliar with the ship's orchestra. Douglas Furber, a regular member of Buchanan's inside circle who was best known as a lyricist and sketch writer of merit, was accorded his own moment onstage and took part in several group efforts. Lawrence, Buchanan and Lillie had only one solo number apiece—Lawrence's laconic "I Don't Know," Buchanan's version of Coward's "Sentiment" and Lillie's excruciatingly funny adaptation of Maisie Gay's "March with Me"—the latter adroitly placed just before the patriotic finale. Blessed with highly clement weather, the *Aquitania* sailed on.

SIX

London, New York and Hollywood, 1924–1926:

Crest of the Wave

The mildly riotous voyage of the *Aquitania* was over. Charlot and his company were enduring various forms of morning-after as they prepared to disembark at the East River docks on Christmas Eve 1923. For Charlot it was not strictly speaking a matter of too much Lanson. Beneath his hauteur, physically dominating looks ("so tall, but with a rather fat tummy" was Jonny's description), characteristic Havana cigar and generally grand manner, he remained mildly uncertain about the prospect awaiting him. What if his lucky streak had finally run its course? The "American project," despite four years of planning, signings-up and re-planning, had slipped away over and over again.

For all his success, the introvert in Charlot knew that invading the United States was on a different scale from conquering the West End. He wondered whether his public relations talk of mid–1923 would be thrown back in his face.

But *tout ou rien*. There had been plenty of opportunities to hedge this bet. American shows coming to London had always wisely "Englished" themselves—hiring plenty of locals, omitting Americanisms and inserting plenty of local allusions. Of course Charlot knew what American revues looked and sounded like—derivations from Ziegfeld. It would have been easy to override his sketch authors, if perhaps less possible to teach his principals the broad humor necessary to milk laughs from Broadway audiences. But he had decided to give Broadway Charlot plain. This would be English intimate revue—Charlot revue—straight or nothing.

He was bringing his show to Broadway during a period of unprecedented theatrical boom. Could he really expect to elbow his way into an environment already overloaded with memorable shows, brilliant talent, and exciting new theaters? The town was feeling its power. Although the birth of *The New Yorker* was still a year in the future, the magazine's creators—the most influential of opinion-makers—were already plying their self-confident and self-indulgent trade. What did they need from the Old World?

In fact, despite Charlot and Wanger's campaigns, the New York theatrical world was not awaiting the Charlot troupe with bated breath. There were plenty of musical shows already—great big splashy ones—and brand names like Ziegfeld as well as Ziegfeld's stars still commanded the market. The mid-war spree of theater building which had completed the creation of Times Square as Theaterland had only intensified the competition among such already successful operations.

Despite all the spanking new houses, so many new productions demanded space that it wasn't unusual for opening nights to take place in the afternoon while companies, coming and going, shuffled to and fro. And there was a strange antipathy toward the rather few British performers who had recently done well in New York, including Leslie Howard (who was actually Hungarian). Successful British playwrights such as Frederick Lonsdale and "Clemence Dane" appeared to be resented. If Charlot did not know about this on Christmas Eve 1923, he soon would.

Though some theater historians later called *Charlot's London Revue* the major event of the 1923–24 Broadway musical season, no one at the time could have predicted it. A host of virtually pre-sold shows were very much in evidence. To begin with, there were two "book" shows underpinned by the songs of the hour's most popular composer, Vincent Youmans. One was *Wildflower*, very much a musical comedy in the old-fashioned European sense. Its star, the bird-voiced Edith Day, was fresh from a record-breaking long run as the prototypical American Cinderella, *Irene*. *Wildflower* had been running a year at the venerable Casino theater, while Youmans's latest and more characteristically flapperish score graced another Cinderella story, *Mary Jane McKane*, newly opened as the first offering of the attractive new Imperial Theater on 45th Street.

It didn't take *Poppy* long to become another surefire star show—just long enough for W.C. Fields, on extended leave from Ziegfeld's *Follies*, to show the public his creation, the bibulous Professor Eustace McGargle. *Poppy* was doing fine business at the Selwyns' nearly new Apollo on 43rd Street. Over at the Globe, *Stepping Stones*, the latest of a series built around the genial Fred Stone which had appeared almost annually since the turn of the century, was in its second year. It boasted the debut of Stone's daughter Dorothy and a score by Kern. At the year-old Earl Carroll Theater at 7th Avenue and 50th Street one of the decade's most illustrious musical comedies, *Kid Boots*, a Ziegfeld show for Eddie Cantor, used the contemporary Florida land boom as a basis for its shenanigans. It settled in for a long run. Cantor, the long-ago honeymooner who played for Charlot at the Alhambra, was now potentially lethal competition. And these were not all the threats. *Sally, Irene and Mary*, a virtual recapitulation of all the Cinderella stories, was in its second theater. Up north at the Colonial, the African-American *Runnin' Wild*, a worthy follow-up to Noble Sissle and Eubie Blake's *Shuffle Along*, was introducing—at least to its white audience—the era's landmark song and dance, the Charleston.

And these were only the book shows. Of perhaps more immediate concern to Charlot were the revues, the market leaders on Broadway since 1907. By the end of 1923 the earlier generation of Ziegfeld imitators had pretty much run their course. Raymond Hitchcock's *Hitchy-Koo* had finished in 1920 when the ragtime craze was truly moribund and the last of the Shuberts' *Passing Show*s would begin a short run just as Charlot's troupe left town in late 1924.

As for Ziegfeld himself, *Kid Boots* provided financial solace for Fields's and

Cantor's absences from the *Follies*, but the *Follies* ran on anyhow. The 1923 entry could not quite match up to the 1922 edition, but what could? That one had run 67 weeks and stormed the road thereafter, creating a national craze for comics Ed Gallagher and Al Shean, who were now arguing with everyone, including each other, about the authorship of their famous song. The new *Follies* still had Fanny Brice (in her last Ziegfeld show) and New Yorkers and tourists alike still knew the well-worn path to the New Amsterdam Theater with its vast panoramas of dazzle and staircases of glamour. The 1923 *Follies* eventually ran for 330 performances, a longer run than any of Ziegfeld's prewar shows. The Ziegfeld magic was still most apparent.

But the tired businessman also had newer, livelier and saucier series to patronize. *George White's Scandals* had been presenting annual editions since 1919, and that old *Follies* dancer had specialized in speeding up tempi and showcasing Gershwin and other snappy new composers. Stylish, by comparison witty and with a good record for showcasing the notorious (the Dollys, who else?), *The Greenwich Village Follies* had also been around since 1919.

A much rawer new strand became evident when in mid–1923 Earl Carroll opened *Vanities of 1923* in his new theater. Carroll posed a lowlife threat to Ziegfeld, the Great Glorifier. He was the great exploiter, and in his shows the nudes (fur coats were good temporary camouflage) and the raucous comics from burlesque were ever present. When Charlot's troupe disembarked, the flagship of another nude, relatively tasteless series, the Shuberts' *Artists and Models*, was also running. Its patrons could look forward to panoramas which might include well-greased showgirls apparently roasting on a spit.

But it was the show at the three-year-old Music Hall, next door to the Imperial, which surely would have seemed most threatening of all, since it inventively blended class and spectacle. The latest *Music Box Revue* boasted a score (though not his best) by the theater's joint owner, Irving Berlin, as well as sketches by two of the wits of the era, Robert Benchley (who also appeared in the show) and George S. Kaufman. More than one member of Charlot's troupe saw this show, later recalling in awe this Broadway version of a "little" revue. It was a sumptuous affair directed by an expatriate Briton, the lighting wizard Hassard Short, and was notable particularly for its $50,000 gold mesh curtain and a number called "An Orange Grove in California," during which Grace Moore and John Steel sang amidst a shimmer of orange while valves under the audience's chairs released the scent of orange blossoms.

How could Charlot's virtually prop-free show or his sparse chorus chosen for versatility over glamour compete? And as for omens, how about *Topics of 1922*? Its star was Alice Delysia, the very same Delysia who carried so many Cochran shows. Delysia had been endlessly hyped in the run-up to a November opening at the Broadhurst, but the show was floundering badly. On the "straight drama" side *White Cargo*, the moody miscegenation epic which made "I am Tondelayo" (often debased to "Me Tondelayo") a catchphrase for two decades of comics, was doing well and *Abie's Irish Rose* had been running in one theater or another for a year and a half. It continued through the decade, prompting the Lorenz Hart line "Our future babies/We'll take to *Abie's Irish Rose* /I hope they'll live to see/it close." This was the competition.

As the *Aquitania* docked, Charlot could certainly have been re-running (and perhaps regretting) his words at the earlier deal-closing news conference with Selwyn. In his beguiling French-English accent, he had said:

> When the American theater-going public is given a chance to see my London Revue, they will understand the difference between this type of show and revue in America, which in some ways, is too subtle to put into words. Over the years, we have developed an intimate understanding between players and audience, such as you do not know in this country. The mixture is hard to define since it depends not only on a company in which everyone—not just the principals—can sing, dance and act, but also on lighting and scenic effects which are simple and artistic. I intend to offer outstanding melody, humor, good taste and distinctive charm.

An intimate understanding? Could it be had with an American audience? After the disembarkation, everyone was quickly engulfed in the anticipated flurry of publicity largely generated by Bobbie Storey. (Storey stayed with the show until April, when Ziegfeld lured her away. Later, she apparently committed suicide in a gas-filled hotel room.) Most of this commotion must have delighted Charlot, but some was unexpected and unpleasant and his mood worsened as soon as the following day's *New York American* hit the stands.

The *American*'s story asserted that Charlot's chorus girls had engaged in all sorts of romantic shipboard escapades and that four of them had simply disappeared upon landing, en route to marrying millionaires. (In fact, one, Marjorie Sexton, did run away to be married to a wealthy fellow passenger.) The *American* further claimed that Charlot had panicked and rushed all over town, making wild accusations in his search for the missing women. Flip Charlot (who according to the story had long since rented an entire New York hotel so the chorines could be under her supervision) was credited with locating the remaining three (one was said to be Constance Carpenter, who ultimately became a successor to Lawrence) and staving off their marriages, as well as talking Sexton back into the show until a replacement could arrive from England. One of the chorus girls who was apparently not involved was Jessie Matthews, who had already made well enough known her unhappiness at staying in the chorus. She also made the point that Charlot had given her the first rights to understudy both Lillie and Lawrence.

For the rest of his life, Charlot remained convinced that the motive behind the runaway story was Ziegfeld's; Ziegfeld would have sent one of his famous telegrams to the *American*'s publisher, William Randolph Hearst, seeking to torpedo the Charlot opening. Although the story was superficially friendly, pointing out the difference between American and English chorus girls—the English type actually *did* something in the show and thus could not be easily replaced overnight, as could the American—Charlot must also have been particularly insulted by the pervasive suggestion that his hand-picked and impeccably groomed "girls" were really gold diggers of the American variety. The story, which also profiled "the Guv," did get one of its details right. As soon as he could, Charlot took to his bed until he had figured out a solution to the problems.

Incredibly, it was even earlier than the morning after docking when the Charlot company received its first rough treatment from the self-appointed newly "most powerful nation." The entire company had attended a Christmas Eve party thrown by one of Selwyn's backers. During dinner the backer gave his ten-year-old son $5. It was, said the banker, enough to purchase his choice of Charlot's leading ladies. Things got worse when the after-dinner speeches began. Most of the American guests found it necessary and entertaining to pooh-pooh British plays and performers in general. Charlot later wrote that they made it obvious that "Broadway didn't *need* people like us. Most of our ladies were close to tears."

The normally even-tempered Buchanan was also visibly upset, barely controlling his anger in a few remarks in which he said he had not invited himself to God's Country, but that he hoped he would not let anybody down. After a few remarks by Lawrence which did nothing to discharge the atmosphere, it was Lillie's turn. Charlot wrote:

> She rose, holding her glass of champagne, and uttered a single syllable: "Oh." That single syllable was uttered so effectively that it seemed to bring our host and his friends suddenly to their senses. Not only was the exclamation effective, but she accompanied it with a swift upward movement of her glass which flung the champagne well over her shoulder. Perhaps it was this as much as the speech which made all the difference.

Once the initial unpleasantries were past, Charlot, his family and principals could renew old acquaintances and see the town. In the Algonquin Hotel, itself a brave choice since it was certainly the focal point for the new and often belligerent New York literati, André, Flip and Philip Charlot sent telegrams home and found things going well, especially with Joan, who was happily spending her holiday with Jonny and the Gladmans.

In New York, Edmund "Eddie" Goulding, he of *Kill That Fly!* and now a well-thought-of film director, joined Clifton Webb, that piccadilly (the name originally meant a dandy) from Indiana, in showing the family around. Some nights were partly soothed by parties fueled from a portable cocktail bar in one of Buchanan's trunks. Charlot did not attend.

The troupe then moved on to Atlantic City and further disappointments. Atlantic City was then resting somewhere between its earlier status ("romantic, enchanting Atlantic City," where one could find love in a rolling chair) and its decline into seediness and subsequent rebirth as the Las Vegas of the Atlantic coast. They were booked into the lavish Ritz-Carlton Hotel, but one of Selwyn's little surprises awaited: he had never bothered to mention that, though at reduced rates, the cast would have to pay their own bills. Learning this some of the chorines moved out straightaway. Across the road from the Ritz-Carlton was a mansion which proved to have a gambling casino upstairs. An ostentatious New Year's Eve party was conveniently ignored by Prohibition officers. At this party, all the Charlot women were presented beautiful bottles of perfume. Charlot, who responded with a gracious speech of acceptance, later discovered that the expense of the party was also charged by Selwyn to the general accounts, so that Charlot was in fact paying for half the tab.

Selwyn-in-person provided many of the worst moments during a week of rehearsal. He kept popping in with suggestions, the most horrifying being to axe "March with Me," Lillie's spoof of Britannia inherited from Maisie Gay. How could, Selwyn questioned, Americans relate to that?

It was not long before Charlot was threatening to take his whole troupe back home. Charlot had dealt summarily with backers before. When a London chancer (and subsequent theatrical impresario) named Jimmy White who had invested in one of his wartime revues insisted upon special rehearsal privileges for his friends, Charlot called his bluff by buying out the backer's share with the help of the Gattis. Now in New York he had to cope with an intransigent co-producer who asked Charlot to stage a complete rehearsal one midnight because some of his friends had arrived in town.

Charlot simply refused; his people had worked hard enough that evening already. This attitude finally cowed Selwyn and it proved a real tonic to Buchanan, that possessor of the most fragile of theatrical egos. It's possible to date Buchanan's conquest of Broadway from this moment of support from Charlot who later wrote, "It was better to be at loggerheads with Selwyn and pull off a brilliant success with the public [and with his cast] than fail with the public by keeping the peace with him."

But rehearsals and early Atlantic City performances of *Charlot's London Revue* were still not to his liking. The New Jersey audiences seemed often puzzled by what was laid before them. And there was Selwyn's reported reaction: "Geez, it stinks." At any rate, during the week at Nixon's Theater, Charlot once again shuffled his running order and streamlined the show.

Running order: the concept was well known enough in variety and its American cousin, vaudeville. But in general the typical vaudeville bill was constructed to build towards the appearance of the star turn. Charlot had quite a different idea and swore by it. It was Noel Coward who wrote most clearly about this:

Charlot (left) and Archie Selwyn in New York, c. 1924.

He would have the names of all the numbers in the revue printed on separate cards, place them on his desk, and then, as though playing Patience, juggle with them and go on moving them about, shifting them again and again until satisfied that they were in the right running order. The finale of the first half would already have been agreed upon, but all the numbers leading up to it had to build, and build to the number BEFORE the finale, and that number, whatever it was, had to be sure fire. The second number in the second half was, still is, and always will be, terribly important. It has to be so strong, or so funny, or so spectacular, or whatever, that the audience, including by then the stragglers from the bar, will settle back comfortably in their seats, happy in the knowledge that the second half is going to be even more brilliant than the first.

All this can be settled with the cards fairly amicably. Then the fun begins. "You can't possibly change the set from so and so straight into so and so." "Gertie can't POSSIBLY make the change from tweeds at the end of this sketch into deep evening dress for the beginning of her big number." And so on and so on: more juggling of the cards until all is set and all will run smoothly.

After his consultation with the cards and with his instincts, Charlot gradually cut six numbers while adding three, reducing the total from 24 to 21. That made it Charlot's shortest show since Alhambra days. He gave particular attention to the disappointing first act, adding Titheradge's "The Green-Eyed Monster." He strengthened the second act by bringing in "Rough Stuff" and "Peace and Quiet." He repositioned nearly everything else.

This reshuffle was particularly designed to make the most of Lawrence, Lillie and Buchanan, whose appeal to the Atlantic City audience had come through clearly. If the reshuffle were to work, its major impact would be felt in the closing numbers. Placing Lawrence's "Limehouse Blues" (previously in the important "second after the intermission" spot) between "March with Me" and Buchanan's suave interpretation of "Sentiment"—this salvo just before the finale—would build terrific anticipation and momentum. Or so went the theory.

When the break-in week was finally over, the train trip back to New York provided further gloom. For reasons which were never explained, the 2½ hour train trip took 6½ hours. The company arrived thoroughly frazzled. And things did not materially improve when rehearsals commenced at the Times Square Theater. Braham, for the first time conducting an orchestra which played American shows, had to keep telling them to play more softly. "But boss," a musician complained, "they won't be able to hear us." And Braham responded, "They won't want to." But no one could be sure how the opening night audience—glittering in a glittering era—would respond at the 1,200-seat house, itself such a clear imitation and evocation of the Music Box.

But if the critic for the *Evening Telegraph* represented the audience's reaction fairly, it must have been beyond even Charlot's dreams:

> When Andre Charlot's company stepped out on the stage last night with their opening "How do you do?" there was an immediate response between actors and audience. [Charlot, who never trusted opening nights anyway, thought the show had started quietly.] That cordial relationship continued throughout the evening and when the curtain fell, the fact was established that in Charlot's Revue, Broadway has something new in the way of musical comedy.

Exactly what was so new about this show? And why had the reviewer called it a musical comedy? It surely had no coherent plot. And being a compilation of Charlot's best, it lacked even the coherence of a unifying theme or motif—no coupons, no alphabetical progression. But perhaps a close look at the twenty-one components of *Charlot's London Revue*, the skeleton of a show that changed the history of musical theater, can provide the answer.

The opening number which so caught the critical eye and ear was one of the few new items. Its music was by Braham, nominally credited as the show's composer. Some lyrics were Jeans's, while others were supplied by the puckish Eric Blore, a man who had been around London revue for awhile and whose own Broadway and Hollywood career as dyspeptic gentleman's gentleman had not yet begun. There seemed nothing remarkable in these lyrics:

> How do you do—How do you do
> We'll introduce ourselves to you
> In a show that we hope will scintillate....
>
> Not a short or over long show
> Bright stuff and just the right stuff
>
> All pretty quick, pretty slick, full of pep
> If you watch your step...
>
> It's revue, it's revue, that we now propose to do
> But different to the ordinary style...
>
> Ready to work, ready to work
> Ready to say who we are
> We never make a fuss,
> Here we are, all of us...
>
> Tidy and trim, and bursting with vim
> Hoping to never grow less
> Any old task, you've just got to ask
> Ready for work, folks, Yes.

Nothing remarkable, but it entranced the audience. It was economical and all the performers did in fact (right after "Here we are, all of us") introduce themselves. They looked fresh—and to a New York audience, they were—and friendly. *This was different.*

Exactly why Charlot commissioned this particular opening has never been explained. For those who rate him an intuitive genius, it's simply one more example of gauging the moment. The Harry Grattanesque notion of directly (or indirectly) addressing the audience had been abandoned before 1920, but perhaps it was Charlot's venture into cabaret which convinced him that quickly establishing intimacy was important. But in any event, it was different. Charlot's troupe just swirled in, looked the audience knowingly in the eye and sang. (In his declining days, Charlot revived "How Do You Do?" with suitably updated lyrics many times, perhaps hoping that the good luck would return with it.)

It may also be worth noting that American revues, which took their time in absorbing the Charlot lessons, did cotton onto this sort of opening number. In *New Faces of 1952*, one of the last American successes in the genre, a small cast swirled out, looked the audience in the eye and sang, "You've never seen us before/We've never seen you before/What a pleasant place to finally meet!/So much pleasanter than a busy street...."

"How Do You Do?," played in front of the curtain, did give an American audience something somewhat familiar to look at: an attractive but not overdressed chorus line of 14, happily centered in immaculate evening dress by Robert Hobbs, a smiling second dancing lead.

The first staged sketch, "The Green-Eyed Monster," introduced Buchanan as well as a theme well suited enough to the times—the trials and tribulations of marriage. It also illustrated "bright stuff." A husband becomes jealous of the dancing master (Cyril Ritchard would assume this role) tutoring his wife in "suggestive" modern dance; the husband's passion mounts and he murders the dancing master— who turns out to be the wrong man! The audience's momentary horror is replaced by delight when the players realize their mistake and by way of erasing the error proceed to play the entire sketch in reverse.

Next came Lillie's fairly straightforward blues-chasing "There Are Times" whose lyrics included "And you'll wake up in the morning/Finding lots of brighter days in store." What was *different* about this number was that it was sung and danced in front of a chorus which was seen only in silhouette—a typical Charlot device, eschewing scenery and saving money. This was followed by "Inaudibility," a sketch which, while minimally staged, spoofed the affectations of modern pre-method actors, as well as the affectations of critics.

Then came the first truly captivating number of *Charlot's London Revue*, Lawrence's "Parisian Pierrot." (It had been a success in London and now it established Coward, its creator, on Broadway.) Though Pierrots were not as well understood in the States as in Britain, they did not need to be. The lilting but sad tale of a contemporary Frenchman's (Pierrot) forlorn love for his Columbine ("Parisian Pierrot/Your spirit's at zero") ends with Lawrence swamped in a heap of gorgeous floppy dolls; these were the chorus, bewigged and furbelowed. That was as lavish as Charlot's show ever got. It proved irresistible.

At this point, most American revues or book musicals would have paused for an encore or two. But that was not the way of *Charlot's London Revue*. The mood of "Pierrot" was not allowed to linger; the show's momentum was not allowed to flag. A spoof of amateur poesy, "The Company Will Recite" showed a clamor of neophyte poets around a lectern, entranced by Lillie's suggestion that each in turn should read one line from their newest work. The "inadvertent" chaos, which also made a crazed kind of sense, carried this lightweight idea through well enough and for just the right length of time before it became wholly predictable. (Its general idea rumbled on for decades; when push-button radios arrived on the market during the late 1930s, comic sketches were constructed about the surreal meanings sometimes achieved by randomly punched buttons.)

"You Were Meant for Me," the only American interpolation into the show, allowed Lawrence and Buchanan to dance lightly together. The sketch "Tea Shop

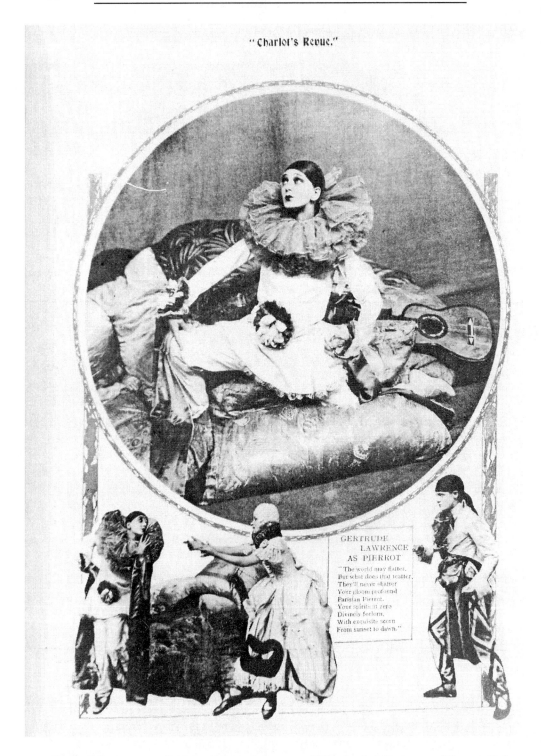

Gertrude Lawrence as Parisian Pierrot (courtesy of Mander & Mitchenson Theatre Collection).

Tattle" had Lillie portraying a malapropistic cockney waitress longing for cinematic stardom; she chats with leading comic Herbert Mundin while ignoring the other patron (Charlot set only three tables), who turned out to be an actor willing to give her a break. Of course few in the Times Square Theater audience would have heard of a tea shop, but Lillie's indescribable presence must have carried the sketch.

Lawrence returned solo before the curtain to sing the flirty song "I Don't Know." ("I don't know if I may have been mistaken/But I thought I saw a flutter of his lid....") The first act finale parodied extravaganza, and although originally created in response to London's version of spectacular revue, it must have come across to New Yorkers as an insouciant burlesque of Ziegfeld. Throughout "In Cigarette Land," whenever Buchanan blew a smoke ring it became—with the aid of some cut-rate lighting effects—a lovely lady. The last and most riotous tobacconite was Lillie, the Scented Cigarette.

Intermission: in those heady days, the smell of success or failure quickly wafted about the theater district during such an interval. Pacing nervously, Charlot (who once wrote, "To a producer, the first night of a play is like a surgical operation; unfortunately, there is no anesthetist in attendance") witnessed a rush of bystanders into the lobby, some offering hundreds of dollars for the tickets of lucky playgoers.

The second half began startlingly enough with controlled raucousness. Lillie became a superannuated soubrette singing Coward's "There's Life in the Old Girl Yet" (another number originated by Maisie Gay, but once more Charlot's substitution was right). The sketch "Incredible Happenings" presented a series of quick scenes separated by blackouts, some only two or three sentences long. Some mattered little to American life—a Scotsman actually buying drinks, an Englishman paying income tax in advance, a telephone caller actually getting the right number the first time. More familiar must have been a wife purposely encouraging her husband to spend time alone with a pretty young thing and a car salesman sending a customer to a competitor—all were fast and deft, maintaining the exciting rush.

Perhaps by this point in the evening what had seemed different could have become delightfully familiar. "I Might" involved Lawrence and Mundin as country maid and stupid bumpkin in love, hanging gawkily about in front of a stile (not the normal habitat of people who hung about Broadway and 42nd Street) and somehow remaining virtually silent for ten minutes while audience laughter and anticipation built up. The evening's most sardonic moments may have come from "The Indicator," a radio-operated lie detector invented by a wise professor ("My advice is—disbelieve the unimportant things and forget them because they're unimportant. Believe the important things, because that saves worry"). The machine, alas, was eventually overwhelmed by lies from just about everyone concerned.

If there was no logic in a segue to "Rough Stuff" it didn't matter; it was a Lillie specialty, a song/sketch in which a shopworn spinster reveals her lusty inner beast ("I want a man to insult me, to beat me, ill-treat me"). Next was the lightly staged and thoroughly lightweight "Peace and Quiet" showing the smoking-jacketed Buchanan, advised to rest from business by his doctor, eventually returning to work because there are so many distractions at home.

No number in *Charlot's London Revue* had worn out its welcome and even late in the show the audience could not really anticipate what might come next—it was the remarkable closing sequence. This began with "March with Me" ("March! April, May and June!") with Lillie as the unsure-footed Britannia-Boadicea overrun by her mignons, barely able to avoid falling into the orchestra pit. The audience roared. Who cared who these legendary figures might have been? Next came what turned out to be the best song ever to grace a Charlot revue, Braham and Furber's "Lime-house Blues," with Lawrence as the melodramatic heroine in a tale of jealousy and murder "in old Chinatown."

During the standing ovation following "Limehouse Blues" (which proved to be Lawrence's ticket to American stardom), up in one of the stage boxes the 14-year-old Philip Charlot turned to his mother and remarked that this was the sort of point in life when one should commit suicide. Then came Buchanan/Coward's sidelong slap at "Sentiment." In silk top hat and tails, carrying a jaunty cane, Buchanan fronted a similarly outfitted chorus in a number supreme in its casual elegance.

Novello's "Night May Have Its Sadness" ("but it's sure to turn to gladness in the day") remains one of the classic revue-closers. The entire company sang directly to the audience sans scenery. Warmly optimistic, it underlined the evening's intimacy and the poignant hour of parting between players and audience.

After the tumultuous curtain calls—the only real halt in the evening's brisk pace—Irving Berlin sat in silence before turning to his guests, who included Elsie Janis and Walter Pidgeon, musing that the whole show had probably cost Charlot less than the finale of the show current at his Music Box.

The next morning's *New York Times* review reported:

> A far more literate entertainment than any American revue—perhaps [terrible thought?]—it is a bit too literate for the general public.... There is precious little concession to Times Square ... it moves rapidly, there is nary an encore.... The chorus is a little below the Ziegfeld-Music Box standard in appearance.... The skits are much funnier than any description would indicate [the common refrain in discussing a Charlot show—we don't know how it works, but it does] ... Jack Buchanan is amiable, lengthy and a first-rate dancer. [Otherwise] it is hardly remarkable.

Otherwise? Percy Hammond, not much taken by the sketch on poetry, lauded the placement and execution of Eubie Blake and Noble Sissle's "You Were Meant for Me": "The gloom was at once dispelled. The music was velvety, the steps graceful and different [there it is again] and the acting was full of subtle charm."

Alexander Woollcott, the preeminent figure of the self-absorbed but potent Algonquin Round Table, wrote:

> It is fair to suspect that Mr. Ziegfeld and Mr. George White must have fairly laughed themselves into a coma at the innocence of this London manager for thinking that any revue so airy and so unpretentious would not be trampled underfoot in New York. Why, the chorus was not half so populous as that of the Follies, and there wasn't so much as a yard of gold cloth in the whole thing.

Heywood Broun added with what the future proved was perception and in fact not terribly good news for Charlot himself: "For the most part, the success of this entertainment rests upon the three principals. Costuming, settings and so forth are quite secondary. From our point of view, Beatrice Lillie, Gertrude Lawrence and Jack Buchanan are worth a good deal more than their weight in gold cloth and velvet hangings."

In April, the *Times*'s John Corbin would write of the show's "discreet loveliness and clean melody, its decorous drollery." He repeatedly compared Jeans and Titheradge's sketches to the cartoons of *Punch*. And he loved looking at the audience, "such as seldom seen since the old days of the Daly-Gaiety shows." This "ultramodern" show, he revealed, was selling seats eight weeks in advance.

Beginning two days after the opening, this advertisement appeared frequently in the New York press: "The Revue Intimate: Something New on Broadway. A Grand Hands Across the Sea Feature. New, Bright, Snappy and Full of Fun. Sang and Danced Their Way Into the Hearts of a Broadway Audience. Exponents of what Barrie called 'That Damned Charm.'"

It was said that young Manhattan blades, wishing to congratulate each other on looking particularly stylish, were soon greeting each other with, "Say, you're looking real Buchanan today." Lillie was quickly a valued party guest—people wondered what on earth she might say next. Soon the Big Three were made honorary members of the Round Table. This was not really the natural habitat of the introverted Buchanan (or for that matter, Charlot himself, who did not become a member). Buchanan, having committed only to the minimum 16-week run, was off to London on April 21 for rehearsals of his very own show *Toni*, the first of a series of "dancing musicals" which confirmed his status as the West End's favorite leading man.

The Algonquin wits liked to dabble in theater themselves and had already staged shows of their own before Charlot's troupe arrived. Still, they proceeded to pay him the ultimate show business compliment: imitation. On May 21, *Round the Town* opened at the Century Roof. Calling itself "an intimate revue inspired by Mr. Charlot's entertainment," it included the performing debut of the personally shambling ("He looked like an unmade bed") Broun and featured contributions from Kaufman, Herman Manckewicz, Marc Connolly and Dorothy Parker. On its own, *Round the Town* made no particular impact, but it began the process of absorbing Charlot's message into the American mainstream.

The impact of *Charlot's London Revue* on stylish commercial Manhattan was also quick and intense. The department store Franklin Simon and Company, Fifth Avenue, was shortly advertising:

> The Charlot suit. Today's Fashion News. The suit is the complete expression of youth and spring! The little boyish coat tied at the throat shows just a bit of the new Paris jabot frill of the satin overblouse. The skirt is a wraparound. It is offered in black and white stripe, navy blue and white stripe, or plain navy blue—with white satin overblouse—or beige, with beige satin overblouse.

Indeed, for Charlot's troupe, part of coping with New York was coping with after-hours New York. This was the great era of the after-theater party, when pianist-composers showed up in the early hours and played their newest, the days in which it was said of George Gershwin's arrival, "The party became freshly oxygenated."

One of the most opulent of partygivers was Jules Glaezner, the head of premier jewelers Cartier. Florence Desmond, a later Charlot star, cited "fabulous stories from Charlot revue girls about the valuable presents they received. It was no uncommon thing to find gold compacts, cigarette cases, and pieces of jewelry placed on sideplates at dinner parties."

At one party thrown by D.K. Wyscop, a Selwyn backer and the head of United Distillers, a 15-year-old named Johnny Green was present because his banker father was a friend of the Wyscops. That was where Green met Gershwin, where Gershwin met Lawrence, where Green met Lawrence and where Lawrence bawled out Green's father for not encouraging his son to become a musician. (Green's friendship with Lawrence eventually led to his composing "Body and Soul" for a cabaret act she was preparing for London. She eventually introduced the song on the BBC, though it never became identified with her. Gershwin's contact with Lawrence soon pried her away from Charlot.)

Lawrence and Lillie (after Buchanan's departure, the show's advertising jingle, subsequently credited to Woollcott, went, "Lillie and Lawrence, Lawrence and Lillie/If you haven't seen them, you're perfectly silly") took a flat on West 54th Street where, according to Lawrence's memoirs, no one ever had time to sleep. Among the regulars were the reigning royalty of the legitimate theatre—Richard Barthelmess, Laurette Taylor, Jeanne Eagels, Estelle Winwood; other impresarios—Charles Dillingham, Alex Aarons, Vinton Freedley; songwriters and librettists—Howard Dietz and Arthur Schwartz, Oscar Hammerstein II, Kern, Bert Kalmar and Harry Ruby, Rodgers and Hart, the Gershwins, Berlin and Youmans. Youmans was a particularly frequent presence; it was said that he composed most of *No, No, Nanette* on the flat's piano. Charlot later claimed that he could have had that show for the asking. But apparently he didn't ask. Were things going too well?

As winter turned to spring, Charlot followed Flip and Philip home to London. The contrast to heady New York success must have been particularly felt by Philip. Stowe, a new and presumably rigorous boarding school, had opened in Buckinghamshire in 1923. Philip was entered for the 1924 summer term. He stayed on until 1927, but his Stowe years were marked by only a single achievement, joining the fencing team. He did not turn out to be ideal boarding school material. He was bullied—in fact, he was once thrown down a flight of stairs. Jonny, his confidant, understood that he was not tough enough for boarding school. Perhaps worst of all, Philip outraged his father by refusing to learn French, clearly a necessity for a cultured man.

Despite the box-office bonanzas of 1924 and 1925, Charlot found it financially expedient to move his family from St. John's Wood to the Prince of Wales itself. There they inhabited a most unusual four-floor living space. One entered via a tunnel from a side street near the stage door. One flight up you came to the kitchen area, another flight of stairs led to Charlot's offices—two large rooms overlooking the side street—another flight to the dining and living quarters and master bedroom, and another to the room shared by Philip, Joan and the cook, Margaret McElwee. There was much less social life than in St. John's Wood. But one thing remained essentially unchanged—Bea was a virtual part of the Charlot family.

Philip Charlot with his parents, possibly 1924.

Although while in New York Charlot had not been on hand to supervise it, his business was still expanding. At the Gattis' Vaudeville, Charlot was listed as "presenter" of a new revue called *Puppets*, largely a collaboration between Novello and Titheradge and Charlot's first opportunity to give Titheradge a show of his own. At the Duke of York's, where owing to a tenancy agreement with its crusty owner, Violet Melnotte, stemming from *London Calling*, he was still contracted, he allowed Archie deBear, till then mainly a journalist, to mount a Charlotesque revue called *The Punch Bowl*. Charlot's only contribution was sitting through one rehearsal and advising cuts, which deBear duly made. Each show ran for more than a year, but *The Punch Bowl*'s run wasn't easy, thanks to Melnotte. According to nostalgist and theater historian W. MacQueen-Pope:

> When fine weather came Charlot put a notice on the board announcing that the curtain would rise at 8:30 instead of 8. Daylight saving time [or Summer Time as it is still known in Britain] had come into force. Madame tore it down and posted one declaring that 8 was the hour. Charlot removed that and said 8:30. Up and down those notices went until Archie deBear—a great wit, besides being a magnificent publicity man—stuck up a notice of his own declaring that 8:30 was right and that "Melnotte shall not ring tonight." That settled it.

Charlot returned to New York after Buchanan's departure and made a few more reshufflings, the better to highlight Lawrence and Lillie and to show how well things were going. Nelson Keys, Buchanan's replacement, proved a much more amenable performer for Charlot this time. The show continued happily at the Times Square and once it was summertime moved to the Selwyn itself. It ran for a total of nine months before heading out on tour. The last New York performance in late September was nearly as memorable as the first. The first two rows were filled with columnists, critics and celebrities. Lillie interpolated a vocal imitation of a banjo and leapt into Woollcott's lap. The entire house stood and sang "Auld Lang Syne" and the cast was escorted by mobs down 46th Street.

Back in London in June, Charlot reported to the Society of West End Theatre Managers on the threat he perceived to be posed by the new British Broadcasting Company. Charlot predicted that the BBC would remain "in its current helpless condition" unless managers unwisely allowed their artistes to perform on the air. He went on to argue that if the SWET were so unwise as to do so despite his advice, it should actually acquire control of the BBC, "making it possible to recoup on the swings what they would lose on the roundabouts." SWET accepted Charlot's report with thanks but took no action on it and soon portions of live London shows were airing on the BBC. They proved the new medium's salvation.

Back in the U.S., the road tour of *Charlot's London Revue* had started well but was suddenly in trouble; Lawrence had fallen seriously ill in Boston. Charlot hurried over and found Matthews (their relationship was now edgy but cordial: he called her "la Petite" or sometimes "Babee") brilliantly performing Lawrence's "Parisian Pierrot" and "Limehouse Blues," so well, he later wrote, that they might have been written for her. This proved a beneficial move for Matthews but a subsequent headache for Charlot, who was eventually forced to demote her to the chorus when

Maisie Gay and Morris Harvey cutting capers in *Charlot's Revue,* **1924.**

they got back to England. Charlot later wrote, "A few months more of apprenticeship would do her no harm. She had to be held in check while she was finding her feet ... she did not always realize that what I was doing was in her best interest."

The American tour concluded happily enough and the troupe headed home to London, where a gala year of *Charlot's Revue* would eventually materialize. Charlot was in New York in the autumn of 1924, already discussing a return engagement. He expressed some reservations about too closely mirroring the original; he hoped to get Hulbert, his wife Cicely Courtneidge and June to star in place of the Big Three. (At the time, incidentally, Hulbert and Courtneidge were enjoying their own New York success on the Charlot coattails.) Many meetings with Selwyn produced multiple disagreements, including one outburst in which Charlot discovered that Selwyn wanted him to sell out to Ziegfeld. It was during these negotiations that Selwyn got Broadway's ticket agents to purchase all the seats for the first 16 weeks of the run. (Since the show eventually ran only 16 weeks, this was a boon.)

Charlot further expanded the business when in September he opened *Charlot's Revue* at the Prince of Wales. Amazingly, this was the first time a London revue had borne its impresario's name, but wasn't "Charlot's Revue" now a household phrase? (This apparently influenced C.B. Cochran greatly; from then on, virtually all his revues bore his name—i.e., *Cochran's 1930 Revue.*) The new Charlot revue boasted all new material by Jeans, music from a variety of sources and a lineup of Charlot regulars and semi-regulars, including the mollified Maisie Gay, Monkman and Haddon. The lure of Charlot's name, now the epitome of trendiness and success, brought regular business to the Prince of Wales. And the best was yet to come.

Phyllis Monkman with Henry Kendall in "Specialty for You," *Charlot's Revue*, **1924 (courtesy of Mander & Mitchenson Theatre Collection).**

By late winter, Lillie was back in London, as was Lawrence, now fully recovered. Buchanan was temporarily unavailable, but Charlot saw the possibilities for expanding his business out of sight. The next version of *Charlot's Revue* would be as much "as performed in New York" as it possibly could be and it would be kicked off by a brilliant burst of publicity.

For some time thereafter, the "midnight matinee" of *Charlot's Revue* (March 30, 1925) was referred to as the greatest single event in the history of British musical theater, and a dazzler it was. Charlot indeed arranged a midnight performance—Lillie and Lawrence in the leads—and invited an audience of the purest British theatrical blue blood, which during the interval was photographed for posterity. The following account is part of a reminiscence by Ronald Jeans:

> Hero-worshipping took place around 3:30 A.M., with a great crowd on the sidewalk. There was a huge ovation for Violet Loraine, a special cheer for Grossmith, in a stage box with Heather Thatcher. Gladys Cooper was there, Lady Diana Cooper with John Barrymore, Zena Dare, Tallulah Bankhead festooned in orchids, Coward with his guest Lilian Braithwaite.... The audience did not want to stop applauding and leave the house, but Charlot got the orchestra to play "God Save the King." Charlot gave a speech at each of the two shows: "I am not paid to do this by the people concerned, but here is a list of the places where those who are hungry can get some food" [it developed that the Lyons Corner House nearby had imported special flour from America to make the specialties]—and he read out a long list of "breakfast" houses. At 3:30 off they went for eggs, bacon, waffles and hot griddle cakes. Some carried on to the 50–50 Club, where they danced to a volunteer band.

The guests were ferried home by an army of taxis and coaches chartered by Charlot. It was a glorious event, undoubtedly marking the peak of Charlot's tenure at the Prince of Wales, and it introduced another Charlot trademark: the "midnight matinee." Even in the darker days which followed 1925, this gala way of launching a new show provided the partygoing aura which characterized an André Charlot production.

It was also 1925 when the revue sketch became a staple of the trade for Samuel French, Inc., publishers of theatrical scripts. For the next ten years the works of especially Jeans and Titheradge sold well to the small groups, professional and amateur, who wanted to seem "up to date." Perhaps the most popular of these was *Charlot Revue Sketches*, a collection of playlets by Jeans.

Charlot's ascendancy was further acknowledged in a journalistic piece called "Andre Charlot, or London, Paris and New York" by the librettist and author Beverley Nichols. Nichols recalled Charlot in his office "lying back in his office chair, for all the world like a prosperous business man—except for one thing. His eyes were agonized." The cause was a pair of rust-colored curtains which were just *wrong*. Nichols used the curtains to help explain Charlot's instincts and intuitions—how he was able to "time" an entire revue without ever timing a single number, for instance, and how "he raised the 'book' of revue from the position of a despised poor relation to the chorus and the coiffeur to a place of primary importance." Charlot included the article in *People 'n Things*.

In 1926, when Huntly Carter wrote *The New Spirit in the European Theatre, 1914–1924*, in general a lament for the passing of the actor-managers and a complaint about the "standardization" of English theater ("The straight theater had become a revue theater") brought about by the efforts of the (American) Trust, he complained that a "big six" practically controlled everything and everybody in the West End. They were Cochran, the variety majordomos Sir Alfred Butt and Sir Oswald Stoll, deCourville, Grossmith (with Laurillard), and Charlot. But Carter

Nerman creates a whirling impression of *Charlot's Revue*, 1925, with Buchanan (left), Lillie, Monkman, Morris Harvey, Lawrence, Mundin and Gay. Charlot calls the tune.

complained least loudly about the last-named, admitting that "Charlot is the aesthetic type—he does not plunge his revues into extravagance and vulgarity." Carter's only favorable description of any show concerned Charlot's earliest intimate revues:

> *Samples* wanders from paradise to paradise, making artistic use of its decorative frame, painted cloths and ingenious lighting ... cool figures in white and neutral

colors sing and dance in rhythm against warm colors ... dazzling. More is staged on a small shallow stage with a black proscenium arch. There's a second false proscenium center stage, a painted back cloth, a dark green one and a dark green curtain for the middle frame.

Now that the New York version of *Charlot's Revue*—called by Charlot the "third version" of this show—was off and running (complete with Lillie and Lawrence's new number, which parodied Brice, the Dollys and various other Broadway luminaries), Charlot was willing to push it to greater heights. Announcing that he would produce an entirely new version every month, Charlot brought in star after star—American "turns" such as Sophie Tucker were included, but at its core, there was always at least one of Charlot's starry regulars. Monkman returned in "A Co-Opti-Clific Impression." The June version headlined Lillie, Lawrence, Matthews and Mundin. In July Charlot brought back Buchanan in exchange for Bea. One of the outstanding sketches was Wimperis's "Methods of Barberism," featuring Mundin as a Sweeney Todd–like barber and Buchanan as one of his victims.

It was at about this time that the Gladman family's foray into show business also proceeded apace. The family stage name had transmuted into "Wynne" and it was as Hazel Wynne that one of Flip's sisters joined the Charlot company. It can be surmised that this

Nerman's deft sketch of Phyllis Monkman's zany appeal in *Charlot's Revue*, 1927.

was a case of nepotism, but listening to Hazel's recording from the show—"The Elevator Belle"—reveals a charming, fey personality. Charlot was not one for being particularly soft on relatives—loyal, yes, but not to the detriment of business. (Hazel's theatrical career would be cut short by a "nervous illness" and she returned to live in the family home after her parents died only a few months apart in 1938.)

Everyone went to *Charlot's Revue,* and the various versions of the revue were simply brilliant. The August version brought Bea back to do many of the best things she had done for Charlot, including her classic "Sealed Feet," in which she portrayed the inept ballerina Wanda Allova. Lawrence's star numbers were performed here, as they had been on the U.S. tour, by Matthews. The September version dispensed with Buchanan and Matthews, but highlighted Bea and Gertie. A significant change was heralded in the October version. The major stars were missing because Charlot had concluded his deal with Archie Selwyn for a return to New York. This eighth version featured Matthews, Dorothy Dickson (in Lawrence's "A Cup of Coffee, a Sandwich and You") and several of Charlot's other regulars. November found Matthews partnered by Cyril Ritchard, a young Australian who rapidly became Buchanan's rival as a principal in dancing musicals. Nearly thirty years later, Ritchard became one of Broadway's great stars.

In one version or another, *Charlot's Revue*, the veritable epitome of 1925 West End fashion, gave 518 performances. At the close of this marvelous year at the Prince of Wales, Charlot presented a revival of *Charley's Aunt*.

The new New York show, tentatively called *The Charlot Revue of 1926*, went to Birmingham and Golders Green for tryout weeks before sailing away on the *Aquitania* (the prophetic rough crossing during which passengers were thrown off their

(Left to right, seated) Hazel Wynne, Jessie Matthews, Sunday Wilshin, (rear) Gordon Sherry, Herbert Mundin, André Charlot, Henry Lytton, Jr., and Harold Warrender arrive in New York for the *Charlot Revue* of '26.

feet and tossed from pillar to post, resulting in many a bruised leg, arm and torso). The *New York Morning Telegraph* for November 15 carried a photo of a woozy-looking group: Mundin, Lawrence, the Charlots, Buchanan and Lillie.

Meanwhile, the London production took off after Christmas from Golders Green on a tour of "the English provinces," alternating four different programs as *Charlot's Repertoire Revue* under the management of various sub-contractors. During this run, which ended in August, Jonny Gladman joined the cast. That was about as successfully expanded as her family and Charlot's business was ever to get.

Matthews, disappointed at being left behind on the second New York invasion ("There was method in it," Charlot later wrote), co-starred on the tour with Mundin, who later became a Hollywood film star (strongly effective in such straight dramatic tales as "Mutiny on the Bounty"), and Elsie Randolph, a newcomer who went on to become a major star as Buchanan's partner in a series of "dancing musicals" and films. Charlot later wrote that Matthews's success on this tour prompted him to star her in what was actually called *The Charlot Show of 1926*. Whatever Matthews may have thought of this latest demotion/promotion, that 1926 show, destined for humiliation in America, was the last time she worked for Charlot.

The itinerary of *Charlot's Repertoire Revue* is worth a glance since it reveals a great deal of expansion indeed. Listed alphabetically from Ashton to York, the itinerary includes a good 120 cities. That these were "reserved" should be taken into account, for no company could really stand up to such a grind. Interestingly, places such as Oxford and Cambridge are conspicuous by their absence (a relatively odd decision, considering how willingly Charlot loaned ideas and material to the university revues and how often university graduates wound up working for him). On the other hand, working-class towns, especially in the north of England, were well represented.

The return New York engagement of *Charlot's London Revue* was most cordial and quite a family affair. (In one sense, this was literally true, since both Hazel and Eva "Wynne" were in the cast, and this time André and Flip brought Joan along— her first transatlantic outing—with their cook, Margaret McElwee. For Eva, this engagement followed her most recent one, as one of "Mr. Cochran's Young Ladies" (C.B. had at last—and with excellent results—decided to employ a Charlot-styled chorus). The Charlots took a big apartment near Central Park and Joan attended DeLancey School. While they were there, the nanny met and married a New York chef.

The run-up to opening in New York proved temporarily happy for the two introverts, Charlot and Buchanan. During the horrendous ocean voyage they sipped champagne and assumed that the resultant delay in arrival meant—thank God!— that they could get away without having to play an opening week in Baltimore. But alas, Archie Selwyn was so determined that he hired a tender to take the battered company directly to Baltimore, where they played three well-received nights which neither enjoyed.

Baltimore was also the place where Charlot played a classic joke on Buchanan. Jack hated one sketch in particular because it was so "interactive" or audience-centered. It offered many possible permutations, depending upon which route the audience chose. Charlot discovered that a particular friend of Buchanan's showed up for every performance, shouting so loudly for one alternative that Jack simply had to play it (it was the only one he had prepared). Charlot finally headed off the friend one night, kept him from taking his seat, and Jack, bereft of help, had to "fake" the version the audience actually chose. This time, even Buchanan laughed.

But an air of unease persisted. By the time *Arch Selwyn Presents The Charlot Revue of 1926 with Beatrice Lillie, Jack Buchanan, Gertrude Lawrence and Herbert Mundin, Dances and Ensembles arranged by Jack Buchanan* opened at the Selwyn on November 10, Charlot was expressing reservations. Could audiences recapture that sense of discovery?

He later recalled, "Unfortunately, Bea, Gertie and Jack were no longer afraid of New York; each had ideas about doing things outside my own material, most not a patch on what I could supply. It was awfully difficult to fight them all along the line…. As I had feared, it was a show which did not discredit us, but which could

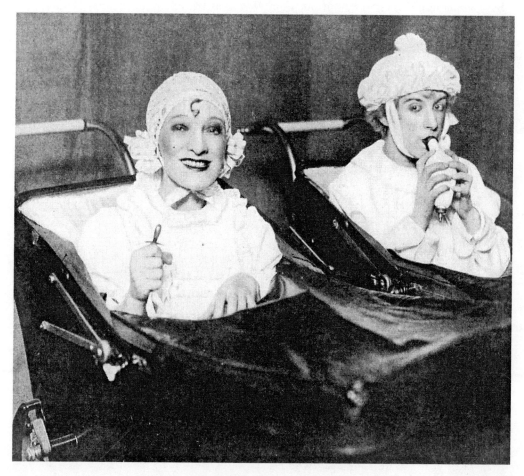

Gertrude Lawrence (left) and Beatrice Lillie in *Charlot's Revue* **at the Prince of Wales Theatre, 1926 (courtesy of Mander & Mitchenson Theatre Collection).**

not be compared to the first." But the new show did produce at least one brilliant moment, when Lawrence and Lillie performed an excruciatingly funny parody of Noel Coward's recent dramas. They called it "Fallen Babies" and performed it in an oversized pram.

The critics were as kind as ever and the Big Three just as lauded. But the sense of something different was clearly lacking. It's possible in retrospect to suggest that the songs and sketches in this show were inferior—after all, this time they were not the cream that had been skimmed from Charlot's London best. It is also possible to suggest that the U.S. had already learned quite a bit from Charlot (the major impact would be apparent at the end of the decade). The learners did not include Ziegfeld or his imitators, of course. But a smaller, smarter American kind of revue had materialized as early as 1924 with the first *Garrick Gaieties*. That breakthrough show for Rodgers and Hart did not allude to Charlot, but by 1926, as part of *The Fifth Avenue Follies*, a nightclub floor show/revue, their score included "Lawrence, Lillie and Jack."

Although the New York run would not be extended (Charlot was at the time grateful to Archie Selwyn for underwriting the 16-week guarantee), that was not necessarily a matter for worry—a transcontinental tour was in the cards—and Charlot, who never had too many qualms about working his contractees too hard, managed to squeeze everything out of the weeks in New York. He took a lease on the Rendezvous Club on West 45th Street and put on a floor show featuring the Big Three. Hearst's *American* described its opening as "one of the most brilliant gatherings of the night club season. Among the celebs present were Berlin, Moore, Webb, Harpo Marx, Ethel and Lionel Barrymore and Marilyn Miller."

After closing the New York run on March 6, the troupe headed west for what was supposed to be a triumphant groundbreaking tour. There were two weeks in Detroit, two in Chicago (where Jack Potter, who was managing the show, said they could have stayed three months), a week each in St. Louis and Kansas City and a week of traveling before arriving in Hollywood, where they discovered that the show's venue, a brand new house designed to be Hollywood's first "real" theater, was not quite ready for business. But on May 3 the El Capitan finally did open on Hollywood Boulevard, not far from the renowned and very opulent cinemas of Sid Grauman, the Egyptian and the Chinese. *Charlot's London Revue* would, for culturally aspiring Angelenos, be a way of showing that "the Boulevard" could offer the best of stage and screen entertainment. The theater critic of the *Los Angeles Times* was typically effusive:

> The plays that will be presented after the first intro-divertisement [!] will be for the most part those that typify the ideas and ideals—for deep-set ideals it truly has—of this community ... the fresh, buoyant and enlivening spirit of the West.

Charlot, who was not with the company at the time, being preoccupied in London with preparations for his next expansion (and, Buchanan noted, having already collected his guaranteed earnings), was not convinced that the film colony was ready for his show. He contacted Archie Selwyn, "who was on the French Riviera gambling away the show's profits," asking that the opening be postponed or even cancelled, but Selwyn did not budge from an idea he believed was timely. Unfortunately, Charlot was right and Selwyn was wrong. The show closed after five and a half weeks.

Although the members of the film colony itself supported Charlot's show from the very beginning, complete with dazzling searchlights, furs and jewels and a megaphone announcing the arrival of one star after another, the general public did not apparently want to make the journey of several miles from the suburbs to the heart of Los Angeles. Sometimes the house was only half full, a situation which was new to the Charlot cast. This was despite its presenting a remarkable mix of the best of Charlot.

The numbers included "Parisian Pierrot," "Early Mourning," "In Cigarette Land" and, of course, "March with Me" and "Limehouse Blues," the latter two billed as by request. The finale was something special, however, being a "Scotch Finale" in which Bea appeared as Bonny Prince Charlie. The closing night finale was pure Hollywood.

> All the British stars and their friends were on hand to give a great send-off. Jack Buchanan [*wearing his own tartan kilt*] staged a stunt that brought the house down. He quietly unlocked the pass door between the audience and the stage, and one by one the screen stars stole through, not letting anybody see them. Soon, Charlie Chaplin, Doug Fairbanks, George K. Arthur, John Gilbert and Rudolph Valentino were standing in the wings. During the finale, all the cast were supposed to appear in kilts. There were no kilts on hand for the stars, but when the music struck up, all romped on in impromptu get up. Chaplin had his trousers rolled to the knees, Fairbanks had a bed quilt for his tartan, and all the rest were trying to be as Scottish and as funny as possible. The audience roared. Never before had so many great stars appeared at once on any stage.

The Hollywood film colony simply fell in love with the Big Three and the feeling was reciprocated. (When Lillie, shooting her first film, awoke one Hollywood morning, she found Buster Keaton asleep outside her door, still holding a bouquet he had brought to show his admiration for a fellow genius.) Charlot's great stars now in various ways began the process of separation and, for some, establishing a nearly permanent residence in the U.S. All Selwyn did to help out was to pay for returning any cast members to London who did not want to stay.

Back in the U.S. to pick up the pieces, Charlot was compelled to cancel all agreements for future shows with Selwyn and sue for fees owed to himself and the various authors. Although he won the case and Selwyn (going bust in the bargain) eventually paid up, all the payoff went to the attorneys. On June 18, aboard the SS *Tuscania*, the three Charlots sailed back to England. Though he was almost always able to conceal his financial turmoil from his family, he was surely uneasy and licking his financial wounds. Perhaps fortunately, he was unaware that the best was over. He had developed diabetes and his great days of gourmet eating also were fast coming to a close. He refused insulin, leaving a strict diet the only option. Farewell, lovely cheeses!

SEVEN

1926–1937:
A Tale of Four Cities

If the disappointments of the second American invasion by *Charlot's London Revue* were not enough to disabuse Charlot of his obsession with American success, the balance of the year 1926—and its hangover into early 1927—could have done it.

The year 1926 was significant in British life. It was preeminently the year of the General Strike, an event that would help cement the national mood in gloom until the outbreak of the Second World War. Building over a long period of time but coming to fruition early in May over the coal industry, the General Strike proved that, contrary to the idealistic predictions of greater democracy and equality following the war, there were still two Britains, and the one with the upper hand was not about to surrender its advantages.

This sad truth was particularly evident in Establishment bastions such as Cambridge, where the well-organized actions of the working class were essentially nullified by the voluntary and "patriotic" actions of the privileged student class, which gallantly kept public services running while the news media looked on, cheering the boys. The General Strike collapsed in nine days, though the coal dispute rumbled on for months.

London theater, of course, tried to detach itself from the whole messy business. It relied, after all, upon the well-to-do. A record number of new shows opened during 1926, although such a figure needs to be qualified. Some were able to open because others had closed. Revue in general continued to prosper, and one very offbeat production—*Riverside Nights*—largely written by the journalist, wit and future member of parliament A.P. Herbert, provided an early preview of the next decade's movement away from music and toward intellectualism. Charlot must have been aware of most of these aspects, but he had his own troubles, which included having a theater to run and a lease to pay. He must have found it harder to concentrate on his own creations.

Even though his great stars now seemed lost to him (Lillie in Hollywood and on Broadway, Lawrence on Broadway, Buchanan with his own London productions with Hollywood beckoning), a new Charlot revue for 1926 had been in development for some time.

Anton Dolin and Henry Lytton caught in mid-leap, Matthews and Mundin on their toes and Mundin seated with a "cuppa" in *Charlot's Show*, 1926.

His ability to spot fresh talent had not deserted him. The new show would feature music by England's future favorite popular composer, Noel Gay, and Richard Addinsell, whose "Warsaw Concerto" became a classic of British light music ten years later. Since Charlot had decided her time in the wilderness had improved her, the mercurial Matthews headed the cast. He, Gay and Addinsell gave her good material. *The Charlot Show of 1926* (somewhat clumsily named, largely to avoid confusion with the title of the recent New York show) also marked the resurfacing of Harry Grattan, back from exile in South America, who helped with the casting and directing.

From the artistic standpoint, the London omens for Charlot's 1926 revue were good. But, still obsessed with success abroad, he seems disastrously to have taken his eye off the actual logistics of London theaters. During Decem-

"Gertie" in *Charlot's Show*, 1926.

ber and January, the British loved their comic pantomimes, which afforded audiences a great opportunity to revisit childhood and have a good laugh at some of the painful elements of the present. So London theaters were normally heavily booked with pantos—and that included Charlot's own Prince of Wales. *The Charlot Show of 1926* opened there on October 5, but it would have to transfer elsewhere within two months. And somewhat unbelievably, nothing could be found in or near the West End.

When he later wrote of the ensuing events, Charlot tended to lay the blame for a crucial debacle largely upon the smooth-talking Earl Carroll and his "gentle, suave manner," but there is little doubt that Charlot already knew enough about the American flesh merchant to realize that the deal Carroll now offered carried great danger.

Carroll's proposal was simple enough: ship the entire Charlot 1926 production to New York and share the stage with Carroll's next offering. An irresistible two-for-one, something different for the novelty-seeking Broadway patron, and of course another outing on the Great White Way for Charlot. There was a flurry of telegrams—Charlot grumbled about "a small fortune on wireless messages"—and very little real discussion of how the joint presentation would go.

In reality, Carroll was clearly preparing to use Charlot's name and gilt-edged reputation to help himself through tough times. Carroll thoroughly suspected that he would be spending the run of this double-barreled monster in an American jail (the day of the opening he went into a series of conferences with lawyers, trying to stay out). Carroll, who was usually exceptionally good at maneuvering law enforcement authorities to his own advantage, had run afoul of Prohibition. In partial celebration of the success of his 1926 *Vanities* (which had achieved a ticket price of $100) there had been an onstage party one predawn during which one of Carroll's "most beautiful girls in the world" had allegedly taken a champagne bath. Somehow the law's chief focus in this farrago had been that very Ms. Hawley, and during the subsequent trial Carroll's lawyer had asserted that he had acted like a gentleman to protect her reputation. Carroll got four years in the federal penitentiary at Atlanta, though he was freed before serving half that sentence.

It was during this clamorous period that Charlot's troupe arrived and soon found itself not so much part of an admittedly strange two-headed entertainment, but demoted to the status of add-on. The show's advertised title was *Earl Carroll's Vanities: International Edition*, and if it had not been for some members of the press, it is unlikely that Broadway audiences would even have known that Charlot's troupe was back. In any event, the press couldn't help much—or perhaps their love affair with Charlot's type of show had already run its course.

The uneasy *International Edition* pitted Carroll's nudes ("Engineered about ... by swinging hooks, rising platforms, and whirling chandeliers") against a typical Charlot chorus threading its way through a half-evening of song and sketch, some of which was so "British" (in one case, faux–Scottish) to have gone over the heads of any but the originally intended London audience. The Charlot and Carroll numbers were unwisely—not to say unbelievably—simply alternated. So occasional flashings of British wit alternated with American crassness. British subtlety jangled alongside the latter-day "coon" or downright racist comedy of Moran and Mack, the "two [not so] Black crows." Even New York audiences who had realized that Charlot was on the bill could not save the show, and it very quickly took off by itself for a road tour (for the predatory Abe Erlander) that proved even worse luck.

Through Toronto snow and Boston tolerance they went, a week or sometimes one night at a time. In locales such as Detroit the tired businessmen clearly wanted what they believed they had been promised: an evening of unchallenging Carroll-type enjoyment, and it wasn't long before they were showering Charlot's performers with coins. The degradation proved too much for the high-strung Matthews, who fled the stage more than once. The road tour shuddered to a halt. Thousands of pounds and dollars in the red, Charlot would not have been able to send his company home unless Bea, Gertie and Jack had sent money. Sunday Wilshin, a member of the chorus, later recalled:

> The show folded and like people are apt to do on such occasions, they all walked away, shall we say, from Charlot, because people do that sort of thing, when they don't get their immediate salaries. He would pay their fares of course to London, but many people—about half—just walked out on him.

A press photograph of March 26 shows "Mrs. André Charlot sailing to England with Miss Joan Charlot on the *Celtic*." It was an agonizing time for Charlot, being left on his own resources in New York for six months before being able to return to

England: "I was as lonely as a man can be." He had one notable success. In the summer of 1927 he joined with Paramount-Publix to present Lawrence in a scaled-down Charlot revue at the New York Paramount Theater. She got $3,500 a week for 30 performances. Finally, having scraped together the fare from this and that enterprise, he was able to catch the *Leviathan* home.

Though it is possible to assert that his emotional state gradually improved, it is even easier to prove that his reputation never recovered and that his ability to mount comebacks was permanently damaged. But he kept selling whatever, wherever and whenever he could. It was early December when a Charlot sketch appeared in *On and Off*, a revue staged in Berlin.

In 1927, according to Sheridan Morley's biography of Lawrence, the star "installed [her daughter] Pamela along with Andre Charlot's similarly-aged daughter at a Catholic girls' boarding school near Margate." Not so; Pamela went to Roedean,

Herbert Mundin in *Charlot's Show*, 1926.

then and now quite a top private school, while Joan was enrolled at The Girdlers in seaside Herne Bay. Even there, one wonders how Charlot swung the deal. It could be that her school fees were offset by her father's giving free advertising space to the school. Joan enjoyed The Girdlers, but remembered even more clearly the annual partings from her family, which would consist of a fine lunch at the Savoy followed by tears at Waterloo Station.

Despite the recent setbacks, the Charlots made one of their regular visits to brother Jean's family in Paris. Jean's daughter Odette recalls "sumptuous parties organized by André which lasted until six in the morning."

There was no 1927 Charlot revue on the London boards. Typical of what was presented that year was a production called *Tuppence Coloured* by "Edward Wilbraham" at Charlot's Prince of Wales. It ran 18 performances, after being described as "unbelievable" by its critics. Edward Wilbraham was actually Lord Lathom and Charlot was bending his principles to return a favor.

By 1928 Charlot had pulled himself back together sufficiently to begin planning another revue, and he joined forces with Grossmith to produce a straight anti-

ANDRE CHARLOT PERSONALLY PRESENTS
THE NEW
CHARLOT REVUE
With of 1927
HERBERT
MUNDIN
JESSIE
MATTHEWS
and
THE
COMPANY
FROM
THE PRINCE
OF WALES
THEATRE
LONDON
ENGLAND

A NEW BOX O' NOVELTIES for 1927

HAZEL WYNNE - SUNDAY WILSHIN
HENRY LYTTON, Jr.
GORDON SHERRY - ALLAN MacBETH
HAROLD WARRENDER - ANN STEPHENSON
and A SINGING-DANCING CHORUS
in
21 Skits, SCENES and Song SUCCESSES
APPLAUDED by LONDON and NEW YORK

Charlot was fortunate to marry into a family with so many attractive and talented daughters. Hazel Wynne featured on this poster and her sisters Eva and Jonny also appeared in versions of Charlot's revues in the 1920's (original artwork courtesy of Peter R. Gay).

war play at the Strand. Next he ventured into a new field with what he called the Sunday Play Society. The SPS was Charlot's once-a-month version of a unique phenomenon, the presentation of plays unsuitable for the West End (on the day of the week that theaters were "dark") in a private club.

Aside from being a somewhat logical extension of the established Englishman's proclivity to take refuge in private clubs of all sorts, the Sunday private clubs were the latest skirmish in the licensing wars. The Sunday private clubs essentially produced plays that were too controversial to be approved by the Lord Chamberlain, whose blue pencil was normally activated by allusions to monarchy and other sensitive public figures, rather than by sexual content.

The clubs also presented sheer vanity productions, which is to say opportunities for well-heeled amateurs, who were often play backers, to see their protégés and scripts on the boards. Predictably, Lord Lathom founded his own private society, the Ventures, and put on three of his own "banned" plays.

Philip Charlot, almost 18, had now put Stowe behind him and was at work in the family business as a sort of apprentice-of-all-trades. Beginning in front-of-house management, he gained experience as a producer for SPS.

Most of those ventures were staged at the Prince of Wales and often offered unplanned humor. Such was the case when Sophie Tucker appeared in an SPS play as Socrates' wife, an unlikely juxtaposition which, combined

Brothers André (left) and Jean Charlot in Barbizon, France.

with her inability to learn lines, resulted in memorable ad libs and shameless raucousness. They also afforded Charlot a continuing commitment to the development of his own stars. A production of the lugubrious (but Pulitzer Prize–winning) Owen Davis play *Icebound* was undertaken so that Lawrence could have a chance at straight drama. As a household drudge faced with the problem of inheriting a lot of money, she showed that there was more to her than flightiness. (She would reward Charlot two years later by breaking her contract for his new revue in favor of co-starring with Noel Coward in *Private Lives.)*

One of the Sunday Play Society presentations in late 1928 was *Nine Playlets*, including works by Coward, Barrie and Titheradge. According to *Theatre World*, Charlot spoke "at considerable length through a loudspeaker at frequent intervals throughout the evening." The reviewer added that he was "aided and abetted by a precocious child named Jane, who should have been soundly slapped and put to bed."

Actually, this was one of Charlot's publicity stunts. "Jane" was one of the principals in a new venture: a weekly radio program. Having made an edgy peace with the BBC, he was about to front 32 episodes of "Charlot's Hour." In typical fashion, he entered negotiations with the BBC (he never really trusted them to his dying day) armed with the unverifiable boast that during the 1927 exile he had prepared "for one of the big American radio companies" a weekly hour-long variety program.

Jessie Matthews not kicking out but kicking back in *Charlot's Revue*, 1927.

The only thing that had stopped him, he insisted, was a last-minute decision to return to England.

In fact, "Charlot's Hour" proved quite a successful retreat from his stated principles. While never quite concealing his contempt for the BBC and its functionaries, but now able to play publicly his avuncular persona as "Uncle André," he put Philip in charge of some of the production, assembled a passable imitation of his famed company, hired Grattan once more as author and performer and was finally able to claim, after the show's last episode, "the largest postbag in the history of British radio."

From January 12 "Charlot's Hour" (55 minutes starting at 9:35 p.m. every Tuesday night on 2LO, the main BBC station) showed a surprisingly astute command of the medium as well as providing, for an audience which was just coming to realize its power, a real revue of the air. The original agreement was for 12 programs but the show was simply too popular to decommission. The BBC's own *Radio Times* magazine accompanied its announcement of the new venture with a classic caricature of Charlot "enchanting the microphone."

Charlot gained a good deal of publicity from doing "Charlot's Hour." In "Celebrities on Toast," *London Calling*, May 19, 1928, H.C.G. Stevens wrote:

> The toast, children, is André Charlot ... pretty well the bitterest opponent of Wireless in all the entertainment world, as well as the manager who on no account would allow any artiste of his to perform on the Sabbath. But ... things and opinions and points of view are liable to change. "Charlot's Hour" is a tremendous success at 2LO and the Sunday Play Society is already beginning to look like a good deal more than the mere thin end of the regular Sunday entertainment wedge.... He is in greater form than ever he was, a possessor of greater

Peter Haddon, Beatrice Lillie, and Gertrude Lawrence in *Charlot's Revue*, **1927.**

strength and vitality than ever. He is simply waiting his chance to pounce upon the public … it really MUST be revue…. Good luck to him—a sentiment that will be echoed by a company of actors, actresses, authors, lyricists, composers (real composers as well as the mere just hum it over to Elsie April and she'll write it down for you type), costume designers.

On radio Charlot mixed items from his theatrical past with new characters devised for the purpose and he invited audience participation via a weekly limerick-writing contest. What listeners heard on March 8, 1928, after the familiar "How d'you do" and "Ready to work" opening, was:

> Hullo everybody, this is Uncle Charlot speaking and very pleased to be with you again. When I left you and the microphone three weeks ago I was feeling quite depressed and wondering how I could get along all that time without you, but thanks to the very kindly consideration of many listeners I have not been alone—I have received so many sweet letters every day and by every post that I have really felt I was with you all the time.

Charlot was interrupted by "Jane," who chided him for being so sentimental. He then introduced a man called Arthur Dorville singing "Over the Hill and Just Beyond," the highly sentimental original work of a listener from Ireland. Charlot had encouraged his listeners to send their own creations. This bit of amateurism was followed by Ethel Baird, one of the Hour's regulars, singing "It's a Matter of Indifference to Me," the comic tale of a malapropistic neighborhood gossip. It would have evoked in listeners a memory of Music Hall days, as well as fitting nicely with the current monologues of Stanley Holloway, an ex–Co-Optimist rushing to the heights of popularity.

Jane returned to express her own "indifference" about the proceedings so far. Further patter between her and Uncle André led to a sketch and song called "No One's Ever Kissed Me," a collaboration between Jeans and Braham. The sketch showed a man of the world trying to educate his shy friend on the best way to treat women—essentially the rough approach. The proof of this "education" comes when the shy one's girlfriend arrives for tea, and he manages to slam her finger in a book so that he has to kiss it better. And she likes it!

Back comes Charlot, stating that Billy Leonard, who's on next, will try to please some listeners who believe the show is not highbrow enough. Leonard performs "Let's All Sing the Lard Song," an absurdity about having a bladder full of lard. Further byplay between Uncle André and Jane precedes the "'normous" (Jane's word) Rex Evans, singing Noel Coward's "Other Girls," in which "sweet simplicity, so full of domesticity" triumphs over the smart, cocktail set (hmm). Further byplay with Jane, who has misunderstood the lyric, precedes a prize-winning (two guineas or about $11 at the time) listener limerick and the announcement of a topic for the next competition.

One of Lawrence's famed numbers, Jeans and Braham's "I Might," was followed by Jane's babbling on about "the funny way they talk." Then came "a concerted number" sung by the whole company entitled "You and Your Li'l Banjulele," a spoof of torch-carrying songs as well as a current instrumental craze. Another sketch by Jeans featured Drake, the "man" (valet) of Philip Cumberland. A know-it-all of the Jeeves persuasion, he is simultaneously helpful and scornful while Cumberland as seducer attempts to deal with a woman who has clumsily revealed their assignation to her husband. After confusion engendered by the valet and master switching identities, the husband gives up his wife, leaving Cumberland with her and the couple's five children.

Further inane dialog between Charlot and Jane precedes "Dirty Work," a comic duet for Leonard and Ralph Coram as two unconvincing all-purpose criminals. Jane is finally sent to bed and the entire company sings the finale, Ivor Novello's "There Are Times," the happifying song providing the necessary upbeat conclusion. About the only thing atypical about the March 8 edition was that it omitted one of the extremely popular Grattan-written dialogues between Emma (Betty Bolton), deft at harpooning pomposity, and the master of pompous philosophical malapropism, 'Erb Grattan himself. "Charlot's Hour" certainly catered to the audience as he envisioned it. And its response proved that his perceptions were accurate.

In 1929 a small book titled *Charlot's Hour Competitions* was published, in the main compiling the best of the limericks submitted by listeners on weekly topics announced by Charlot. In the preface, he was in avuncular form:

> Hello, Everybody, this is Uncle André calling…. It is exactly six months since I was privileged to address you for the last time in this way—but it feels like six years—you see, I miss you.

He went on to say that like most people, he kept an address book "with the names and addresses of my friends" and that he had at his last broadcast asked those who had enjoyed the show to send a postcard with their name and address to add to his book. Thus eventually 24,000 letters and cards arrived.

> Now, do you wonder why I miss you? I cannot pretend that I managed to read everything myself, but I read as many as I could, others helped me to read the rest and reported on them, and this little book owes its existence to the fact that a number of my correspondents expressed the wish that there should be a lasting record of our competitions…. I hope it may bring pleasant recollections to some of you, and, feeling that I must not outstay my welcome at this microphone—I beg your pardon, I should say outstay my welcome as "announcer" of this book, I will once more, for the last time, perhaps, say "Good-night, Everybody, good-night."

Although he refused to mortgage his future to radio—he had scraped together enough backing for a new revue which would open in late 1928—he had once more broken ground and in fact established a new trend. Before the last episode of "Charlot's Hour" had even taken air the *Radio Times* was announcing a "new radio revue"—by Albert deCourville. But it proved not to have the panache of Charlot's show. During these times, Charlot took advantage of his relationship with the BBC by giving a preview performance of *The Charlot Show of 1928* on radio. In the subsequent *Manchester Empire News* articles which later ran under his byline, Charlot explained using "show" this time instead of "revue"—because the public had come to think of "revue" as implying "a stupid form of entertainment" (a slam at everyone else's kind of revue?).

Alas, the new Charlot stage revue had very little panache of its own and signaled a clear decline in its impresario's fortunes. It's possible to say that the real stars of that short-lived venture were the Charlot "contract girls"—a technical name for those half-dozen which were the core of the typically versatile chorus: Betty Oliver,

Betty Frankus, Nina Presley and Joy Spring, who formed the basis for the sub-revues which characterized Charlot's next two unhappy years. Several of them reen-listed for Charlot's theatrical comeback in 1933 and stayed until the end of his English career. One of them, Trixie Scales, thought there was a reason: "We all had very deep affection for him. He was kind and lovely. He used to take so much trouble with the understudies. He would see as many as eight in a day. He would have one or two understudies for each number. He was a gentle man."

It was never clear to what degree he might have been, like his great rival Cochran, a Lothario as well as an impresario. There may have been a "favorite of the run" but nothing substantiates this. Charlot appears to have been a synonym for discretion—and Flip, perhaps, a model of tolerance and forbearance. Before leaving St. John's Wood, he had received a most unusual note—which he kept for the rest of his life—from a French aviator in Casablanca. The aviator implored Charlot to find him a "frolicsome" chorus girl with whom he could correspond. One reason he kept it is probably the note on the back of the envelope from Flip, who had read it by mistake: she said she did not know he had taken up this kind of thing as a side-line.

Flip was, in fact, a frequent visitor to rehearsals of *The Charlot Show of 1928* and most of Charlot's shows, leaving behind an image, as Scales put it, of a "soft and gentle lady, who always stopped and talked with you." Charlot was occasionally on the receiving end of his wife's silent treatment and over the years there were separations not necessarily connected to business.

It was during one of these separations that Joan accompanied her mother for a lengthy visit to "Oncle Jean, Tante Raymonde and cousin Odette" at 114 Place Lafayette in Paris where she went to day school in the old Charlot neighborhood.

In July and August of 1928 Charlot "told his life story" to the *Manchester Evening News*. It was another way of keeping his name before the public, though he professed dislike of having a "ghost-writer." After the collapse of the 1928 production (100 performances and going-away weeks in Golders Green and Brighton) there were no more Charlot revues in the 1920s. It is a typical irony that to youthful London theatergoers circa 1930, the name Charlot mainly meant a troupe of talented chorines.

At least he kept his girls working. There were new cinemas where they could appear. A trimmed-down Charlot show accompanied the Al Jolson film *The Singing Fool* during its week's run at two London houses. There followed a week in a south London cinema and a six-week tour of Paramount houses in Newcastle, Liverpool and other northern cities.

Charlot kept his business going. Throughout 1929 he assembled "floor shows" based upon "The [Ten] Charlot Girls," working with transatlantic choreographer Barry Oliver, for two London hotels. The shows were quite similar to *The Midnight Follies*: the girls were fronted by a major star from one week to the next. These included Charlot regulars McLeod, Claude Hulbert (Jack's brother) and "Billie" Barnes, who upon finding a glittering film career became "Binnie."

The first of these cabaret/floor shows opened in April 1929 at the Splendide in Piccadilly. In July it transferred to the Grosvenor House in Park Lane. By October

Charlot had enlarged and divided the company, so that shows could proceed at both hotels simultaneously, with two shows nightly at nine and eleven. (Some of these shows found their way onto those film roundups of current West End entertainment.) Most of the material was provided by Rowland Leigh, with music by Harry Revel, a Londoner who would shortly make a minor name for himself on Broadway but a major one in Hollywood. Charlot modestly noted that his floor show was Revel's first full score. From this point on, Leigh was one of Charlot's chief collaborators and supporters.

Among those regularly attending these floor shows were the Prince of Wales (later King Edward VIII) and the Duke of York (later King George VI). Charlot records that his chorus girls eventually grew quite blase about the presence of royalty, recording an incident in a *London Sunday Express* story in 1931:

> "The Queen of Norway is in tonight," I told them.
> They said "H'm."
> "And Prince Olaf and his young wife," I added.
> Again, "H'm."
> "The Duke and Duchess of York, too," I ventured.
> A slightly more interested "H'm"—but that was all.
> "And, look here, the Prince of Wales and Prince George are also coming," I said.
> Then one of them asked, "Isn't there anyone else?"
> "Well, there is Clive Brook," I suggested.
> That stirred them to the depths. "What, Clive Brook the film star?" they shouted. "How terribly thrilling. Oh, do let us see him. Where is he?"

He also records a conversation with Queen Alexandra, when she complained that she had heard that some of his program had been altered because she was coming. Since it was a Grand Guignol moment, with excessive bloodshed, he told her, it would not have been suitable for either her or her young daughter. The queen was mollified.

Having now had firsthand experience with radio, Charlot considered himself authoritative enough to hand out advice. In May 1929 a number of newspapers carried his article "How I Would Run the BBC." Prefacing his remarks by stating that he would voice no criticism of the "present administration" until "it is given more rope, more scope, and more money," he offered his prescription:

> I should scrap the composite programme [*"programme" served as the British word for "format" or perhaps "outlet"*] ... I should have three programmes.... First, I should have a station broadcasting dance music from noon until midnight. That would give every dance enthusiast the chance of arranging his radio party whenever he wanted to, and would, I think, greatly increase the number of listeners. Next I should have a station which, from noon until midnight, would broadcast nothing but serious music.... The third station would be ... general ... broadcasting this, that and the other, and meeting the needs of the large body of listeners who consider jazz fiends and highbrow musicians equally hopeless cases.... That one, too, would run for twelve hours of the day, if not longer.

In subsequent years, the BBC essentially adopted all of Charlot's ideas and the present BBC Radio 2, Radio 3 and Radio 4 correspond almost exactly to his suggestion, though they now transmit 24 hours a day. Charlot concluded his manifesto:

> I should pay the most meticulous attention to correspondence and criticism from listeners…. As an impresario, I regard the need of the broadcaster to keep in touch with listeners as paramount. In the theatre, the box office and your study of the audience give you an immediate answer to your question, "Do they like it?"

Charlot was offering an oblique critique of the paternalism which the BBC's first guiding light, Lord Reith (who had recently been knighted), had practiced and would continue to practice. He was also pointing the way to audience research, the rating systems which now virtually govern broadcasting.

In the late summer of 1929 Charlot returned to New York in search of a way to reverse his recent decline. His weakness for cinema surfaced once more. Having observed the success of talking (and singing and dancing) motion pictures, he was well disposed when Jennie Jacobs, an agent, suggested, "Why don't you do a 'talkie-revue?'" When Jacobs promised to introduce him to Heinrich Schnitzler, the New York head of RKO Radio, recently formed to produce talking pictures, Charlot set about imagining how to use his best material on the screen.

The meeting with Schnitzler went well, and when Charlot realized that Lillie, Lawrence and Buchanan were all due in New York shortly for three different Broadway shows, things got even better. All that seemed to be missing were the actual scripts and songs.

Charlot promised to return to Britain immediately, collect the scripts and the songs and discuss things with the Big Three. All went moderately well, though on the return trip to New York, Charlot nearly had to stow away, there being at first no apparent room on the ship. Back to Schnitzler went Charlot, laden with material that included production photos which could help illustrate the film's likely continuity. Schnitzler said he would have to discuss everything with the producer William LeBaron, who was in Hollywood.

So off by train to Hollywood went Charlot and his material. LeBaron listened intently and said he would discuss things with Schnitzler. When LeBaron returned to New York in the near future all of them could get together.

After 24 frustrating hours in Hollywood, Charlot returned to New York, determined to get aboard the *Olympic* and return to England. But Schnitzler insisted LeBaron would be there soon. Two weeks later, LeBaron arrived but no conference ever occurred and Charlot went home. The talkie-revue was never done and he put the whole business down to learning the Hollywood runaround.

But the Charlot business did get into the movies. In the first British musical film, *Elstree* [a film studio] *Calling* (1930), "The Charlot Girls" performed a charming number called "A Lady's Maid Is Always in the Know." The film, co-directed by Charlot, Jack Hulbert and Alfred Hitchcock, was basically another roundup of West End talent within a hastily concocted story line and featured current stars of the London musical stage, including Hulbert and Courtneidge. Charlot received credit for staging the dances and ensembles. He proceeded to plan a film of his own,

"André Char-lot's sound film revue *The New Waiter*," but although sheet music for songs by Leigh and Reg Casson exists, the film was apparently never made.

It was 1929 when Charlot's last three Sunday Play Society productions trod the boards at the Prince of Wales, a house whose lease had two years to run. These included *Hunter's Moon*, an adaptation of a Danish original; *Let's Leave It at That*, a three-act comedy by a recent Charlot regular, Jeanne deCasalis, and her partner Colin Clive, who played the leads; and *The Donkey's Nose*, another three-act comedy starring Sybil Thorndike. All things considered, it was impressive stuff for a private club.

1930 saw Charlot rolling the dice once again in all-out attempts to regain his ascendancy in the musical theater. *Charlot's Masquerade* was hatched amidst a brave general effort on the part of West End theater to combat the twin perils of the Depression and the talking, singing and dancing film. Charlot looked at a new theater, the Cambridge, quite a lovely Art Deco house close by the scruffy Seven Dials neighborhood of Covent Garden, not far from Leicester Square. Here he planned a return to form.

To underline his intentions, he lined up Lawrence, whose legitimate career had begun to prosper. The show had sketches by Jeans (of late a regular for Cochran and Hulbert) and attractive songs by Leigh. There were some of Charlot's new "regulars" and even the work of dancer-choreographer Anton Dolin. (These were the heady early days of native English ballet, whose new talents had often already worked for Cochran. Original ballets created for revue by Dolin, Frederick Ashton and others are rarely included in their *oeuvre*.)

But Lawrence proved to have other ideas—or at least Coward gave her some and she took them. In *People 'n Things*, Charlot told part of the story:

> During London Calling, I said to Coward, "Noel, one of these days you must write a play for me, with you and Gertie to play in it." "I'll do it," he promised.... After one or two setbacks ... his stock went low, but I still believed in him and looked forward.... All the time I waited for this play.... He did it in 1930, but not, alas, for me.... When I reminded him two years ago [probably 1935] that he had promised to write the play for me, he said, "that was very naughty of me, wasn't it?" My motto is Figaro's: "Let us laugh about everything, lest we should have to cry about it."

Lawrence informed Charlot that she would break her contract with him in order to do *Private Lives* with Coward. The decision was, of course, the making of the rest of her career. By 1931, "everyone" was writing plays like *Private Lives*—even Jeans (*Can the Leopard?*) and engaging Lawrence to star in them. But it was a bitter blow to Charlot, who responded in the best way he knew—which was to force Lawrence to pay him—to buy out her contract. Although she was bankrupt herself, partly because of the failure of her recent *International Revue* for Lew Leslie in the U.S., she raised the money—£2,000—and the show, minus its intended star, went on.

That was not the end of pre-production woe. Charlot had engaged Sir Seymour Hicks, by then a legend of the West End, to co-star, but when Hicks learned that Lillie was to replace Lawrence, he refused to take the stage opposite her. The wrangling eventually caused Charlot to give Hicks £500 of his windfall.

A retrospective glance at *Charlot's Masquerade* shows a first-class production. Florence Desmond, scouted by Charlot during her nightclub act at the Café Anglais, became the nominal co-star with Lillie. Desmond advanced her own career as a glamorous impressionist with stunning numbers which wowed the audience and the London theater world. Constance Carpenter, the quintessential substitute Lawrence, took over some of her material.

The highlight of the evening was the first act finale, staged on a small but genuine skating rink, in which Desmond—as the currently popular and wholly outrageous American, Tallulah Bankhead—stopped the show. Entering in an outfit identical to Tallulah's in the recent play *Let Us Be Gay*—white leather motoring coat, white beret, large flame-colored chiffon hankie—she threw open her arms and shouted to the audience, "Bless you, darlings," at which the audience "rose as one." (At a party after the opening, Bankhead herself swept in to give advice only to discover that "She speaks like me off stage—the bitch!")

But the show's box-office numbers never suggested a long run and Charlot, who had fended off the offers soon made to "Dessie" by London's best cabarets by doubling her salary, was truly up against it.

Perhaps he could re-scale the heights with *Wonder Bar*, an unusual musical comedy which had arisen in Europe and eventually would find Broadway and Hollywood success as a vehicle for Al Jolson. Charlot saw it as perfect for the Savoy, a theater which was, after all, located in one of his favorite refuges; lunch at the Savoy could almost always put things right, and during the show's run, he enjoyed many a happy supper there with the show's Danish star, Carl Brisson, who had touched off some fireworks early in the run by bickering onstage with co-star Joan Dickson during their love duets.

Wonder Bar was the most expensive production of Charlot's career. In order to make it work, the theater had to be transformed into a semblance of Sam Wonder's Bar, so that the audience would at one and the same time be in an actual cabaret bar (complete with "real live" cocktail bars on each side of the auditorium) and witnessing a drama being played amongst itself. The modifications were expensive; so was the cast, headed by Brisson and Dickson, the reigning queen of British musical comedy. Adaptation of book and new English lyrics came from Leigh and very good they were.

Another of the London stage's attempts to cope with the onslaught of musical motion pictures was a drive toward *bigness*—something overwhelmingly engulfing onstage which the still small and not entirely convincing cinema screen could not offer. (This prefigured what happened twenty years later when film itself grew bigger in order to compete with the tiny new television box which was keeping audiences at home.) And Cochran, still Charlot's chief rival, was willing to go as big as it took to get the audience.

Cochran's *Evergreen*, with music by Rodgers and Hart and starring Matthews, was due at the newly refurbished Adelphi in the Strand. The refurbishments included huge revolving stages, which could make *Evergreen* the biggest and most technically advanced show ever to play the West End. As the shows neared their projected opening dates near the end of 1930, anticipation heightened. Cochran finally stole the march by suddenly advancing the opening date of *Evergreen* at short notice. Charlot had no option other than to move his opening later in the week. Two of his principals then caught colds and missed the rescheduled opening at a cost of £800 a day.

By a margin of two days, *Evergreen* made the running as London's biggest stage show. Though *Wonder Bar* (boosted by a July outing on the BBC—"Wonder Bits from Wonder Bar") eventually gave more than 200 performances, a more than respectable showing during a nearly impossible theatrical era, it had no chance of recouping its cost. That and the loss of the Prince of Wales leasehold, sold for £700 though Charlot had refused an offer of £105,000 a year earlier, made him bankrupt. The Official Receiver listed his liabilities at £60,000.

Bereft of Charlot's taste, the Prince of Wales would go on to house "non-stop revues." The bankruptcy finished off his plans for a 1931 revue which would have featured the rising monologist Reginald Gardiner, Betty Frankiss and Gertrude Musgrove, later Mrs. Alexander Korda.

Cochran, no stranger to bankruptcy himself, surely knew that such a fate might befall whoever lost the battle. He probably believed, as did many, that Charlot would simply shrug off bankruptcy as part of the impresario game and soon be back in business at the same old stand. Buchanan, who was by then riding high, gave Charlot a helping hand with a check for £600, together with an encouraging note from himself, Lawrence and Lillie.

Charlot was still a soft touch for any friend who was in trouble, still the spendthrift who could not deny himself, and still the sensitive boy who could visit a dark place in his soul where no one else could reach him. He mused, "When nations are on the verge of bankruptcy, when they are really bankrupt, they go off the gold standard and all is well. When individuals go bankrupt, they acquire a stigma difficult to shake off in the years that follow—unless they take the precaution to feather a hidden nest before taking the great step."

He was not the only troubled entrepreneur during this period. The definitive listing of annual London productions by H.P. Waring shows that during the calendar year of 1931 no fewer than 555 different attractions opened at London theaters—not including the variety houses. This was the largest number on record and it did not imply success. Plays and musicals went on—and came off—with deadening regularity. In 1932 the total was 472, the second largest on record.

Cochran had always responded to bankruptcies by writing a book of memoirs. Charlot now re-entered (halfway, at any rate) the autobiographical realm, although the *London Sunday Express*'s William Pollock did the actual writing. A short series running over the holidays in 1931–32 was filled with bits like, "It's nice to have your own car waiting outside, but taxis are less bother and the tube is quicker" and "I used to play bridge for a dollar a hundred … now I play bridge for a penny or two pence a hundred," its overall tone was implicit in "…as Mr. Micawber might well have remarked, although I am 'down' financially, I am not 'out' in spirit." But he also delivered a prediction in *The Argonaut*: "There is still an enormous public for the kind of intimate revue and musical comedy entertainment with which my name has always been associated." He eventually showed that he was a better writer than his ghosts.

He did not entirely sit out his bankruptcy, which in Britain was tantamount to exile as the bankruptcy laws then as now were admittedly creditor-biased. To be made bankrupt was to be "hammered." At least it gave him a chance to visit his French family more often.

The Charlot family spent a good deal of 1931–32 across the channel. Charlot worked for London Films, the company headed by Alexander Korda, an up-and-coming young filmmaker to whom he was introduced by Grossmith. His own debacles in Hollywood notwithstanding, film had made an impression on Charlot and he welcomed the chance to learn more. André Charlot is credited as director of a French film (Pallas Films, 1932) called *Le Jugement de Minuit*, also titled *Le Venguer* and *Mystère de la Dame Blonde*. He also welcomed working in Paris once again. Though he'd been a British subject for 15 years, it may have been hard for him to believe he'd ever been away.

With no specific job description ("Korda told me I was a yes man who said no"), he learned a good deal about the medium while working on the French and English versions of Korda's *The Lady from Maxim's*. And when the opportunity arose, the Charlots and Kordas holidayed in Tenerife together.

The Korda connection—Alexander, Vincent and Zoltan, producers, directors, designers—would prove valuable in other ways, including providing some backing for one of his later comeback attempts. But it also helped Philip, who became a sensitive cutter of film. Philip would work for the Kordas for several years as assistant editor, editor or supervising editor on some well-remembered films, including *The Private Life of Henry the Eighth*, *The Private Life of Don Juan* and *The Man Who Could Work Miracles*. As an increasingly talented editor, he eventually cut special sequences on other films, including *The Ghost Goes West*, *Sanders of the River*, *Elephant Boy*, *The Shape of Things to Come* and *Pygmalion*. He also performed a good deal of second-unit directing for Korda, though always without on-screen credit.

It was in 1932, while working for Korda, that Philip met the stunning Mary Musgrave at a nightclub. She had survived a brief marriage and on this evening was out with another man, who turned out to be an acquaintance of Philip's. Visiting their table, Philip made the first move and she responded positively, though nothing came of it at the time. When a few months later Mary came to Korda's for a screen test, they met again at the studio canteen. By 1934 they were living together and in 1937 were married.

Mary recalled Philip's parents being delighted by the match, although she observed how nervous Philip was around his father and how little he sought to compete with him. She added that the father, "very *grand seigneur*," was probably never conscious of putting his son down. The couple's attendance every week at Sunday lunch was mandatory: "Attention would have been drawn if we had said we couldn't for some reason be there."

One of the high points of Philip's film editing career came in the area of the short subject. *The Private Life of the Gannets*, a John Grierson production about seabirds written by Ronald Lockley and which would set the tone for later wildlife films, won the 1934 Academy Award for best documentary. Later, for Korda, he cut *Moonlight Sonata*, a short subject about the famed pianist-statesman Ignace Jan Paderewski.

In 1932 Charlot was back in London where he produced two "legit" plays in association with other entrepreneurs. His return to revue proved pretty big news and when he arrived in Manchester that April for the break-in week he was mobbed by the press. As it turned out, however, Girlie, the latest of his Great Danes, got a share of the publicity when Joan's sketch of the dog ran in a local paper. A Manchester columnist did predict that Charlot could do well up north if he brought his "penetrating wit to bear upon Northern life."

The comeback show was *How D'You Do?*, staged in 1933 at the Comedy Theater. Charlot and his friends had almost literally passed the hat for the money (Sir Peter Saunders, the producer of the legendary long-run champion *The Mousetrap*, said that the total was only £1,000, for which Charlot delivered an entire show). The reward was encouraging. The show went through three versions and, according to reviewers, was a reincarnation of the "party of good friends" atmosphere of old.

For *How D'You Do?* Charlot assembled a fresh company. Its nominal star was Frances Day, an expatriate American singer he had first spotted doing a cabaret act in London after her return from working for Texas Guinan in New York. A singular performer, she was capable, he wrote, of everything from circus to Shakespeare but guilty of always trying to improve on her last performance. Blonde and gorgeous, Day sang with a little-girl voice that could be quite irritating, but what a treat for a male audience she proved! Saunders recalled dropping in two or three times a week just in time for her big numbers: "She was magic!" Her fox terrier shared the wings with Girlie.

She and Charlot experienced a brief estrangement over her refusal to do one number, "A Cabaret Artiste," but the break was patched up quickly. She left before the end of the run to appear in a British film, *Two Hearts in Waltz Time*. During those days, West End producers were often caught up in competition with films and usually lost out because even in depressed Britain, the movies had more cash on hand. Thus during her peak years, which lasted through World War II, Day was only an occasional presence on London stages and never appeared again for Charlot, though later he made his first film appearance—as a theatrical manager—in one of her films. He noted with some hauteur: "Salary nil, supplied my own cigars, champagne was ginger ale."

Day was joined by Arthur Macrae, a performer, composer, lyricist and sketch writer who was almost immediately called the poor man's Noel Coward. *How D'You Do?* did approximate the panache of the Jeans-Titheradge efforts, partly due to original sketches by Herbert Farjeon, who would be a major revue figure during World War II. Macrae's comic song "Cads" proved a standard of Charlot's later career. Although a youth named Dennis Van Thal was not a major presence, Charlot had recently put him under contract and Van Thal provided the music for almost all of Charlot's remaining shows.

Charlot met Van Thal in a way both typical and atypical for a man gifted in spotting new talent but risk-prone when it came to managing money. Van Thal's uncle Bertie Helbron wanted to put money into the forthcoming show and one day, with Van Thal in tow, he visited the Charlots' flat in Albemarle Court. (After the loss of the Prince of Wales, there was no such thing as a permanent Charlot home in London.) Though Van Thal had written no music professionally, he was hired. It was the beginning of a major career for the young composer, though by the time Charlot left for America Van Thal had already discovered that being a theatrical agent came naturally to him and paid a lot better. Charlot disapproved of that choice strongly.

To Van Thal, Charlot was a great hero who was responsible for "the best times of my life—the most wonderful years." He recalled him as a stern taskmaster, always at the theater by 9:30 in the morning and expecting everyone else to be there too. When Charlot finally abandoned London theater, Van Thal mourned: "[He] left so abruptly. It was a great tragedy for me."

Other principals in *How D'You Do?* included Edward Cooper and Queenie Leonard, who had been performing a successful London cabaret act for several years. Leonard, another transatlantic who eventually found a film career in Hollywood, remembered Charlot a bit differently from many who had worked for him. "His shows were fun. He could always say 'Oh, all right, you silly cow' or something like that and get a laugh. Working for Cochran was different; he was pompous." Leonard helped to develop the London branch of Actors' Equity and on a matter of principle over actors' rights left the cast in mid-run ("I always kicked myself for that") but returned for other Charlot productions.

When Leonard left, her spots went to Doris Hare, who could not be counted a discovery, since she had already proved herself a fine comedienne with Cochran (she went on to be awarded an Order of the British Empire honor). Decades later she recalled being flattered by Charlot's reaction to their interview. In *Words and Music* (Coward, 1932) Cochran had been paying her £25 weekly. She was so charmed by Charlot that she forgot to mention money and got £15. "He paid terribly. But his shows were so pretty. The 'gels' looked like 'gels,' not like boys with their bums hanging out."

One of the highlights of *How D'You Do?* was a performance on May 28 for Paris commercial radio. Charlot divided the cast in half—he wouldn't want to lose them all at the same time—and put them on two planes from Croydon, south London, self-proclaimed as the world's first international airport. The flight took hours and there was champagne and brandy for all and, once in Paris, sumptuous dining in the Bois du Boulogne. Charlot, of course, did not fly. Not strictly *tout ou rien*.

Throughout the bankruptcy, he had managed to keep his family's pleasures pretty much intact. Joan was by now enrolled in the girls' school at Boston House, near the seaside in Eastbourne. She seems to have had a better time at school than Philip, recalling:

> We played tennis and cricket in the summer and hockey and lacrosse in winter. We'd go on nature rambles on the Downs and to the beach to swim. We also

studied hard. I took my Oxford School Certificate exams there and passed, but never went to college.... We walked in a crocodile [in single file] to church on Sundays, and the vicar was great fun!

In the summer of 1933 Flip and Joan, accompanied by Girlie and Gin the Scottie, spent a while with Bea Lillie at Lady Peel's country home in Hatfield Heath. There were horses in the stables, young foxhounds being walked, sows with many piglets, a duck pond, a tennis court, and acres of land.

Compared with Bea's Pekingese, the Charlot dogs were pretty sedentary. The lionhearted Peke rambled the fields with Joan and Bobby Peel. One day Joan and Bobby had gone roller-skating in the squash court and let two dozen piglets free. They even saddled up a mare and rode her about, leaving her in a paddock occupied by a stallion. With perfect early-adolescent insouciance, they stole a honeycomb from a hollow tree without getting caught. It was "sheer heaven, and much more fun than London."

Lillie, an expert on double-talk, might say, "Joan darling, would you mind going into the study and getting me the (unintelligible word)?" With a straight face, of course. "She caught me every time," Joan recalled. During the same summer Charlot's wife and daughter also stayed in Lawrence's rented house at Sunbury-on-the-Thames.

It was around this time when animosity—never directly at the time nor thereafter alluded to by either principal—broke out between Charlot and Coward over the Actors' Orphanage, of which Charlot remained a director. Coward was nominated for chairman while Charlot, a director, was for some reason bitterly opposed. Later speculation had it that he was hostile to Coward (who got the job) because of Coward's homosexuality. In Charlot's defense, there is no other evidence and much to the contrary of any homophobia. It is just as likely that the digs by Coward in the occasional volumes of autobiography he began to issue later in the decade were down to a clash between two strong personalities.

Later in the year Lillie returned to headline *Please*, another (but much more frugal) outing at the Savoy. The show was largely written by Titheradge, with music mainly by the highly lyrical Vivian Ellis (who was later to explain his preference for Cochran: the most scenery he could count on from Charlot was a single palm tree). Some songs from the Dietz-Schwartz American success *The Band Wagon* were added for zest.

Dietz and Schwartz, who had been watching and listening closely during Charlot's 1924 conquest of Broadway, had since 1929 been creating Broadway revues of an intimacy and wit which would have been impossible without the prior example. Their revues often starred Bea Lillie, and it is possible to assert that, because of this double dose of Charlot, the 1930s represented the golden age of American intimate revue and in fact the time when intimate revue became the international standard.

Back in England, this phase of Charlot's comeback was capped by *Hi-Diddle-Diddle*, another outing at the Comedy which was notable for the first theatrical performance of Cole Porter's "Miss Otis Regrets" done by the bluer-than-blue singing actor Douglas Byng. Byng later recalled that Charlot always insured his performers against illness, but in Byng's case, against death. Something that made a terrific impact on Byng was the barrel of oysters and crate of champagne which arrived at the theater destined, of course, for Charlot.

All these shows had respectable runs. *Hi-Diddle-Diddle* also heralded the connection between Charlot and Robert Nesbitt which would continue until Charlot left Britain in 1937. Nesbitt and William Walker wrote book, lyrics and music for the show and soon Nesbitt, who had staged his own mordantly successful revue *Ballyhoo* in 1932, was Charlot's disciple, learning "the business"—and especially Charlot's lighting trickery—and in general becoming the active part of his remaining team.

Everything suggests that these revues were entirely up to Charlot's earlier (and, as always, nearly impossible to describe) standard, but London theater was losing out to films to such an extent that virtually all its leading lights were available only when a better job in the movies wasn't on offer. In late 1933 Charlot returned to the BBC. Twelve new "Charlot's Hours," not quite along the lines of the earlier series (they were "specials" because the BBC now refused to allow connections between the individual shows), elicited good responses such as the following:

> Thanks for the return of Charlot's Hour. Charlot has the great gift of putting over clean humor, tuneful melodies and topical numbers without that terrible shadow of badly played pianos and jazz. He does allow "revue" to fade quietly into the background.

The first new "Charlot's Hour" was built around Lillie. In general, these programs featured his new "company"—various combinations of Macrae, Leonard, Cooper, Hare, Edward Chapman, Day and Dolores Dalgarno. In the *Radio Times*, Charlot likened his leave-it-until-late method of readying a new radio program to the mixing of a cocktail—you wouldn't want it sitting around for weeks going flat, would you?

He traveled to Vienna in 1934 to stage *Der Verlebete Koenigen* (the beloved little king) starring Gitta Alpar and contributed quite a learned article, "Producing Revue in England," to *Theatre and Stage*. In his "encyclopedia for amateurs," he traced a good deal of revue history, explained the role of the French *compère* and *commère*, thus providing a key to his own Alhambra shows, and gave Grossmith the honor of being the father of English revue. The article remains a valuable source on the subject of musical revue.

Charlot was back with the Gattis at the Vaudeville in 1935. His return was accompanied by considerable ballyhoo, including a redecoration of the walls of the stalls (the orchestra) and of the upstairs bar. Downstairs, the walls were now covered by the reigning theatrical cartoonist Tom Titt with caricatures of all the famous Charlot discoveries and stars. Upstairs, the walls of the bar were festooned with Titt's impressions of the reigning critics of the musical stage—it was, after all, their natural habitat. Decades and many refurbishments later, it remains possible that under the wallpapering and paint, these relics of Charlot's great years still exist.

Charlot was back at the Vaudeville because he had struck a multi-year deal there. His first effort was *Charlot's Char-a-Bang!*, which turned out to be a puzzling failure. Of judgment? Of taste? Then came a more ambitious outing in cooperation with Sir Oswald Stoll, *Dancing City* at the cavernous Coliseum—an expensive and quite lovely star vehicle for Lea Seidel, but a money-loser despite its 200 performances.

A rather ingenious revue along the old familiar lines, *Shall We Reverse?* at the Comedy, was one of three more productions in quick succession. In it Charlot again demonstrated his ability to spot new talent, in this case a 17-year-old Australian named Alan Davis. Though not much of a singer and dancer—Davis's assessment of himself—he became Charlot's assistant manager on the show and eventually one of his era's most successful theatrical directors and producers. The (very) long-running farce *No Sex Please, We're British* was his most "renowned" show in a very long career. Davis was still putting on shows into the mid–1990s.

Charlot's notes on the development of *Shall We Reverse?* display a man still in hopes of return to glory. He saw the finale, for example, as "too intellectual, not sufficiently climactic for New York—it would have to be built up." For New York, he envisioned a current leading man (who had British credentials), Jack Whiting, though "He would have at least three or four additional songs and of course some important dancing." *Shall We Reverse?*, a fairly ingenious show in which the passage of time was shown to be quite a fluid thing, featured most of the recent regulars, including Leonard and the "contract girls."

The headliner was June, recently Lady Inverclyde, given a comeback chance by her mentor from *Buzz-Buzz* days. And yes, he paid her £100. ("More Surprise Pink for Miss June," he was heard to call out at one rehearsal: Surprise Pink was a lighting gel particularly friendly to no longer youthful performers.)

The show, ingenious and apparently very attractive, was notable for its bad luck. Once more, another show's opening trumped it. *1066 and All That*, an adaptation of a currently popular spoof of English history, made it a pre-sold ticket. A fire in Charlot's theater destroyed costumes and delayed the opening. The result was that *Shall We Reverse?* was branded by some critics as an imitation of the other show and never had a chance. No wonder he hated critics.

The last of these 1935 efforts, a pantomime featuring the regulars called *Sleeping Beauty—or, What a Witch!* starring Nellie Wallace, an old-time music-hall comedienne, ran on into 1936 and received real acclaim for its way of renovating panto. It dispensed with the principal boy (always played by an attractive woman) and pantomime dame (always a burly male). It was really, one critic noted, "a typical Charlot revue," and, as another perceived, an endearing burlesque of pantomime complete with sophisticated *double entendres*. It would have a well-deserved revival during the next Christmas season.

However innovative these shows might prove to be onstage, they did not fit well in the contemporary theater climate, which was generally hostile to almost everything. Upon the death of George V the public mood darkened further. The exceptions seemed to be the amazing shows circa 1935–41 authored by and starring Novello. These mixed all theatrical forms—operas inside musical comedies, musical comedies inside operettas, etc.—and drew record crowds. The only other successes of the era were in the realm of variety.

In 1936 Charlot presented *The Town Talks*, a collaboration with Nesbitt at the Vaudeville, as well as a touring show assembled by Nesbitt from various bits of recent revues. Still striving for elevated taste, he presented other genres at the Vaudeville, including a season of Trudi Schoop's ballet. But not very many people were interested. It seemed that everything had hit bottom, though the revival of *Sleeping Beauty* allowed the year to die with some dignity.

In perfect harmony with his policy of denying himself—and usually his family—none of the good things, he managed a summer holiday in 1936. Aboard the ship on which they sailed to Algeciras, Spain, were Colette Leveaux, the wife of the son of his old ex-partner, as well as a well-known cricketer of the time who was now an importer of Spanish sherry. On the itinerary was a visit to Gibraltar. It would be the last European vacation for the family but not the end of pleasure for them. Odette recalled in particular a month spent at Ascot where Charlot had somehow rented a big house:

> The family was together there: my aunt Flip, my cousin Philippe and his wife Mary, and of course Joan, as well as the dogs Girlie the Great Dane and Jeanne [Gin] the Scotch Terrier. The house was welcoming and the weekends we invited numerous friends. My uncle enjoyed the pleasures of life—he could devour a whole chicken and was very gay, very joyful. He enchanted us by playing piano.

By 1937, when theatrical advertisements such as Duggie Ascot's for his school of stage dancing tended to refer to him in the past tense, Charlot's financial position was desperate. In February, as part of a series in the *Sunday Chronicle* which had begun the previous year (when he described the young Coward as having "a martyr complex"), he set down a few thoughts about the BBC:

> I see no reason why, when relating some of my experiences in Broadcasting, I should not touch with good humour on some of the BBC's idiosyncrasies.... In 1923, when listeners numbered only a few thousands, I made a report to the Society of West End Managers, predicting that radio would do irreparable damage.... Today it is more dangerous than ever. The damage that I predicted has been done. Then why did I allow myself to be swallowed for a time ... by the radio octopus? Because ... I realized how much pleasure broadcasting could bring to invalids and to people who lived 50 miles or more from a theatre or a cinema. I shook hands with the enemy....

Recalling the huge postal response to the last edition of "Charlot's Hour" in 1928, he added that a BBC official had commented, "We pay no attention to correspondence of that sort." Charlot added that since then the Corporation had learned a few things and now even had a public relations officer. Not only that, its lofty attitude had brought some good results, including a spread of interest in symphonic music. He noted that his own direct-to-the-listener comments during "Charlot's Hour" were at the time directly opposed to BBC policy and practice.

So, he confessed, were his "idiosyncrasies" during rehearsals—having his hat and coat at hand, instead of in the cloak room, having his tea in the control room rather than breaking off work to take it in the canteen (he had to provide a doctor's certificate for that). Then he returned to his main theme, extrapolating from it:

Actually the radio has kept millions of people away from the theatre and has given them a cheaper substitute. Lectures, concerts, music—light or serious—these are things that the radio does well, but in any other form of entertainment it is bound to be imperfect. I think we have a perfect parallel in the moving pictures situation. There was always something unsatisfactory in the silent films.... In the same manner broadcasting plays lack something, and I am very strongly of the opinion that when television comes into its own, the broadcasting of an entertainment without television will ultimately appear as futile as the silent films are appearing today.

He wasn't always right, obviously. He wound up with several anecdotes about "prophylactic" BBC censorship, including one in which he had his cast rehearse a "blue" number which they never intended to use, just so they could disconcert the BBC.

In March he produced for the fledgling BBC Television a version of a Charlot revue, then had to wait and wait for payment. (A letter from him as chairman of *Plays and Players*, a theatrical publication, shows his exasperation.)

He produced whatever was possible. An *André Charlot Cabaret* with Ronald Frankau, noted for his very blue humor, opened at the New Bristol in London. It was bereft of any of Charlot's regulars and Frankau's presence indicated how badly things had gone wrong. The fastidious impresario had given in to a particularly crass trend, the non-stop revue.

The genre can be seen as a response to continuous-showing cinema programs. After all, many London stage shows, and not all of them variety, musical comedy or revue, had shifted to a two-a-day policy, the better to lure the fickle consumer. But the non-stop revue, whose origin can be traced to a Soho venue called the Windmill, was mainly an excuse for onstage nudity which vaguely passed the contemporary licensing rules and *double entendre* comedians. To steadily declining audiences, Charlot presented three of these shows in 1937, all starring Frankau. The last one stayed on the boards for only a week.

Charlot, pleading illness, left Britain for good. Flip, Joan (who was working as a girl Friday for a London architectural firm) and Gin, along with Philip and Mary, moved to a cottage in Great Missenden, Buckinghamshire.

Trunksful of books, paintings, years of memorabilia were put into storage. The departure—ostensibly for a vacation but seen by many as an escape from creditors—took almost everyone by surprise, including Edgerton Killick and Victor Payne-Jennings, his hosts at the Comedy Theatre, who for some time handled his business affairs. Charlot's longtime stage manager went through the piles of material and finally sent some to the Gladmans and the rest abroad to Charlot.

His co-workers and friends—Leonard and Van Thal in particular—always believed the move was a great mistake. Nesbitt, who may have had the only notice of Charlot's intentions to go to California, agreed. After all, didn't producers always recover from bad times?

EIGHT

Hollywood, 1937–1956:
Trying to Repeat the Past

Exactly why André Charlot left for America—and in particular, Hollywood—remains open to question. He certainly could be seen as on the run from creditors (doing a "moonlight flit" in the English vernacular), though he had never really "stiffed" any of them before. Regardless of the blows it had dealt him, the United States surely remained the site, in memory at least, of the peak of his career. And a lot of his friends, including many of his theater family, now lived in the U.S., most of them in California. He said he was on vacation, but he must have thought he could find help there, could find a new start in some way or other.

Like many an immigrant before him, he came on his own, leaving family behind until he could properly provide for them. He came in style, of course, sailing on the *Queen Mary* on July 21, 1937. When he arrived on the 26th, his 55th birthday, his New York greetings did not echo the good old days. This time there was no cut and thrust of making a living, no exhilaration. For all intents and purposes, he had been gone for a decade. Regardless of the success of post–Charlot revue on Broadway, his influence was nowhere admitted. He was no longer even mentioned in connection with his starry creations. There seemed no place for him in the rather more serious theater of Roosevelt's era. They just didn't know him any more.

He must have understood all this, must have felt the irony of the situation. He stayed awhile with this and that old friend through sticky August. Then came the long train ride to California.

In September and October he stayed with Rowley Leigh, whose screenplay the previous year for *The Charge of the Light Brigade* had elevated him at least temporarily into the upper echelons of film society. These were also the months of grief and commemoration for George Gershwin, so recently and prematurely dead, but Charlot's archives contain no mention of the man who had been so much a part of his own past.

Throughout November and December Charlot sojourned in Beverly Hills with the Hillmans. Mrs. Hillman was none other than June, the selfsame former chorus girl from *Buzz-Buzz* who had become Lady Inverclyde in the early 1930s, only to find herself in a loveless, sexless marriage, with most of the peerage ranged against her. Charlot had rescued her at her lowest with that role in *Shall We Reverse?*

Though carrying a torch for Robert Nesbitt for some time ("He was one of those men who can make a woman bloom"), June had pulled herself together, rejoined society and met (at the coronation of George VI) and married a wealthy American oilman. By 1937 she was presiding over a mansion in Santa Barbara in addition to the showplace in Beverly Hills. The Hillmans' doors were always open to Charlot, through the subsequent years when he was "down on his luck and playing bit parts in films but still holding his head high."

June was quite well connected in the show-business circles of southern California and she was gradually able to introduce Charlot around (*nobody* lived in Hollywood any more—Beverly Hills was the new Hollywood) as is demonstrated by some of the photographs of parties in her autobiography *The Glass Ladder*. Eventually Charlot, who had by then taken a great many mental notes on life in Movieland, was well enough to leave and began a desultory round of house-hunting, perhaps inspired by a need to be close to his acquaintances in Beverly Hills.

He settled into lodgings at the Villa Madrid Hotel on the Sunset Strip, a hostelry remarkable in California terms, in that at this writing it's still there. Not long after his arrival, he adopted Zaza, a German shepherd with a penchant for walking away and being brought home by taxi. Zaza was finally pensioned off to a ranch, to be replaced by Shep, a cross between a Saint Bernard and collie who had been found abandoned in a local backyard by one of Charlot's friends. Shep, too, was a wanderer and when Flip and Joan arrived at the Villa Madrid in the summer of 1939, the dog had already established a personality for himself along the Sunset Strip. He immediately took up the job of protecting Gin.

Charlot's journals are remarkably silent on an aspect of life which must have affected him—the weather. Certainly, what he found in southern California, then as now essentially a desert made to bloom by imported water, would have made it possible to say that he had lived in one climate heretofore, even if it was labeled Paris, London or New York.

Arriving in September, he would surely have wanted to hide from the 100-degree days characterizing that time of year. He was suddenly in a place where nothing was old, where tradition might have a dozen years' pedigree. It would have seemed especially new and raw since the 1933 killer earthquake had caused so much damage, demolition and rebuilding. Within a couple of years he would experience one of L.A.'s periodic deadly floods. A stranger in a strange land, indeed.

He did what he could to establish himself in this ultimately indifferent if not hostile environment. He drew upon his past and prepared a lengthy radio script called "The Charlot Revue: February 19, 1938." Echoing that earlier West End program, it emphasized the importance and sheer busy-ness of Charlot himself.

The script opens with hotel employees discussing the new arrival, André Charlot, "popularly known as the 'Ziegfeld of England'" (!!!). Famous ex–Charlot stars come calling, one after another (all of them—June, Myrtil, Mundin, Evans, etc.— were actual local residents at the time). All go up to Charlot's room, where other friends have already gathered. Charlot says that he'll be in Hollywood a week at the most, that he's here to gather up the English talent to take back for his next revue. A telephone call convinces him that, if he stays a while, a sponsor will put up the money for a radio show. The friends are so enthusiastic that they "put on a show" then and there—June sings "A Cup of Coffee," Evans "K-k-k-Katy," Myrtil "Lime-house Blues."

Charlot remarks that most American radio shows are elevating and proceeds to unearth "La Plume de Ma Tante"—or, as it was onstage and on the BBC, "French as she is learnt." (The skit hilariously applies the typically lunatic methods of learning a foreign language to a real-life situation.)

Myrtil's song "If I had only said to him in English what I thought about him in French," followed by patter about the letter B ("You know what 'The Bee' did for Jack Benny") introduces Mundin's comic song about bees. Chatting about contemporary Hollywood use of Shakespeare leads to the need for a guest star. Herbert Marshall appears and agrees to perform the Jack Buchanan sketch "The Green-Eyed Monster," which had got the New York show off to such a rolling start.

Tea was served with byplay on the difference between British and American English, and June's "We Speak the Same Language" from *Shall We Reverse?* There are further reminders of Charlot's gifts to Hollywood—Colman, Cantor, Barnes, etc.—and the show closes with all reprising "We Speak the Same Language." But no real-life sponsor came forward and the script was never aired.

Charlot quickly understood the obvious—that Hollywood was a movie town. But it never seems to have occurred to him to use his talents and experience to write screenplays taking advantage of contemporary fascination with "The Good Old Days." Who knew more about the subject?

Still, by early 1939 he was highly hopeful of a commission from the Works Project Administration's Federal Theater Project. It is possible that when the deal fell through, the reason was that the FTP chose to produce *Meet the People* instead. That revue became one of FTP's most successful done outside New York. But it is even more likely that Charlot, like hundreds of other hopefuls, was let down because the FTP itself was abandoned in 1939, the victim of long-term censorship and contemporary congressional sniping at its real or imagined political bias. Whatever the truth, he felt quite betrayed when he didn't get the commission.

A first draft of *The Charlot Revue of 1939* suggests that it might originally have been done with the FTP in mind. The "How D'You Do/Ready to Work" opening is shortly followed by something called "WPA Time Clock." Most of the rest of this "book" is made up of existing, but relatively unfamiliar sketches and songs from his shows of the 1930s. If it was in fact submitted to the WPA, by contrast to the quite proletarian *Meet the People*, it must have seemed the relic of a bygone era.

Whatever blind spots he may have had, he proved himself a sharp-eyed observer of the environment. When in the early 1950s he turned to writing those autobiographical essays, he recalled early days in Hollywood and Beverly Hills brilliantly. His evocation of the wide, eerie, pedestrian-free streets of Beverly Hills stacks up favorably alongside any other author's; perhaps only Scott Fitzgerald's "Crazy Sunday" cuts quite so incisively to the essential, insecure but brutal hollowness within "movie stars," these ferocious egos inflated by publicity and the neediness of a deprived mass audience. "Beverly Hills, 1937" and "A Quiet Game of Bridge" are essential reading for anyone seeking to understand the insides of "the industry" of

Hollywood and in fact seem hardly dated. There exists no evidence that he ever tried to market the stories separately.

He must also have believed that his Hollywood friends could revive his theatrical fortunes. He clearly believed that Leigh best understood him and his work—at one point years later he commented that he would trust only Leigh to put on a "Charlot revue." Hollywood as the focal point for a film career was tough enough, but possible. But Los Angeles in general (and after all, Hollywood was—and is—only a district in L.A.'s 450-odd square miles) was quite another challenge.

The Los Angeles theater scene had not really advanced since Charlot's 1926 visit, although the public transportation had improved and would continue to do so until it was sabotaged after World War II by automotive interests. The El Capitan itself remained the only legitimate house on the boulevard, and even as such, it was only limping along. In short order it would become a movie theater, the Hollywood Paramount.

The Pantages Theater (named for Alexander Pantages, a would-be Ziegfeld of the West Coast), east on the boulevard just beyond Vine Street, had already reverted from its original status as a film and variety house to become the first-run home for RKO, Columbia and Universal movies. A couple of blocks beyond that, the glitzy Florentine Gardens (the Los Angeles enterprise of flesh merchant Nils Thor Granlund—NTG) offered titillation and food. In a remarkable piece of irony, Charlot's one-time evil genius, Earl Carroll, was building a theater-restaurant a few blocks farther south, on Sunset Boulevard not far from the main studios of CBS and NBC radio.

Every other theater in Hollywood was a movie house, whether palatial (the Boulevard) or second/third run. Towards downtown Los Angeles, things were no better. On Broadway near Ninth Street, in an area dominated by large department stores, the Orpheum Theater stood as the last L.A. outpost of vaudeville, and even at the Orpheum the crowds would not come unless offered a movie as part of the bill. Most of the original movie palaces of downtown had fallen into neglect and were either closed or offering sleazy material. Raucous skin houses such as the Burbank (in downtown Los Angeles, not in suburban Burbank) offered burlesque—fan and bubble and fireball dancers and comics with greasy stains on their trousers.

The second generation of downtown movie palaces existed in tandem with Boulevard partners; what was playing at the Pantages would also show at the RKO Hill Street. Halfway between downtown and Hollywood existed the Theatre Mart, a club-sized theater (its later incarnation was as the home of the Los Angeles Press Club) where a faux Victorian melodrama called *The Drunkard* ("with olio acts") was beginning a run of several decades.

Around downtown's Pershing Square, a rare example of anything Old-World-ish having even momentary success in L.A., could be found the city's only examples of respectable live theater. Thrust into one side of the Biltmore Hotel was the Biltmore Theater, the regular L.A. stopping place for touring versions of New York shows that made it this far. A few hundred yards distant, fronting directly on the Square, was the Philharmonic Auditorium.

Nominally the home of the Los Angeles Philharmonic Orchestra, which summered three nights weekly at the open-air Hollywood Bowl, this auditorium actually fostered the most original stage productions mounted in the city. It was the home of the Los Angeles Civic Light Opera, which generally did opt for operetta, but under the directorship of Edwin Lester presented touring or entirely local versions of recent Broadway musicals, as well as (in tandem with the San Francisco Light Opera) commissioning the occasional original. Subsequent to 1937, two of the LACLO's hit originals—measured by what happened to them when they transferred to New York—were *The Song of Norway* (Grieg sentimentalized) and *Peter Pan* (a new romping version for Mary Martin).

Maverick small theaters such as the Las Palmas, tucked away on a side street just beyond Grauman's Egyptian, lived from hand to mouth, or not at all. Clubs such as the Masquers occasionally put on live entertainments for the benefit and amusement of their members. And that was it, the paltry theatrical scene surrounding André Charlot.

In fact it did not take him long to learn that movies were the only game in town, and for a brief time he served as a technical advisor at Paramount Pictures. Unfortunately, his advice was required for only a single film, *Zaza* (named for the dog, or vice versa?). Presumably he was thus engaged when in 1938 an old acquaintance, Eric Maschwitz, himself on a Hollywood tour shopping for assignment, encountered him.

Maschwitz was the lyricist of many British songs popular in the United States, among them "These Foolish Things" and "A Nightingale Sang in Berkeley Square." Upon his return to London, Maschwitz said that Charlot had advised him, "Go back to London; your roots are in Europe, which is as far away from this circus as the planets." In his 1982 autobiography Maschwitz portrayed Charlot as essentially broken and lost: "in a tiny apartment to which he had retired like a wounded tiger, to lick his wounds ... I can still see him standing in the doorway, a frail spectacled figure."

Charlot was on his own in Hollywood for almost two years and he did not see his son again for longer than that. When war broke out in September 1939, Philip, who had become a father in January (Sargine—soon nicknamed "Nini" because she couldn't pronounce her real name), joined up from Great Missenden. Philip eventually had a distinguished military career, ranging from the Duke of Cornwall's regiment through the Oxford and Buckinghamshire Light Infantry, where he rose to the rank of Lieutenant, and thence to India, where in June of 1942 he transferred to the Royal India Naval Volunteers. In India he ultimately achieved the rank of Lieutenant Commander. His service totaled five years and nine months when he was finally released in February of 1946. By that time Mary had met another man, written Philip a "Dear John" letter, and gone off with Nini to live in South Africa with her new love.

Charlot had wanted to bring Flip and Joan to live with him for some time and by the late spring of 1939, when he was hopeful of the WPA commission and sure that war would break out soon in Europe, he sent for them. But it turned out that Flip and Joan were none too eager to leave England. (Flip was probably never reconciled to life in California, especially as there was never much choice but to live in it.) Joan, who, like her brother, had worked in her father's office and briefly as a script clerk in the Shepperton Studios, had just completed her course at Queen's Secretarial College in London and had an Oxford University certificate which qualified her for entrance to the university. She was fluent in French and had taken Berlitz courses in German and Spanish. At least in terms of a career, England seemed to offer greater opportunity than America.

Flip's sister Jonny had married but, sadly, Tillie had just died. For Flip as well as Joan, England seemed more than ever where they belonged. But they got on a ship with Gin and headed for a reunion with the head of the household. Even as they traveled, the WPA was calling off the project that was supposed to pay their way.

The transatlantic passage was not gloomy, however, partly because the passengers and crew were so fond of Gin. Their cabin steward also happened to be the restaurant's carver and regularly turned up with prime cuts of beef. The voyage seemed to have upset Gin's digestive regularity, and despite brisk walks on the deck, he remained

Flip, Joan and Gin embarking for the U.S., 1939.

quite a constipated animal. From their deck chairs, other passengers regularly inquired, "Has he yet?" One day, possibly stimulated by the singing of a deckside canary, Gin got rid of the problem to a collective sigh of relief.

On arrival in New York, the travelers were met by Velma Deane, who had appeared in Charlot's shows as early as 1922, and her husband Ted Knox. They stayed with the Knoxes briefly and then set out for Pasadena, where the transcontinental trains then stopped. Flip, Joan and Gin moved into the Villa Madrid while the reunited family looked for a more permanent place. Many of Charlot's long-time associates from Britain helped them get acclimated. Binnie Barnes, for instance, had them down to her beach home in the Malibu Colony, a star haven still in its infancy. Joan made her first foray into the Pacific Ocean, winding up knocked

The Charlots on the balcony at Crescent Heights with Shep and Rolette.

down and washed to shore by the big waves, only to find herself side by side with a seal.

They found their first real Hollywood home not far from the Villa Madrid at 1432 Crescent Heights Boulevard, a broad avenue that connected Sunset Boulevard with its parallel main street to the south, Santa Monica Boulevard, in what might be called lower Hollywood. During its westward migration, a large proportion of the film community—in particular its expatriate and literary components—had settled within this amorphous area just west of Fairfax Avenue stretching several blocks above and below Sunset Boulevard. It was far enough west in the L.A. area to get some hot-weather relief from sea breezes and its air was at that time free of smog.

Within these precincts (just a block away from Crescent Heights, in fact) could also be found the Garden of Allah, which was originally meant to be Alla for the imposing star of stage and silent screen Alla Nazimova. Its older rival the Chateau Marmont Hotel was across the street. Schwab's drugstore (shortly to enter Hollywood lore), as well as a well-patronized Jewish delicatessen, stood a block away from Crescent Heights near where Laurel Canyon came down from the Hollywood Hills, so often the site of devastating brush fires.

Just below Sunset on Laurel Drive, the self-doubting F. Scott Fitzgerald was trying to restart his screenwriting career. All unknowingly he was preparing for work on perhaps his best (but unfinished) novel. When the Charlots moved into Crescent Heights, they were back to back with the house where Fitzgerald lived. They never met.

Although a substantial expatriate colony had grown in Hollywood during the 1930s, especially after *Kristallnacht,* an "English colony" had existed there much longer. Essentially focused on the beach city of Santa Monica, which at the time deserved to be known as Hollywood's access to the sea, this was a community very much devoted to its own enthusiasms. These included cricket and golf, as Sheridan Morley's *Tales from the Hollywood Raj* points out in some detail.

In the true Hollywood manner, "English" could include Errol Flynn the Tasmanian as well as Douglas Fairbanks, Jr., son of perhaps the most impossibly American of all celebrities. As World War II loomed, more and more British film people came to Hollywood where they would sit out the war, earning scorn from those who stayed home. Eric Blore had been a member of the colony since 1933 and was puzzlingly said to act "more English than the English." (But he *was* English.) Charlot, essentially a solitary, never became part of the colony, and apparently never tried to.

Life at 1432 Crescent Heights must have seemed pretty tame. There was a small store not far away on the Strip that delivered groceries, a good thing because Flip and Joan had followed Charlot's lead in never learning how to drive. None of them ever did learn. And, except for one brief hop by Charlot, none of them ever flew.

Friends such as Odette Myrtil lived nearby but they entertained rarely and, when there was some mild triumph to celebrate, they did it with Cook's champagne rather than Lanson '28. (Charlot always dispersed the bubbles with a swizzle stick.) He spent a great deal of his day in his bedroom/study, writing and considering his options. There were many evenings of bridge, though without Flip or Joan. Among his bridge set were expat Connie Lupino and her daughter Rita. Connie was the wife of Stanley Lupino, a major star of the English stage, and the mother of Nina's sister Ida. Whenever he could find someone to play bezique with, Charlot played that, too.

The Charlots went out rarely. One exception was when Queenie Leonard, now thoroughly launched on her film career, opened a cabaret act at the Deauville Club on the Strip. Charlot startled her by offering negative criticism of her number "Elizabeth," which he deemed disrespectful of the long dead Tudor queen.

The family read the daily papers in an unenthusiastic manner, though the local *Hollywood Citizen-News* held some attraction. All of them were avid radio listeners during that golden age, having as favorites Jack Benny, Fred Allen, George Burns and Gracie Allen. Although Joan read *Variety* and *The Hollywood Reporter* at the jobs she got in "the industry," Charlot was never apparently particularly interested. Flip and Joan often went to the movies, but Charlot rarely joined them, even for the films in which he eventually appeared as a performer. One of the pluses of his slight movie career was the free passes that went with it, which made enjoying the indoor national pastime that much easier for the moviegoers in the family.

For some time, the family was made up of André, Flip, Joan, Gin and the lovable Shep, still a wanderer who liked nothing better than a daily stop at a Strip butcher's where he could count on getting a fresh bone, and a nearby florist, where he was assured of a drink. One day he showed up on the doorstep of 1432 with a freshly cooked leg of lamb; on another he arrived with a note tucked into his collar: "The lilies are in."

When Gin and Shep departed their doggy lives, they were inadequately replaced by Rolette, an apricot-colored standard poodle from Leigh. Rolette, alas, was subject to repeated false pregnancies, which required repeated taxi jaunts to the nearest vet's.

Feeling guilty about leaving London in wartime, Joan first managed to get a job with the British consulate in Los Angeles where for some time she worked in the confidential unit established for war purposes. She was helped in getting the job by Alan Mowbray, the unacknowledged head of the British film colony. For a time thereafter, Mowbray figured prominently in the Charlots' California saga.

In November of 1939 Charlot almost staged a revue in Los Angeles. This was *Hit and Run: The Revue of Wit and Fun*, written by Leigh, Gene Stone and Jack Robinson, the latter two said to have authored the Federal Theatre's local hit, *Two-a-Day*. Handbills announced "a topical satirical musical ... staged by Andre Charlot and Kurt Robitschuk." It was to include several of the performers from *Meet the People*. The show was set for a small Hollywood theater at Sunset Boulevard and Cahuenga Boulevard called the Montmartre which was soon the site of the Hollywood Canteen and later, as things went almost inevitably in L.A., a parking lot. The show was banned by the Board of Fire Commissioners after one private showing to 400 invited and very Hollywood-style guests. It finally did open at the downtown Mayan Theater in May of 1940 but did not last long.

Robitschuk was actually the financier of *Hit and Run*, according to Charlot's actor friend and cast member Peter Garey. Robitschuk once wired Charlot saying that he was "among my best friends." Garey later related Charlot's response: "I wouldn't want to be among your best friends even if there were only two of us."

However, with England fully in the war's firing line, Hollywood turned its attention to making films that portrayed the English spirit of endurance and to various relief projects for the doughty Brits. Despite the town's apparent indifference to theater, Charlot saw a chance here and began planning what eventually became the *Charlot War Relief Revue of 1940*. He received much verbal encouragement but little actual cooperation from Mowbray, an actor particularly skilled in portraying overbearing and insufferable Englishmen.

Charlot's efforts for British War Relief were to prove notable. By now, he had in his possession all his scripts and musical scores, and so he decided to stage a gala recapitulation of his best work—allowing, of course, for his judgment on what the southern California market could understand. He began to lay the groundwork in early August, when Carroll was opening a new show and *Meet the People* was still running at the Hollywood Playhouse.

Though Charlot's contribution was uncredited, *Tonight at Eight-Thirty: Noel Coward's Famous Plays*, offering "the greatest cast ever assembled," was the first offering in a short season at the El Capitan which remains remarkable in Los Angeles history. The productions got some useful publicity when the British film director Michael Balcon was quoted as saying that British players in Hollywood should be considered deserters. Mowbray, the self-appointed public voice for this project, was thus able to criticize this "unwarranted smear.... Most of them served in the last war."

For the first series of three plays (of the total of nine) of *Tonight at 8:30*, a notable cast was indeed assembled: the consummate villain Basil Rathbone, Gladys Cooper, ex–Charlot performers Barnes and Gardiner, child star Freddie Bartholomew, glamorous Constance Bennett, dashing Douglas Fairbanks, Jr., and many others. Directorial chores were shared by Eddie Goulding, George Cukor and Dudley Murphy.

It was with Murphy that Charlot had made his connection and through him, his behind-the-scenes contributions. The *Los Angeles Times* for August 3 crowed, "Hollywood has taken the spotlight away from Broadway ... all eyes are on the El Capitan ... theatrical history is to be made." The *Times*'s drama critic Edwin Schallert called it "The most interesting aggregation of people ever to be assembled on the stage here."

In mid–August, when the second series opened, the local competition included something called a *French Follies* (bearing no relation at all to the real thing) at the Orpheum. The singing cowboy Gene Autry was featured and the show was publicized by a baseball game between the Comedians and the Leading Men at 10,000-seat Gilmore Field.

Onstage for the Coward plays were the venerable Dame May Whittey, the recent Academy Award winner Claire Trevor and the young star Joan Fontaine, the bemustached super–Brit C. Aubrey Smith, comedienne Zazu Pitts, tragedian Judith Anderson, starlet Isobel Jeans and Melville Cooper, recently a Merry Man alongside Errol Flynn. When the remaining three Coward plays were presented, they featured Marshall, female stars Rosalind Russell, Heather Angel, and Greer Garson (her *Pride and Prejudice* had just opened), character actress Una O'Connor, ex–European stage heartthrob George Metaxa, actor Brian Aherne and Elsa Maxwell herself. This ambitious enterprise was for the actors without stage experience demanding and dangerous ground.

With the London Blitz by now in full and terrible flow, Murphy announced his further plans, which included creating a West Coast version of the Theater Guild dedicated to quality productions (this never happened) and a September opening of *Charlot's Revue* for the Motion Picture Relief Fund. The competition for this would include a "carefree comedy" at the somewhat moth-eaten downtown Mayan, Thornton Wilder's new play *The Merchant of Yonkers* at the Pasadena Playhouse and F. Hugh Herbert's comedy *Quiet Please: A Comedy of Hollywood* at the Biltmore. Of much greater importance, the latest Hitchcock film *Foreign Correspondent* opened at a midtown cinema.

On September 16, a newspaper advertising campaign featuring Fanny Brice hit the streets and on September 21 the revue opened. Schallert reported a "good show, rough in spots, a throwback to an age of comparative innocence when 'social consciousness' was still a bookish turn." The show, he added, was for "people who want to laugh, or cast fulsome eye on beauty in dress and undress." Charlot "has not lost a certain continental smartness, a kind of ingenuous charm."

The printed program *(The Playgoer: The Magazine in the Theatre)* highlights, amongst the advertisements for restaurants and self-help advocates, some of its cast, a remarkable blend of sheer Hollywood (Bartholomew, Charles Farrell, June Lockhart, Mischa Auer, Jackie Cooper, Buster Keaton, Mowbray, J. Carrol Naish, singer Billy Daniels and Hanley Stafford, (well known on radio as the daddy of Brice's Baby Snooks) and the transatlantic musical theater (Connie "Emerald," Mary Brian [a star of one of Charlot's mid–30s revues], Richard Haydn, Neagle, Brice and Blore). Among the "turns" singled out for praise was Gardiner imitating, as he had done for Charlot and in American revue, trains, wallpaper, lighthouses, steamships and floating buoys. The "young people" headlining the show were Bonita Granville, Simone Simon and Rita Hayworth.

The "Who's Who" number which proved the regular showstopper was Macrae's "Cads." (The permanent "cads," including Henry Fonda, George Sanders, and director Mitchell Leisen, would regularly be joined by guest cads.) Audiences glittered as only movie audiences could: Betty Grable, Burns and Allen, Irene Dunne, Hedda Hopper, Janet Gaynor, Merle Oberon, the Kordas, the Zanucks, Charles Boyer, Goulding, etc. They all came to the El Capitan. As bombs rained down on London, *Charlot's Revue* promised "Two and a half hours of continuous laughter."

According to the *New York Herald-Tribune*, theater people in New York were watching with great interest. The paper reported that after its El Capitan run, a

Backstage at Charlot's Revue, 1940 (left to right): Mary Brian, Charlot, Bob Hope, Gertrude Niesen, Rudy Vallee.

transfer to San Francisco was likely. *Daily Variety*, transfixed by "the mobs out front," reported that "Cads" had received eight encores.

Charlot's still lively genius for publicity took over. There were "two shows nightly—one outside the theatre as stars alighted from their limousines." Charlot had hired boys and armed them with peashooters to ward off any obnoxious autograph-seekers.

The El Capitan was treated in subsequent weeks not only to a further parade of Hollywood stars who had graduated from Charlot's London "school" but the film and radio stars of the present who had no Charlot connection. Abbott and Costello, Gertrude Niesen, Rudy Vallee, Jack Benny, Harpo and Groucho Marx, Bob Hope with Jerry Colonna and their radio friends, and the gossipy switchboard-operators "Brenda and Cobina" did their current specialties or just showed up as a surprise.

The opening of this *Charlot's Revue*

Nini with her mother Mary and her paternal grandparents (courtesy of Nini Hitchman).

was followed by many radio and print reviews which expressed hopes for what the show might imply for the future of theater in Los Angeles. Even the boosterish local scribes, however, worried about the prospects of the show's losing money—"this is not a theater community"—and more than one radio/film guru thought the show should really be filmed. What a loss for the history of popular culture that it wasn't.

The combination of Coward plays and Charlot revue raised a lot of money for war relief, but for Charlot they did virtually nothing. Thereafter, he retained a significant grudge against Mowbray, who had apparently agreed to back the show himself but then managed a financial razzle-dazzle involving phantom corporations that left him free of accountability.

In 1941, not a propitious year for transatlantic travel, Philip's wife Mary had taken Nini to visit her mother in New York. Apparently Philip was not sending money home and, after a trip to Bermuda, Mary brought Nini to Hollywood, where they spent a year in a bungalow court across the street from the Charlots. Mary was introduced to their Hollywood friends and while working on charitable projects such as Bundles for Britain, she became particularly close to Mrs. Ernst Lubitsch, whose children were about the same age as Nini. His grandchild had created a new nickname for Charlot—"Deeda"—but her mother met a naval officer and severed the relationship with the family.

In 1942 Charlot decided to do professionally what he had been doing for years anyway. He became a teacher, holding classes and offering practical training at the Walter Anderson Laurel Workshop, just around the corner from home. A publicity story in the *Citizen-News* asserted that in so doing, Charlot was achieving a lifetime ambition. In other publications came the news that Charlot was offering six girls scholarships if they were selected for his forthcoming new revue.

Once more out of the trunks came scripts and scores, an "orchestra" of two pianos was hired, and the Charlot "Revuettes," at least on paper resembling the unproduced 1938 show, proceeded to showcase a number of youthful hopefuls, none of whom went on to any particular success on stage or in film.

These shows did, however, garner some familiar-sounding critical praise: "brisk and volatile … gayly sophisticated and piquant." And the Laurel Workshop did provide Charlot the entree to the last stage of his career. He was performing onstage as *compère* (a review noted that he "at times dominated the show in person, adding *esprit* with his every appearance") when his old friend and former employee Goulding dropped by to see the show. Goulding apparently liked what he saw and suggested that Charlot could make a living from film acting. And so, as a doctor in Goulding's *The Constant Nymph*, he began his career as film bit player.

Although tall and imposing, at 60 he made quite a different personal impression than in the glory days of his forties. He made a definite impression on the camera which, combined with his slight accent, made him easy to typecast. Though his eyebrows were still fiercely black, his face had thinned and sharpened and he seemed made for sinister roles.

In *The Song of Bernadette*, one of his earliest parts, he dominated several scenes late in the film by investing his character, the unforgiving Bishop who sealed Bernadette's fate and assured her martyrdom, with an implacably menacing nature.

He didn't always play a villain. Other roles included a mys-

Charlot on Hollywood Boulevard, 1940.

terious, dilettantish gentleman on a train in the Astaire vehicle *Yolanda and the Thief*, M. Philippe, a theater manager, in *The Dolly Sisters*, the president of France in *Annie Get Your Gun* and a café manager in *Above Suspicion*.

He took his motion picture acting seriously. But his perception of his position was acute. In his long story *Sandy Sutton's Sorrowful Saga*, a successful theatrical actor is signed up for films, begins with great gusto and winds up understanding that he has received the same run-around which Charlot himself had experienced in 1929. Having seen his major part finally reduced to one line, at story's end Sandy Sutton heads back to Broadway.

Joan recalled her father's readying himself for a day on the lot by getting his makeup case

As a chief in *Here We Go Again*, 1942.

just so. "Though the income did help, it hurt me to think of Pop sitting around for hours on the set. He didn't complain, but I apparently got it fixed in my mind that it was not appropriate for a genius to be treated that way."

A typical day on the set would ordinarily begin with a bus trip from Hollywood north through the Cahuenga Pass to some hot though air-conditioned enclave in the wilds of the San Fernando Valley. In the B-film *Thumbs Up* (1940), Charlot must have been on hand for several days, since he had several scenes as—what else?— a theatrical manager. Though Queenie Leonard was one of the movie's principals, they never ran into each other on the lot, and appear never to have realized that they were in the same film. It's also possible that Leonard was being tactful.

Among his other B-picture roles were three in the "Falcon" series starring Tom Conway, George Sanders's brother (and, at the time, Queenie's husband). In perhaps the best one, *The Falcon Strikes Back* (1943) he played Bruno Steffen, a wheel-chair-bound intended victim of a bogus bond scheme.

He was pleased with his role in *Wilson*, a renowned biography of the president. In this lengthy and perhaps overly serious work, he portrayed the Cardinal Archbishop of Paris. On the film's infrequent reshowings, however, you will look for him in vain. His entire sequence wound up on the cutting-room floor—shades of Sandy Sutton. He continued acting in films until 1954, when his health no longer permitted such work. Among the last of his fifty-odd roles was a French priest in the Cary Grant comedy *I Was a Male War Bride*.

He also worked at studios dubbing films into French. His sixteen credits included such disparate projects as *Yankee Doodle Dandy*, *The Sea Hawk*, *Random Harvest*, *Tarzan*, (!!) *Destry Rides Again* and *Woman of the Year*. He also dubbed four radio plays, including *Holy Matrimony* and *Abe Lincoln in Illinois*. In 1947 he was technical advisor on *Ivy* and coached actors during *The Bishop's Wife*.

Throughout the war, the family regularly scoured the shelves of their local supermarket for items to send back to relatives in France and Britain. (They once sent soybean flour because it was high in protein; Gladmans used it to make an ersatz marzipan.) These packages were loaded with Spam, Jello, Royal Pudding, Bisquick, nylons, adult and kiddy clothes (including "nappies"). Fondly remembered were the canned sausages coated with what Jonny described as "a lovely white pork fat which we used for frying bread."

These were also the years of the Hollywood Canteen, now in the former Montmartre site. Along with a group from the studios where she worked, Joan spent some time at the Canteen, where she never quite learned how to jitterbug. The Canteen was not quite his sort of thing, but Charlot approved of it anyway.

In 1945, in her autobiography *A Star Danced*, Gertrude Lawrence paid him a belated and unexpected tribute:

> Gaiety, nonsense and lighthearted fun: that was a Charlot revue. They were characterized by exquisite economy, camaraderie between all players and a voice not known up to this time.... The mental closeness was hard to define and immediate in its appeal. Every girl in the line was chosen to give an intimate individuality.

She went on to paraphrase Charlot: "*I do not engage an artiste and then find a place for her.... First I have the place, then I find the artist to fit it. I never buy names. What I pay for is personality, charm and talent.*"

In 1946 he became a naturalized American citizen. It was also then that Philip, demobilized and divorced from Mary and separated from their daughter, boarded the Liberty Ship *John L. Elliott* in Fowley, England, and joined his father, mother and sister in Hollywood. For a time he had rooms with Lilian Sloane, a family friend and a voice teacher. He filed his intention with the French authorities to become Philip André Jean Charlot, an

This time a scowling doctor in *The Foxes of Harrow*, 1947.

Playing the part of a Bishop in *The Razor's Edge*, **1946.**

American citizen, though this wouldn't happen until 1952. Later that year he was married in Las Vegas to Shirley Agin, one of Sloane's pupils.

The marriage did not last and later Philip wrote a poignant story ("Cry Wolf") about her self-destructive tendencies. In the story, the husband calls the suicidal wife's bluff. Philip eventually married Terry Fry, a union which lasted until his mysterious death.

Why had Philip come to the unknown territory of California? He may have believed there was nothing left for him in England or perhaps it was a matter of giving in to pressure from his rather overbearing father.

Philip fairly quickly found himself a part of the motion picture business. During the part of his naval career that had been spent in India, he had been director of services cinematography, in charge of official films in the Eastern theater of war. In Hollywood, his first job came at Universal-International in 1946 as associate story editor.

As story editor at Columbia, where Barnes's husband Mike Frankovich was in charge, he contributed original screenplays to several of the majors, including Twentieth-Century Fox, was involved in the production of several films, and wrote with his friend, screenwriter Albert Duffy, a number of screenplays and television pilots. (Duffy, an acquaintance of Charlot *père*, would be responsible for sending misinformation to the British press after Charlot's death.) Philip also wrote several short stories, largely for English publications.

Joan's movie career was solid as could be in tumultuous times. She was lured from her job with the British consulate by the Alexander Korda company and, since the Kordas had long been family friends, she was somewhat able to convince herself that she had not harmed the war effort by such a move.

There were happy times at the Kordas', including the interlude during which *The Jungle Book* was filmed, when Joan made friends with many of the animals, in particular Jiggs, the famous orangutan. She once borrowed him and sat him down with pencil and pad at the head of the table where a production meeting was taking place.

The increased income was a crucial element in the family's survival. From the Kordas' at 1040 N. Las Palmas, a fair trip from Crescent Heights by "shank's mare," bus, streetcar or (borrowed) bicycle, she moved on to the nearby Samuel Goldwyn offices at 1011 N. Formosa. By 1941 she was private secretary to David O. Selznick (she found that dealing with this man *was* a job), then to Basil Bleck, the Goldwyn general manager, and later in 1942 to Universal-International, where she was the private secretary to William Goetz, a son-in-law of Louis B. Mayer and a "prince of a man" who was destined to democratize moviemaking while undermining the studio system. She stayed with Goetz (and with her "Pop") until she married in 1955.

Family life, at least during the day, was almost nonexistent. Joan would be off to her job, Charlot very likely to one film set or another, and Flip to some volunteer work. Breakfast was a sometime thing, each to his own taste and at his own time. Charlot would have to have his Earl Grey tea (a tea not usually served with milk, which he could not tolerate) while the women of the household drank strong India tea.

The main family meal was dinner, with Flip generally in charge (with an eye on the needs of a diabetic) and Joan frequently a weekend substitute. Charlot, in a pinch, could whip up a mean omelet. He was not much of a drinker—champagne always excepted—which left Flip and Joan to enjoy in tandem a regular before-dinner cocktail.

The relationship between Joan and Philip continued to mature. Joan didn't appreciate his willingness to push her into ventures she didn't truly relish—for example, the time he decided to teach her to drive. Joan was dating the photographer Robert Capa, and they borrowed his Lincoln and Philip had driven to the beach. When they came back to the vicinity of the Beverly Hills Hotel, he told his sister to take the wheel. She managed to get into reverse and to mistake the accelerator for the brake and straight as an arrow they shot, backwards across more than one intersecting street. Well, the tragic and comic are not far apart. That finished Joan's attempts at driving.

Various temporary encouragements continued to come Charlot's way. In the New York edition of *Variety* on February 6, 1946, Jack Pulaski, introducing the publication's choices of Broadway's all-time top shows, acknowledged *Charlot's Revue* as the best of all New York revues. On June 10, Irving Hoffman wrote in the *Hollywood Reporter*, "At this time, a revived, revised *Charlot's Revue* would do well on Broadway or in Hollywood."

Briefly heartened by such mentions—and by a proposed show to star Lillie and Lawrence, *The Best of Charlot*, which was apparently Bea's idea, Charlot headed east in 1947, carrying with him stacks of material from past revues. He was buoyant enough about it to allow Los Angeles newspapers to state that there would be a new Charlot revue on Broadway next year—if not this one—perhaps one starring Hermione Baddeley, who had been a great star in wartime London revue.

While engaged in discussions with Lawrence's financial amanuensis, Fanny Holtzmann, Charlot stayed in familiar surroundings, the Algonquin. But when Holtzmann delivered her verdict—"It would not be feasible for Miss Lawrence to do this"—he was crushed. He decided to pack up and go home—but there was a problem. He had no money to pay for the suite he had inhabited for four hopeful weeks.

Peter Garey was commiserating, when Charlot asked him, "Old boy, would you go downstairs and fetch my billet-doux?" In a few minutes, Gay reappeared with a very elegant Algonquin envelope. Charlot opened it and found a message from Frank Case, the hotel's legendary majordomo. It began, "The Algonquin and I would be most honored if you would consider...." Case had made a gift of the stay, and Charlot was nearly reduced to tears.

It was also 1947 when the avant-garde English director Norman Marshall brought out his book *The Other Theatre*. Commenting upon the small revues he himself had staged beginning in 1932 at the tiny Gate Theatre in London (where Haydn, the great imitator of fish, had starred), Marshall began by noting with slight inaccuracy that "the long line of brilliant intimate revues produced by Charlot and Archie deBear had come to an end."

Unspoken but obvious to many readers was the implication that during wartime or indeed immediately thereafter in Britain, Charlot could have regained his greatness. But there is no evidence that he ever entertained such an ambition. He had cut himself off from old friends and associates—Nesbitt, then approaching his own zenith of power, was one—and presumably saw no way back.

After returning to Hollywood in late 1947 still determined that his revues would not die, he incorporated a company called Revue Properties, Inc., in order to close any loopholes which would prevent or hold up his use of past material. In some instances, this meant tracking down authors and their representatives who had not been heard from in decades.

The minutes of RPI's regular meetings include some fascinating detail. For instance, those of August 8, 1949: Noting that the 1924–25 and 1925–26 *Charlot's Revues* were financed and presented by Archie Selwyn and that their association was dissolved in 1926, the minutes go on: "Since then, whenever Selwyn has heard that Mr. Charlot may be planning a revue, he has consistently tried to muscle in.... In 1939 he tried to force himself in on a deal with the WPA. The theater section of the WPA then collapsed. In 1940, Selwyn had written to Mowbray that no Charlot revue could be produced in the United States without Selwyn's permission." Did a man as proud as Charlot really still fear that Selwyn would try to make trouble and frighten possible backers? If so, perhaps it says something about the weariness that was overtaking him as he approached 70.

In 1948 Lawrence was in Hollywood filming *The Glass Menagerie* in which she was cast against type as the faded southern belle and overbearing mother. Like many others would do, she later wrote of the sadness of seeing the impresario turn into a mere extra.

Charlot, still irrepressible (or desperate) and seeing possibilities in the runaway popularity of television, wrote as part of his presentation to RPI: "I have been approached to prepare a series of telecasts to be known as 'Charlot's Tele-Revues' and the time has come when in order to submit a budget to any prospective sponsor, I must be in a position to submit a budget."

He asked RPI if it was possible to recoup $2,000 spent since forming the corporation, a great part having been incurred "on the trip to New York made in the performance of his services to the corporation." But RPI had no money. By 1949, he had again regrouped his forces and in "Notes and Estimates on the Preparation of a Revue" envisioned rehearsing a show in Hollywood, opening in San Francisco for four weeks, and then jumping to New York. In the same year came the sad news from London that Paul Murray had committed suicide with his wife in a "gas tent." Thus the fate of a financially strapped producer? It can't have made Charlot feel good.

In 1951 he (finally?) gave his blessing to Leigh's outline for a screenplay called *The Charlot Girl*. Although no copies of this outline seem to have survived, the title suggests a romantic comedy evoking "the good old days." But the time for such a screenplay was a decade and a half past and *The Charlot Girl* was never produced. Charlot now saw Leigh as "possibly the only person who could do a Charlot revue: Only Mr. Leigh combines his idea of the two essential qualities—humor and taste." He increasingly pinned his hopes upon Leigh (and his hopes for a good game of bezique on Leigh's mother, who occasionally visited from England).

Late in the year he received a letter from Lawrence: "Dearest Guv ... from Clapham Common [a not very distinguished park in London] to Columbia, eh?" She had just been named professor in charge of the dramatic school at Columbia University. She was asking for his help, soliciting the use of some of his sketches but also hoping he might write a paper so that she could share his wisdom with her students.

He responded immediately ("Professor darling..."), noting that what he had "taught" and she had "learned" came directly from audience reactions. He eventually created a full-length book ("The most important thing in my life right now"), later cut down to a 25,000-word essay called "Tips to Budding Actors and Actresses." Learning that Lawrence herself wanted to write a textbook on acting, he offered to allow her to co-author his own. But Holtzmann once more intervened, proposing to Charlot that if he wrote the book, it would be published under Lawrence's more saleable name. Finally, there was no book and Charlot could not afford to travel to New York ("The Court of Siam") where she was making her triumphal return in Rodgers and Hammerstein's *The King and I*. Her sudden death finalized the loss.

"Tips to Budding Actors and Actresses" is not a scholarly work; it is quite like what he called it in a foreword—advice from a Dutch uncle. The essay is highly practical and obviously derived from personal experience, yet it is almost completely free of name-dropping. Perhaps its greatest charm is its emphasis upon the performer as ethical and thoughtful *whole person*, doing unto others as he or she would be done to. It's a serious piece of work which suggests no shortcuts or arcane theories; something farther from "the method" can hardly be imagined!

Whatever the sadness of this book's failure to live, the experience seems to have convinced Charlot that he still had something to say. He began to write *People 'n Things*, and from then on there were occasional rumblings in the London press

Charlot's 70th birthday with (left to right) Richard Drake, Flip, Rowland Leigh, Joan, Lillian Drake, "the Gov" and Queenie Leonard.

regarding a book in preparation. Oscar Hammerstein II wrote a friendly preface and for a time there was hope that the project would see print.

In 1953 Charlot was dickering with the American Federation of Musicians for a revue planned for the small Ivar Theatre. The show never materialized. In that year Jack Buchanan came to visit him while filming *The Band Wagon* in which he co-starred with his transatlantic smoothy rival, Fred Astaire. Buchanan found Charlot's dream of TV success still alive, as well as a belief that he retained his old power and authority and that a revival of revue was just around the corner. Buchanan wrote a friend:

> He wanted to produce, control and receive a massive sum for the sketches. I can't explain to him that TV is a different medium and one in which he has no experience … this way the whole deal will go out of the window, and actually much of the stuff has dated very little and would be perfect for the material-eating monster that is TV. But he'll never change, the dear old boy, and you must remember he's a Frenchman and careful with his francs.

Charlot also received an on-the-set visit from another former star, Desmond, who wrote, "It was all wrong for Charlot to come to that after all those wonderful shows … and the number of stars of today who owe their success to the start Andre Charlot gave them in his revues." Back in London, the critic Cecil Madden lauded Charlot's revue manner and called his version of revue "A polite anthology of the arts in which beauty and wonder have equal place with sentiment and humor."

In 1952, Charlot discovered that Lillie had used "References," a Titheradge sketch from the second New York revue, in a version of her highly popular show An Evening with Beatrice Lillie. Suspecting that things had not been done properly, Charlot advised Lillie and her companion, John Philip, to deal with Samuel French's, the executors of Titheradge's estate. It was in 1954 when Lillie, after visiting the ailing Charlot, sent RPI a check for $1,000, "for certain rights"—but really as a prop to a financially broken man. Apparently Buchanan did the same.

That year Charlot had incorporated in RPI's minutes the following instructions:

> Dead or alive, I would not expect anyone to condone a screenplay which contained extra-marital episodes to make it more attractive. On no account should you allow anything that could hurt my wife's feelings; and should she have passed away, if and when the time comes I would still expect you to rule out anything that might be offensive to her memory.

It is characteristic that these orders suggest that such "episodes" would be fictional. Without any firm evidence that he was not a model of fidelity, he has to be allowed the presumption of innocence, keeping in mind that he was only human and a Frenchman at that.

Charlot's animosity toward the BBC surfaced one last time. Asked to write and record a speech (he always hated giving speeches) for the corporation in honor of Lillie, he agreed, but eventually wrote of the "same phony baloney," especially about its refusal to allow him to discuss the autobiography he was then finishing.

Old friends, Charlot and Bea Lillie.

He told a London representative, "If I ever hear again from the BBC ... you will tell them to go where they belong." In regard to the same broadcast, the *London Daily Mail* also pestered Charlot for an interview which he reluctantly gave.

In 1955, Charlot was feeling (or at least thinking about) his mortality and enlisted Leigh as editor on the latest deal he was hoping to strike with NBC television, requesting that Leigh take over the entire project if Charlot predeceased him. Fruitless discussions with the network dragged out humiliatingly. The runaround would go on for another year. A local newspaper stated that he was now a "French instructor."

One last roll of the dice with Leigh manifested itself in a show called *Four Dolls on a Dime*. He made a disgusted notation in his papers about having completed an "audition for a backer" (Russell Lewis, "pleasant, complimentary") and Leigh. He was particularly angered at the suggestion that he should be responsible not only for directing the show, but for finding the financial backing. Garey has said that the show had a brief run in a small New York theater but there seems no evidence to support this claim. It is more likely that Leigh was still trying to interest backers and producers up until Charlot's death.

Charlot's general anxiety level was further raised when in July 1955 it was revealed that RPI's vice-president, Syd Cassyd, who had helped found the Academy of Television Arts and Sciences in 1948, had placed all of RPI's documents, which included the sketches, musical scores, etc., in his own office, which had no doors! And Cassyd would be away in New York for a month! The possibility of losing so much material in a fire, earthquake or other typical California event weighed heavily on the frail Charlot. Not much later, Cassyd resigned and agent Charles Collins, who had replaced him, took the material to his ranch in Encino.

Joan, by then greatly depressed about the family's fortunes and her own future, was given some time off by Goetz for rest and rehabilitation. She traveled to Hawaii and there met expatriate Englishman Douglas Midwinter, an executive with the Matson Lines, who was rehearsing his part in a community production of *My Three Angels.* They hit it off and after she returned home "a blizzard of correspondence" took place. They were married March 18, 1955.

After a honeymoon at the Beverly Hills Hotel, they returned to Hawaii. Joan worked for the Hawaiian Broadcasting System as secretary to its television and radio program director until Matson relocated Doug to San Francisco, where they found a place in the Marina overlooking the Palace of Fine Arts and, subsequently, a house not far from Golden Gate Park, complete with fireplace and garden.

They were happy in San Francisco, where Joan became the executive secretary for the general manager of Westinghouse Broadcasting. It is a measure of their contentment that they were devastated when orders came through for Doug to return to Hawaii. However, they found a house high above most of Oahu which they would enjoy until the late 1960s.

In the closing years of his life, Charlot wrote an essay for *People 'n Things* called "Could This Be a Self-Portrait?" Near the beginning, he said, "I am afraid that if I had to live my life all over again, I would still resent criticism, still be self-opinionated, still be obstinate; only more so." He added:

> I maintain that when a man's aim in life is to accomplish some creative work— which is what I have always attempted to do—he is doomed to artistic failure unless he makes decisions for himself ... I am no megalomaniac; I have always listened to experts' advice when I could not find out for myself the answer to some of the problems that were facing me.... It is far less painful to tell oneself: "I was wrong, don't forget the lessons," than "Why did you allow someone else to influence your judgment—you would have avoided that blunder."

Revealingly, he continued:

> I have known a number of men in my calling, who could never take a decision, or form an opinion, about the value of the shows they were preparing, until they had consulted a dozen friends—they were not creators; just entertainment merchants.
>
> I have been accused of being vain—nothing is farther from reality—the truth is that I am too deeply sincere in my work to allow anyone to kid me; also that, being as sensitive as a "teen-age" girl, I "feel" too deeply to kid myself.... I am fundamental and embarrassingly shy; I am lost in a room where more than eight people are present.... Making a speech—and I have had to make hundreds—has always been agony to me; in short, I am a complete introvert.

Although my mind is active to the point of restlessness, my body is equally lazy. Except for horse-riding, ice skating and tennis—all in moderation—I have always detested any form of physical exercise.... My doctor ... pretends that my taste for "good living" may have caused the diabetes which I have managed to keep under control for twenty years. I have a gift for which I am thankful: a sense of humor, but my wife, in spite of 46 years of married life—or is it because of that—pretends that it is sometimes distorted!

Last ... I am afraid that extravagance has been one of my worst failings ... life is no longer what it used to be. The question is, if I had to start my life all over again, would I live differently? I doubt it! At the time of writing this, I have turned 72, I have lived a lot, enjoyed a lot, paid a lot—sometimes too much.... No, I am afraid I would find it difficult to reform—and I am not sure I would want to. I would still be self-opinionated, obstinate, allergic to criticism and physical exercise, fond of good living, and ... well, what about extravagance? Well, I am not sure I would be successful, but I might try to save a little. Life is tedious, and somewhat painful, when extravagance is no longer possible in one's old age.

Having suffered not only diabetes but phlebitis since 1953, he progressively weakened. His blood pressure's systolic average had risen to 212. Still, he carried on with daily life. In his last year of life Charlot, increasingly debilitated, convinced RPI to make Philip his "deputy" and through Collins continued to push his television ideas to no avail.

Garey, then living in Los Angeles's Venice, recalled Charlot's requesting of him one day, "Old boy, I want you to drive me to take Rolette to the vet's." Dickering for "a most important television show," he wrote to ASCAP to secure material by their authors.

Charlot believed that the show had been okayed by "Mr. Wile and Mr. Kemp, who have the last word in Hollywood for NBC." In February, his associate Lillian Small traveled to New York to finalize the deal, only to be turned down there. Thereupon ensued weeks of farce, including the apparent loss of the show's script. Then once more, the deal was allegedly on, and the newspapers said so. But there never was a Charlot revue on television.

Hating the insults to his body which were accumulating day by day, he wrote, "Scientists and doctors do not stop telling us that they are prolonging human life; their boast is slightly exaggerated, so far, they have not managed to prolong life, but merely old age."

On May 20, 1956, only days after an emergency operation for cancer of the sigmoid colon, a heart attack at the Motion Picture Country Home and Hospital in the San Fernando Valley ended Charlot's tribulations.

There was only the briefest notation in the *Los Angeles Herald-Express* and none at all in the *Los Angeles Times*. The London obituaries ranged from condescension to downright inaccuracy.

The (London) *Times* emphasized his bankruptcy and the six-night run of his final revue. The *Daily Telegraph* gave him credit for *Wonder Bar*: "Making the stage a kind of continuation of the auditorium to give the appearance of a huge night club." The *Daily Mail* said his last film role was as a doorman ("Such was the world's reward for Charlot's enterprise"). It described his later Hollywood days as "mooching around a vegetable market with an old collie dog doing his own shopping in a carpet bag."

It went on to say he had died "at a private Hollywood nursing home a few days after an operation for a stomach complaint" and that he had "helped found the modern Hollywood trend in musicals." The *Daily Express* called the place of his death a "charity hospital" and added that he was financially supported by his son and daughter. The *Evening Standard*, noting that he had been writing a book in Hollywood, claimed that Charlot was "Anglo-Russian." But it got the place of death right.

Among the few to give Charlot his due was W. MacQueen-Pope: "Charlot reigned as a king of revue, one of the best of them all. There have been few managers with a greater flair for spotting talent than he. He stands second only to the great George Edwardes in that respect."

Charlot had left one specific instruction about what to do after his death—none of his "girls" were to have any responsibility for dealing with his remains or with his will. Everything was up to Philip, who may well have been overwhelmed by the task. Charlot was cremated on May 23 and his ashes were placed in Valhalla, a raw pseudo-cemetery on a bend of Victory Boulevard, where North Hollywood and Burbank blend anonymously.

The last segment of *People 'n Things* is dated November 15, 1954. "Cavalcade" begins with a disclaimer of the "ghost-written" series in the 1928 *Empire News* and 1934 *Sunday Chronicle*, giving his dissatisfaction with them as a reason for essaying this semi-autobiography. But in writing this series of essays he was troubled by the thought that he had left out many people important to his life. These "appeared in a dream ... or was it a nightmare?" when "a crowd of my former associates was surrounding me, closing on me with pain in their eyes."

To put the record straight on his behalf, below is a selection of many who have had only passing if any mention in Charlot's own version of an autobiography and the biography here:

"Miss Philip"—starting with Alhambra days, for 14 years his secretary.

Hilda Brighten—"*who tried to impress me by writing the lyric of 'Mouse! Mouse!' but did not have to make any effort to be one of the best friends my wife and I ever had.*"

Ralph Lynn—"*The only comedian whose 'gagging' always delighted me.*"

Ronsin—"*When he brought his partners Marc Henri and Laverdet to London, I did not allow him to take them back, and kept them busy in London for years. Ronsin asked me to take him backstage at Drury Lane Theatre to look at English scenery; he was amazed by the quality of the canvas and the timber they used but could not refrain from saying 'What a pity they paint with—dung!'*"

Cyril Scott and Eric Coates—"*who each wrote two remarkable ballets for me.*"

Mistinguett—"*The only way in which I could dissuade her from 'borrowing' my musical numbers was to give them to her.*"

George Benda—"*who had been my comrade at Condorcet as far back as 1898, and eventually designed hundreds of beautiful costumes for me.*"

John Tilley—"*the most naturally amusing of comedians.*"

O.D. Harris—"*my dear old friend and manager.*"

Harris, generally known as "Odee," has a specific role in the dream—he closes the gates, since so many hundreds are still waiting outside—Brisson, Oscar Shaw, "Pat" Dolin, Frank Lawton, and many more, including all the people who worked at building sets, etc.

His dream is ended when Flip wakes him by announcing that it is past his usual breakfast time. Learning from him that in honor of the dream he will now call the last chapter of his book "Cavalcade," she reminds him, "But that's the title of a play by Noel."

"Is it?" he replies.

Flip has the last word: "You old fraud!"

• NINE •

Epilogue

Flip was not to outlive her husband by more than a few short months. She died suddenly on August 19, 1956. This left the doubly bereaved Joan and Philip to deal with Charlot's archive, a massive holding that existed essentially in two parts. These were eventually disposed of in a fashion characteristic of those who administered them. Joan came into possession of most of her father's writings and photographs, as well as all the documentation from those final years when he was so desperately trying to make sure of his rights to long-unused material, just in case his hour would strike again. Philip held many boxes of scripts and musical scores, contracts and miscellany which had been passed on to him while his father was still alive.

In 1959, in a state of depression, Philip wrote to his sister suggesting that they burn everything or give it away or sell it and share the profits. In the same year, RPI held its final meeting. After that, Joan kept all her holdings in the firm belief that Charlot would eventually be rescued from obscurity. Philip (perhaps wishing to unburden himself of an oppressive father and probably to save himself from storing an oppressive amount of material) gave almost all his holdings to the special collections department of the library at UCLA. That collection runs to 46 boxes, although no single category seems to be complete. He wrote Joan that he had given away some other items to people who might enjoy them, a likely explanation for the collection's gaps.

In 1960 Philip, then living on Holloway Plaza Drive just off the Sunset Strip, became acquainted with his daughter Nini, then 21. She stayed with Philip and Terry in Hollywood for a year and finally got to know her father as much as he allowed himself to be known. In 1965 Philip wrote to Fanny Holtzmann, who was now guarding Lawrence's legacy, "Joan and I care very much that [Charlot] be correctly and sympathetically portrayed, and that his part be played by an acceptable actor.... The casting of Julie Andrews is a stroke of genius."

This letter referred to *Star!* the motion picture biography of Lawrence. With the contemporary critics and, to a lesser degree, the paying public of the time, the finished film never quite lived up to its promise, though as the years have passed it has gained stature, as has Andrews's portrayal of "Gertie" and Daniel Massey's of Coward.

The screenplay of "Star!" demonstrated Hollywood's way of playing fast and loose with the facts. So well, in fact, that Lillie refused to be portrayed at all! (This hole in history is reminiscent of the astonishing film biography of Jerome Kern, *Till the Clouds Roll By*. Its screenplay omits all mention of Kern's great collaborators, Guy Bolton and P.G. Wodehouse. The screenplay was written by Bolton.)

The portrayal of Charlot in "Star!" was also typical—both accurate in the sense of control conveyed by the actor, Alan Oppenheimer, and inaccurate, as Jonny would indignantly point out years later. The expert ocean swimmer Charlot would never have been shown floundering in a pool, and the "majestic" Charlot ("not a *Darling!* type of theatrical person") would never have been caught clowning atop a bus in London.

On November 11, 1966, Philip died of "a coronary occlusion" under mysterious circumstances in a Mexican hotel where he had gone for a vacation. He left behind no will, but a letter which was not in acceptable legal form with his bank. His few assets were left to his wife Terry with no mention of Nini. The Mexican authorities were never forthcoming about the matter and over the years the speculation grew that Philip had committed suicide.

The Matson Lines abandoned their passenger services in 1972 and Doug, the unfortunate division's manager, landed a job with Princess Cruises based in Los Angeles. After a tearful farewell to Hawaii and a temporary sojourn in an L.A. apartment, he and Joan found a house in Pacific Palisades where they lived together until Doug's death eleven years later.

In 1975 the British Broadcasting Corporation was in the midst of a series of hour-long radio programs called "The Impresarios," dealing with the major producers of London theater's illustrious past. Doug Midwinter's brother Jack, who was living on the south coast not far from Bognor Regis at the time, contacted the "Beeb," complaining about Charlot's apparent omission, and he was hastily added to the series.

A number of voices contributed to this portrait, but the overall program leant so heavily on the connection with Coward that Charlot himself seemed a supporting player. The show also included a hidden insult. His career was allotted only the program's closing half-hour. The first half went to J.L. Sacks. Sunday Wilshin, one of Charlot's 1927 New York chorus, was interviewed for the show, but when she discovered the Sacks connection ("Like comparing hamburger stalls to French charcuterie") she withdrew her contribution.

Charlot had in fact dealt with Sacks on one occasion. In 1916 the two had agreed to produce a revue starring Harry Lauder. Charlot wrote, "It was soon after I had left the Alhambra, and I wanted to build up my business." He never got over marveling that Sacks, who could neither read or write, had managed to get the canny Scot to sign a contract.

Charlot had a certain amount of respect for Sacks's ability to make money, as well as his skill at cards. They had discussed cooperating on a musical comedy with Gaby Deslys which never materialized and Charlot withdrew from the Harry Lauder revue, *Three Cheers*, but not before it had been produced.

Nearly twenty years after Charlot's death, the Londoner J.C. Trewin, one of his era's leading critics, confessed that he had been guilty of forgetting Charlot's accomplishments and innovations: "We all knew Andre was not a businessman! But this had nothing to do with his genius for finding and creating stars—afterwards always pinched or borrowed by others—particularly C.B. Cochran." The apparent flurry of interest in Charlot and in revue led to no real re-discovery of either, although over time a body of allusion accumulated:

The American theater historian Gerald Bordman wrote, in the first edition of his chronicle *American Musical Theatre* (1978), "*Charlot's Revue* helped point the way to the more intimate, literate and fast-paced revues that later dominated Broadway. In after years the show would be looked back on as a milestone."

In 1982 R.B. Marriott, writing in *The (London) Stage and TV Today*, recalled an

> ...elegant man, who looked at first as if he dressed very casually but was in fact exceptionally smart.... As a manager, as distinct from producer, Charlot was financially all right; as the revue producer he was continually in financial trouble ... because ... Charlot was personally extravagant.... He wanted the best ... talent and taste.... He was a perfectionist and a go-getter, a man-about town ... friendly yet something of a loner. He died, his shows remembered, but the man virtually forgotten.

A 1993 BBC Radio 2 series on the centenary of revue (assuming that Hicks's *Under the Clock* was in fact a revue) written and presented by Richard Anthony Baker included a significant segment on Charlot.

Later in the same year, also on Radio 2, "Buzz-Buzz: The Lives of André Charlot" featured a number of surviving voices from his later London years. In the course of the program Nesbitt recalled Charlot as "very relaxed, I can't remember him ever getting particularly excited about anything, he had a sort of rather fatherly attitude to most of the cast and staff that worked for him." As for what Charlot taught him:

> Most shows were very simply presented in a permanent set with various droppings and pieces and therefore the most vital thing for the effect was lighting. I mean, you had a cyclorama and maybe three or four sets with nice curtains and a few built pieces ... but the lighting had to create the atmosphere and the effect.

In the program, Hare recalled that in doing the 1933–34 radio series it was necessary for all the performers to get into full evening dress. Charlot, she recalled, "had the air of an impresario. He wore a kind of cowboy hat thing, and he would come in with this dog, a sort of signature thing. Girlie used to come in and Guv would take a bow." Davis suggested that Charlot had finally "got into the hands of moneylenders." His daughter Joan remembered the Charlot Young Ladies, her father's club for chorus girls, with Flip as president. "They had uniforms like royal blue shorts and white shirts ... I had my own uniform and it was really a lot of fun."

A live 1996 series on revue under the general direction of Ned Sherrin at London's Theatre Museum (a branch of the Victoria & Albert Museum) included one episode on Charlot which featured a number of anecdotes, not all of them strictly accurate. The series was subsequently aired on Radio 2.

If Charlot had created and defined the most distinctive form of British revue—the intimate—he was one of the most important figures in 20th-century theater and certainly the most unjustly forgotten.

He was a man of great strengths and weaknesses. His training and vision placed him perfectly to create a theatrical form ideally suited to its time—and thereby made history. When that time had passed, he may not have trusted his creativity enough to abandon its shimmering earlier product. He was stuck, albeit benignly, in the past. As a man, particularly in his most intimate dealings, he may never have escaped the characteristic and stereotypical French duality (at least as seen by Anglo-Saxons)—that imperfect fusion of cool intellectualism and utter, passionate abandonment.

Aware of both sides of his nature and perhaps more than that, he nevertheless always placed his trust in himself. It usually worked. But not always. *Tout ou rien.* But what a joy it must have been, being entertained at home and abroad by André Charlot!

Beverly Hills, 1937
by André Charlot

Very often, we travel thousands of miles to gaze on sights attractive in their novelty, or surprisingly strange. Sometimes, although we do not realize it, there are such things right under our nose, and we do not see them, we do not even know they are there.

I was born and bred in Paris, but it was not until I had visited dozens of other famous cities that I was struck by the fact that, standing on the Place de la Concorde in Paris, and looking around, specially in the direction of the Champs-Elysées and the Arc de Triomphe, one was encompassing a panorama which, as far as I am personally concerned, has few equals in the world. So, today I do not intend to tell you of the cruises that took me to Turkey, or the Canary Islands. I will simply pilot you to a land which is only a few miles, possibly a few hundred yards from your own door—that land of make-believe—Beverly Hills and the surrounding areas that have become the home of those who shine in the Film Industry.

I would take a bet that lots of you who travel daily along Santa Monica Boulevard, or Sunset Boulevard, on your way to and from the Beach and Los Angeles, have never been curious enough to explore the chunk of land which, between those two main arteries, constitutes the heart of Beverly Hills. I can assure you it is worthwhile, and if, on your next afternoon of leisure, you decide to roam up and down the various streets, all called drives in that district, you will probably agree with me that you have never seen anything so attractive in your life.

In 1929 I had taken a lightning trip from New York to Hollywood. I had only stayed there twenty-four hours. I had crossed Beverly Hills a couple of times, but my impression was, of necessity, a fleeting one.

When I arrived in California in 1937 to spend a much-needed vacation as the house guest of a friend of mine in Beverly Hills, I was allowed to relax, possibly for the first time in 35 years. What I saw bewildered and delighted me, because let us face it, the little city called Beverly Hills is an enchanting sight, once you have recovered from the first shock caused by the various and sometimes ill-assorted styles of architecture used in its construction. It presents an harmonious and delightful crazy-quilt pattern, with the houses limited to two stories and the beautifully kept lawns and gardens to be seen everywhere between the road and the houses.

Another extraordinary feature to the newcomer is the complete absence of beggars, of visible police and of pedestrians. This last aspect specially struck me as weirdly fantastic. Surely, there were some automobiles, roaming occasionally here and there, but those who were not just passing had an extraordinary knack of disappearing into the private garage drives—and, under the warm summer sun the apparent absence of human life was giving the whole place the eerie atmosphere of a dead city, an atmosphere emphatically contradicted by the spick and span appearance of the houses, of the trees and of the gardens.

My greatest delight, during my first weeks in Beverly Hills, was to stroll from drive to drive, just looking round and dreaming that I was in some extraordinary new world.

I had seen only very few things that compared with that serene beauty; one was Bruges, "the dead city" in Belgium; another was a stretch of the river Thames, at Maidenhead, 20 miles from London, where, when boating on the river, there was for a few miles a charming panorama of old country houses with enormous lawns that had been kept to perfection for centuries, sloping gently to the water's edge. I was imagining, too, that before it had become merely a sight-seeing spot for tourists, Venice, in the days of the Doges, must have presented a similar picture of peaceful repose.

If you have not already been there, this impression I got on my arrival in Beverly Hills is yours for the asking—that is, if you have a little imagination, and a heart easily moved by the outer appearance of things that are only a combination of vegetable and mineral products, without the apparent presence of a soul. All you have to do is jump in your car, and roam around.

Seeing what is on the other side of these facades is not, however, within the reach of all—but—I was among the lucky. I knew the occupants of many of those dream houses and I was positively amazed by the degree of luxury and comfort that had been attained in their construction. It was then that I first got acquainted with the playroom, the home-bar, the barbecue, the patio—all novelties to a European. The pools, too, fascinated me, and the tennis courts lighted for playing at night left me speechless.

I must admit that, at first, the purpose of the playroom rather bewildered me; if you just stop to think for a minute, the basic reason for its existence is positively insulting. It just means that, having built and furnished your house with love and care, you do not sufficiently trust your friends' manners to allow them to make use of it. Therefore, you have installed a sort of super pig-sty deluxe where they can upset their glasses and throw their cigarette ends on the floor. It is not altogether complimentary, but it is extremely practical and as I was soon to find out, completely justified. Common sense was responsible for the existence of the playroom.

The next thing that struck me was the extraordinary laziness of the inhabitants. No one walked a step. I was told that the distances were so great that everyone had to have an automobile. The tremendous area of Los Angeles was already an obvious fact to me, yet I was finding it difficult to understand why people had to use their car when they were going to a friend's house no more than two blocks distant. What absolutely amazed me, though, and irritated me "more than somewhat," was the way in which people called the operator to get them a number they could have dialed themselves. I felt there was something stupidly decadent about that expression of moronic inertia. I am glad to say that since the war, the Telephone company has got wise to that habit; they are too busy to coddle the subscribers to that extent, and those who were taking such unfair advantage of the operators' good-will are now compelled to dial for themselves—indeed a colossal effort—but a good job, too.

Just as strange as its appearance, the home city of the Film Industry has a way of living, idiosyncrasies and private codes of customs that are baffling to the new-comer.

During my first week among them, I had acquired only a summary amount of initiation. I knew already that no self-respecting person lived in Hollywood; that only a low form of life was to be found in Los Angeles, and that anyone blessed with any standing, reputation and pride, dwelt west of those two benighted com-munities.

I had discovered, too, that the western portion reserved for the chosen few, was itself divided into four sections. They were the commercial district of Beverly Hills, which is south of Santa Monica Boulevard; the section limited by Santa Monica Boulevard in the south and Sunset in the north; and the slopes between Sunset and the Hills; the fourth section was all the area comprised between Beverly Hills and the Beach.

The first section, south of the tracks, was reserved to those who were aspiring to the dignity of living north of them, and to those who could no longer afford the northern portion; they were the fallen ones, but they could not bear the idea of an address that was not Beverly Hills. Besides, their phone number being a Beverly Hills one, could fool those who did not know where their residence was located. In that less dignified district were also the restaurants, the shops and some offices.

In the second section, between Santa Monica Boulevard and Sunset, were to be found the bodies who were "somebody."

The two other sections, north of Sunset and west of Beverly Hills, were the privileged grounds of the super elite. True, they were rubbing elbows with a num-ber of peasants and other primitive Angelenos, but this proximity added some dig-nity to their superb isolation—because—when your next door neighbor happens to be a member of your own profession, you are more or less compelled to acknowl-edge his existence, but when you have the luck to be surrounded on all sides by indus-trialists, business men and bankers, you are allowed to ignore them and you are entitled to a satisfaction only comparable to their ownership of a private island.

Curiously enough, when later, I met industrialists, business men (but no bankers), I was made to see that there was a fellow-feeling about that craving for isolationism. They, too, preferred to be surrounded by Film people. It made it pos-sible for them to keep themselves to themselves.

Another anomaly that I want to relate to you is the strange craving people have to live in furnished houses. It goes somehow like this: no sooner has someone spent thousands and thousands of dollars on the equipment of a house, then, fascinated by the house of a friend, the owner of the new house rents the house of his friend and sublets his own; sometimes the reverse process operates. The new house owner gives a house-warming party, and someone must get his new house from him at any price, so he sublets it, and rents someone else's house for his own use. No one seems to be able to resist that constant mania for shifting and changing. Some people go as far as just swapping houses for a while. I suppose it is due to the fact that in the studios, they constantly go from set to set, and they must do the same in private life.

It is sometimes most confusing when you want to locate friends, or when you are asked to a party. You are never sure whether or not you should go to the house where you were the preceding week. It gives the whole community a curious hotel atmosphere. The place is occasionally turned into a sort of super-bungalow-court where people seem to be unable to stop playing a crazy game of Musical Chairs.

I must now take you inside one of these houses, and tell you the story of the night when my friend Tom, a very successful Actor, took me to the house of Dick, a very successful Writer, for a quiet game of bridge with Harry, a famous Producer.

I cannot forget that night. It was my most illuminating introduction to the mysteries of Movieland.

A Quiet Game of Bridge
by André Charlot

First of all, I would like to tell you—in case you think I am a snob—that I know a large quantity of people who are neither famous nor successful. Luckily for me, I escaped the curse of ever "going Hollywood."

Secondly; my story was taking place many years ago, when circumstances had landed me, for a short stay, in the whirl of Movieland's Merry-Go-Round.

Third; that I have completely recovered from that experience, and that it left no scars, but I *HAD* to mention the fact that Tom, Dick and Harry were famous and successful. The cause was probably mechanical and subconscious. You see, I was in the midst of celebrities. Maybe I should explain:

You probably have some poor relations, some poor friends, and I am sure they are welcome in your home, and at your table. There is no such weakness of feeling in Movieland. The successful only invite and meet the famous. When giving a party, the host who makes a list of guests is solely guided in his choice by the importance of the names he is in a position to select, not by any sentimental reason. It is considered embarrassing to ask one's acquaintances to rub elbows with people who do not matter. It simply is not done.

I have never come across this attitude anywhere else in my wanderings, but it did not take me long to realize that most of those people who were living so regally, and in all appearances, so happily, were all under the spell of some awful fear of anything that did not have the ring of success. With them, it was a kind of superstitious phobia.

Most of them had had hard fights to get where they were; many of those eating caviar had known days when a chunk of bread would have been welcome, but that belonged to the past. No one could laugh, or even smile about it—that stigma was not to be revived—and the only way to keep it at bay was simple. The successful only met the successful. Those who were not favored by Fate were kept at a safe distance.

When Tom and I reached Dick's door, I was rather horrified by the noise that was reaching our ears. I had been promised a quiet game, and the sounds coming from what was obviously the playroom, indicated that a party was in full swing. I must confess to you that I do not like parties. When there is a crowd in a room, I lose all my faculties.

The butler reassured us; there was no party going on, but we soon had the explanation. The radio and the phonograph were both belching forth, at their loudest. Dick and another man were having most animated conversations on the two telephones, and a Great Dane and a Pomeranian were welcoming our entrance with strangely contrasted barks.

Dick was the proud owner of one of those magnificent radio-phonographs that can be switched on in all the rooms of the house at the same time. I was informed that every day, his secretary, under his instructions, prepared a list of records for the following day, and it was one of the butler's jobs, at the appointed times, to empty the machine and refill it. Thus, Dick, a writer who could not stand silence and communion alone with his soul, was insuring a constant background for his creative mental energy. That was my first surprise, during an evening full of novelty as far as I was concerned.

I must confess another weakness to you. I find it impossible to concentrate enough to answer the phone, if a radio, or even a conversation is going on in the room—and—on being told that the Capehart never stopped from the time of Dick's awakening to the moment when he turned off his light at night, I was thinking, with terror of the kind of bridge I was going to be able to play with this noise going on.

I hope you do not think I do not like music. I am very fond of it really, and I am very eclectic in my appreciation of it. As a matter of fact, I am so fond of music that I can never accept it as a background. When I am hearing something I really like, it is utterly impossible for me to listen to anything else. Every other sound becomes background to me—and I hate background when music is being played.

I found that the second instrument responsible for a portion of the cacophony which was filling the room was the latest thing in radio-portables. In front of it, a lovely little blonde was sitting admiringly, listening with rapture to "The Umbrella Man" song, completely oblivious to the fact that the house phonograph was playing at the same time Tschaikovsky's thundering ending to "1812."

At the same time, Dick was blasting down a third instrument—a telephone— pouring insults addressed to his third wife who was about to divorce him.

Tom introduced me to those who were in the room. There were four of them besides Dick. I am afraid I was not sufficiently prepared for what turned out to be surprise No. 2.

Two of the ladies, Edna and Pamela, were playing backgammon. Edna was arguing, rather violently, against the ethics of Pamela's last move of her men. They were Dick's first and second wives. The third lady, who was so engrossed in the radio, was Betsy, Dick's fiancée, whom he was supposed to marry as soon as he had managed to induce his third wife, Josie, to go and spend six weeks in Reno. From the conversation going on over the phone, it was clear that Josie was making sure of having enough cash to bust all the banks of Nevada's gambling rooms.

The other man was Jack, a Movie big-wig, and he was having a violent and most offensive argument on the second phone with a man who must have been his bookmaker.

To say that I was taken aback by these various situations would be to put it mildly. Happily, I had sufficiently recovered my self-control when I was told by Tom that, since they had both divorced Dick, Edna and Pamela had become the closest of friends, and that, knowing of his approaching third divorce, they had expressed the very natural wish to meet the lady who was to become his forth wife—so—Dick had asked the three of them to dine together.

Of course, I am speaking of many years ago. In those days it was considered bad form to be on too friendly terms with a wife from whom you had only *just* parted. I understand things are slightly different now, and that the lady who has just divorced you is the one entitled to the maximum of your attentions.

By the way, I want to follow this slight interruption with another one. I hope I am not conveying to you the impression that every home in Movieland is patterned on that of Dick, and that the story I am telling you represents the rule—the only way of living in Beverly Hills. Nothing of the kind. The majority of homes there are as normal and peaceful as yours and mine, but I am not inventing a fairy tale in the hope of amusing you. What I am telling you may be the exception, but it is based on facts.

Going back to Dick's house—Tom, mistaking the expression on my face for a fear that their presence might interfere with our quiet game of bridge, thought he had better reassure me. Jack had just preceded us into the room, and he was only waiting for the arrival of Bobbie to take Edna and Pamela dancing at the Clover Club. Betsy had to leave in a few minutes for the Trocadero, where she was doing an Adagio dance number with Paolo, her former husband. Jack had previously been married to Edna, after her divorce from Dick, but they, too, had divorced after two years of stormy bliss.

I hope you have managed to follow me in this matrimonial maze, but if you have not, don't let that worry you. We should not take those people's marriages more seriously than they did themselves.

Within a moment, Dick had finally agreed the price of his freedom with his third wife, and Bobbie arrived.

Bobbie was a curious character. He was an actor who had played in various theatres and night clubs and, wherever he was, whatever the hour, he had to act ... that is, he felt a curious urge to entertain and to have an audience.

Let me say that Bobbie had talent—that he had reached a position where it was not necessary for him to make an exhibit of himself, but ... he could not help it ... he still had to sing.

Bobbie had not seen me since my arrival, and welcomed me with that gushing and perfectly rehearsed enthusiasm, with which I am, alas, only too familiar, and he immediately offered to let me watch his latest specialty. Happily for me, I knew him well enough to be blunt, and I reminded him that two ladies had been waiting for him for half an hour, and that I had come to see Dick for a game of bridge. He took it nicely and left with Jack and the girls. His parting farewell was a jovial "Let's get together...."

"Let's get together...."

Somehow, these words were becoming a red rag to me. I was finding them the most irritating form of courtesy yet invented in the English language. Why? Possibly because I was not used to them. We say daily things like: "So glad to see you" … "You're looking fine" … "I have enjoyed your party tremendously." When six times out of ten, we really mean just the reverse. Somehow, we are used to these daily lies, we were born and brought up with them, but to me, "Let's get together" had the ring of a new and unnecessary from of hypocrisy.

Since my arrival in California, I was meeting many people I had not seen for a long time. I was getting acquainted with lots of others I had never met before, but it had not taken me more than a few days to realize that, on parting, it was one of two things—either a date suggested for a meal, or merely a visit, which meant a form of welcome to this part of the world, or—it was said: "Let's get together" which, translated in truthful words, expressed the thought: "We could not help this meeting, could we? Well, let's leave it at that."

I know perfectly well that hypocrisy is one of the basic elements of civilization, that tact, diplomacy, tolerance, restraint are all forms of hypocrisy without which life would be unbearable. I know we can't tell people "This pimple on your nose is really hideous," or, "I don't care if I never see you again" or, "I could not cross the street fast enough to dodge you." I know we can't stand people who make a point of being literally frank in their remarks to us—and—I am positive George Washington could never have become the most popular President of the United States if he had always spoken the truth, but somehow it sounded so unnecessary to me, with so many expressions of indifference already current in the English language, to coin a new one. There is something so pleasant about getting together with the people you like that, to me, "Let's get together," when it is not meant, is a most offensive form of desecration.

Another cute idiosyncrasy to which I had to get used was the manner in which one always had to guess the last name of every person mentioned. It was always Tom, Dick or Harry—never a last name.

Within a few days of my arrival in Beverly Hills, I had been sharply reproved, by some friends who were taking a filial interest in my social education, for telling them that I had met Norma Shearer and Helen Hayes at a preview, and that I was going to Mrs. Rathbone's party the following week. I was accused of being utterly provincial. "For heaven's sake, André, forget that Victorian way of expressing yourself. Say that you saw Norma and Helen, that you are going to Ouida's party. Unless you can acquire that habit, and quickly, people will think you are nothing but a dope."

"That's all very well," I replied, "but if I say Charles, for instance, how will you know that I mean Boyer, or Laughton, or Chaplin?"

There was some logic to my question, and I thought I had them floored, but I was informed, with a sneer, that in Chaplin's case, I was to say Charlie; Laughton was "Butch," and Boyer a very French "Sharl." That was the end of that.

I must make another confession to you. I am not given to familiarity. It took me a long time to get used to it, but now I expect I am completely callous about what I used to consider "bad manners." I even got as far as referring to the First Lady of the Land as Eleanor.

Going back to my quiet game of bridge—the other guests had departed, and we were now left in comparative peace, except, of course, for the Capehart which was crooning César Franck's symphony, my most revered musical achievement, as a conversation background.

Dick welcomed me charmingly, but appeared surprised to see us. He had entirely forgotten our game of bridge, arranged only the previous day. My presence suddenly reminded him that, during the morning, he had had a message from Harry's butler, informing him of the latter's sudden departure the previous night. He had flown to New York to be present, this very evening at the opening performance of Tootsie Toots' season at the Rainbow Room, so, we had to find another fourth.

Normally, this might have been a simple problem. All you have to do is to call your bridge friends, and you usually find one who is sufficiently anxious to escape from himself—and there you are, but, remember, we were not exactly normal. We were in Movieland, and we were faced with a real puzzle, the exclusive rights of which belong to the Film world.

Remember, you and I are simple folk. We are phone subscribers, and our name, our address and our phone number are to be found in the directory. That is far too ingenuous for our make-believe industry, and the reason is really most amusing.

There are in the Film colony a certain number of stars…. Let's be generous and say about one hundred, who, continually pestered by autograph hunters and beggars, find it necessary to ask the Phone Company not only to refrain from publishing their names in the directory, but, also, not to disclose their numbers to inquirers. Although most inconvenient to their friends, and sometimes to themselves, this craving or privacy can be understood. There simply is no other way out.

What happens to the stars is this: They give their private number to a restricted number of friends, who in turn disclose it, confidentially, to an unlimited number of their friends, the number soon ceases to be private property. The Star gets a new number from the Phone Company, gives it to a limited number of friends, and the process is repeated, ad infinitum.

The hilarious side of this situation is that, since the *important* members of the Film colony have to resort to this form of protection, no one, connected with the Movies, can afford to admit that he, or she is not important, and, as a result, thousands, from top executives to junior writers, refuse to come down to earth and recognize that no one would really bother them if their phone number was published in the book. Furthermore, it is considered smart, from time to time, to change your telephone number in order to convince your acquaintances that your fame is getting positively overwhelming; that your private number has reached too many people, and that you are being pestered to death.

You can imagine what a job it is to keep a private telephone directory under those conditions.

Dick's private book was in pretty good order, and he decided to call Jim—another writer—but on calling, he was informed that Jim's number had been changed that very day, and the new one was not to be given. Then he thought of Dave, a song writer who was only living two blocks up his street. Somehow, the number could not be located, and Tom had a bright idea. It was nine p.m. in California, therefore midnight in New York. Harry was sure to be at the Rainbow Room at this time, and Harry never moved without his pocket phone book, the most complete in the community. Dave's number was sure to be in it, so a person to person call was immediately put through to New York.

Meanwhile, I was sitting next to a pile of books, one of which was the phone directory. I knew Dave to be an eccentric individual, and I felt it was worthwhile making a colossal effort and I looked in the book. Sure enough, Dave's number was there. My sense of humor was so tickled, though, that I wanted to find out to what extent Tom and Dick would waste time and money, so I kept the information to myself.

Owing to the magnificent efficiency of the American telephone system, ever a wonder to a European, Harry was at the end of the wire in less than two minutes. Dick started to tell him about a whiz of an idea he had for a picture. Harry, not to be outdone, gave Dick the outline of a situation that had struck him on entering the Rainbow Room. A long controversy ensued, on the respective merits of their brain-waves. Harry told Dick that Tootsie had been swell at her first performance. Dick asked him to give her his love, and put the receiver down, having completely forgotten the reason that had prompted him to call Harry, at that hour, and three thousand miles away.

By that time, my keenness for a game of bridge, quiet or otherwise, had more than left me—but I would not have given up my armchair for a thousand dollars. I had not watched such a good show for a long time.

Tom had not been able to grab the phone fast enough to ask Harry himself for the all important information, so, as Dave's house was only a hundred yards away, and time was getting on, he got up from the davenport, with a supreme effort of energy and told us that he would jump in his car, he knew Dave was home, and he would bring him back within five minutes for our quiet game of bridge.

When we were left alone, Dick asked me if I intended to work for the Movies when I considered my vacation had lasted long enough. Before I could answer, he told me all about his last assignments, the picture, not yet released, which had caused him so much trouble with an impossible director; the picture, just released, which had almost broken his friendship with an unbearable producer; the picture, now in the process of being shot, and the daily rows with a temperamental star who was driving him crazy.

Then, Dick remembered that he had promised a friend to listen to a girl who was singing with a prominent dance band, so he switched on the portable, and having made sure that he was on the right station, and of course, without switching off the Capehart, he forgot all about the girl singer and proceeded to ask me if I had a good agent. I was just about to open my mouth for the first time in half an hour, but before I could do so, Dick was giving me a lot of good advice on the subject. He had skillfully torn to pieces half a dozen of the most important firms in the business and was going to give me the name of his agent—the only agent in town—when the telephone rang.

It was Betsy, his fiancée. She had forgotten her portable radio and, as she was going straight home after the performance, she must have it and would Dick be a lamb and bring it to her himself, because she had something of importance to tell him. It could not wait until the following day.

There was still no sign of Tom, so Dick begged me to remain in the room—it would only take him five minutes to go to the club and come back. He put a box of excellent cigars in front of me, shouted an order to his butler to bring me a cuba libra and rushed out of the room before I could say a word. I am glad to say that he was taking with him the portable, on which the girl singer he had promised to listen to was crooning a mournful torch song.

The butler, Okito, was a Japanese. He put the drink in front of me and smiled, the kind of smile you can only see on a Japanese face. I could not tell whether it was expressing happiness, contempt, disillusion, or if it was just a friendly invitation to conversation. I felt it was just as well to accept the latter possibility.

I asked Okito if there was any objection to his turning off the phonograph until his master returned. The instrument was playing the "Nutcracker Suite," which I abominate as much as I love Tschaikovsky's symphonies.

Okito smiled, broader than ever, told me he usually did the same when left alone, and we had a most interesting conversation about the reactions of surroundings on one's powers of concentration. Then, we discussed the influence of stimulants on mental clarity, which naturally led us to the psychopathic results brought about by excessive use of alcohol. Then I discovered that Okito had graduated in abnormal psychology at the University of Tokyo.

After the conversations that had taken place in the same room, Okito's knowledge was almost disconcerting, and although he was discussing one of my favorite subjects I was finding it difficult to keep up to his level. I was wondering, too, what a student of his caliber was doing as butler in a Beverly Hills home.

He told me his greatest relaxation was chess. I know enough about that game to get some enjoyment out of it, even if I am beaten, so—as there was still no sign of Tom and Dick, I felt the courteous thing to do would be to suggest a game. Okito proposed we should play for a dollar a game. We played five games. I lost five dollars.

It was now three in the morning. No word from Tom. No word from Dick, so Okito, noticing I was looking tired, offered to drive me home. I was glad to accept.

Just before we left, Okito switched on the Capehart, and in so doing, gave me another of his cryptic smiles, a very broad one.

The following morning Tom called me. Not, as you might think, to apologize for failing to return the previous evening, but to tell me what a good time he had had after leaving me at Dick's house.

He had found Dave alone and very depressed. Dave had written a whale of a good song, but on playing it to his publisher, the latter had been compelled to point out to him that Jerry Kern had written exactly the same tune three years before. That was too recent to fool the public, and Jerry Kern.

Dave did not feel like playing bridge. The only thing that could cheer him up was backgammon. There is only one other player at backgammon, and you can talk and wail while playing. You can't do that at bridge. Dave wanted to talk and wail. Naturally, Tom could not leave him alone in that state.

In the middle of their second game, they had been interrupted by the welcome arrival of Kay and Frannie, two show girls appearing in a Metro musical. Immediately,

Dave's mood had changed. He still wanted to talk, but no longer felt like wailing.

After a couple of drinks, it was decided to go and laugh at Betsy's Adagio turn at the Troc. Kay got in Tom's car, Frannie in Dave's, and they drove off. On the way to the Troc, Tom thought it would be fun to stop at the Clover Club for a few minutes and join Dave and Frannie at the Troc a little later—but they had soon forgotten them. I already knew that, because Dave had called me before Tom to say he had not seen me the previous evening. After he had left his house with Tom and the girls he had felt, on his way to the Troc, that the peaceful darkness of the Beachcombers was more suitable for the kind of chat he wanted to have with Frannie. Yes, he'd had a wonderful time, and do you know why he was calling me? He wanted me to come to his house to dinner the same evening with Tom and Dick, and after dinner … we would have a quiet game of bridge.

Selected Bibliography

Unpublished Material

Charlot, André, essays, journals, other uncollected writings and miscellaneous papers (Family Collection, Pacific Palisades, California).

Special Collection

Scripts, sheet music, duplicate sketches and lyrics, publicity and programs, company papers, contracts and miscellaneous papers (Collection 1318, Papers 1910–1944, Special Collections, University of California at Los Angeles).

Playscripts in the Lord Chamberlain's Collection, The British Library

Kill That Fly! (1912)
Eightpence a Mile (1913)
Not Likely (1914)
Odds and Ends (1914)
Samples (1915)
Bric a Brac (1915)
More (1915)
5064 Gerrard (1915)
Some (1916)
This and That (1916)
See Saw (1916)
Cheep! (1917)
Bubbly (1917)
Tabs (1918)
Buzz, Buzz! (1918)
Bran Pie (1919)
The Co-Optimists (1921)
A to Z (1922)
London Calling (1923)

Published Single Theatrical Sketches (London: Samuel French)

Jeans, Ronald. "A Cabaret Drama," "Great Expectations," "Mixed Methods: In Four Examples," "The Old Lady Shows Her Muddles," "Game to the End," "Four to Six-Thirty," "Grand Guignol," "The New Education," "Counter Attractions," "Pleasing Everybody," "Incredible Happenings," "Peace and Quiet."
Titheradge, Dion. "The Altogether," "The Indicator," "Tea-Shop Tattle," "Midnight Oil," "Waiting," "The Stoic."

Collections of Published Theatrical Sketches (London: Samuel French)

Coward, Noel. *Collected Sketches and Lyrics.*
Jeans, Ronald. *After Dark, Black Out Sketches* (1941), *Follow the Streamline, One Dam Sketch After Another, Review of Revues, The Stage is Waiting* (1931), *Sundry Sketches* (1924), *Charlot Revue Sketches* (1925), *Odd Numbers* (1927), *Vignettes from Vaudeville* (1924).
Titheradge, Dion. *Out of the Box* (1925), *Ups and Downs from Revue* (1926), *Written on Foolscap, Behind the Curtain* (1926), *From the Prompt Corner* (1925), *Exits and Entrances* (1934).

Books and Articles

Agate, James. *Immoment Joys: A Survey of Light Entertainment on the London Stage, 1920–1943* (London: Jonathan Cape, 1945).
Aldrich, Richard. *Gertrude Lawrence as Mrs. A* (London: Odhams, 1954).
Allen, Robert C. *Horrible Prettiness: Burlesque and American Culture* (Chapel Hill & London: University of North Carolina Press, 1991).

Appignanesi, Lisa. *The Cabaret* (London: Cassell & Collier, Macmillan, 1975).

Baddeley, Hermione. *The Unsinkable Hermione Baddeley: An Autobiography* (London: Collins, 1984).

Banham, Martin, ed. *The Cambridge Guide to World Theatre* (Cambridge: Cambridge University Press, 1988).

Barber, Peter, and Peter Jacomelli. *Continental Taste: Ticinese Emigrants and Their Cafe-Restaurants in Britain 1847–1987* (London: Camden History Society, 1997).

Bloom, Ken. *Broadway: An Encyclopedic Guide to the History, People and Places of Times Square* (Oxford: Facts on File, 1991).

Bordman, Gerald. *American Musical Comedy: From Adonis to Dreamgirls* (New York: Oxford University Press, 1985).

_____. *American Musical Revue: From Passing Show to Sugar Babies* (New York: Oxford University Press, 1985).

_____. *Jerome Kern: His Life and Music* (New York: Oxford University Press, 1980).

Burke, Billie, with Cameron Shipp. *With a Feather on My Nose* (London: Peter Davies, 1950).

Carter, Randolph. *The World of Flo Ziegfeld* (New York: Praeger, 1974).

Castle, Charles. *The Follies Bergere* (London: Methuen, 1982).

Castle, Irene. *Castles in the Air* (New York: Doubleday, 1958).

Charlot, André. "Producing English Revue" in *Theatre and Stage* (London, 1934).

Clunn, Harold. *The Face of Paris: A Record of a Century's Changes and Development* (London: Simkin Marshall, 1933).

Cochran, Charles B. *Cock-a-Doodle-Doo* (London: Heinemann, 1941).

_____. *Secrets of a Showman* (London: Heinemann, 1925).

Coward, Noel. *Autobiography* (London: Methuen, 1987).

_____. *The Lyrics of Noel Coward* (London: Methuen, 1983).

Damase, Jacques. *Les Follies du Music Hall: A History of the Music Hall in Paris* (London: Hamlyn, 1970).

DeCourville, Albert. *I Tell You* (London: Chapman & Hall, 1928).

_____. "The Story of Four Revues" in *Theatre Programme*, London Hippodrome, May 1915.

Forbes-Winslow, D. *Daly's: The Biography of a Theatre* (London: W. H. Allen, 1944).

Gaines, James R., *Wit's End: Days and Nights of the Algonquin Round Table* (New York: Harcourt Brace Jovanovich, 1977).

Gardiner, J. *Gaby Delys: A Fatal Attraction* (London: Sidgwick & Jackson, 1986).

Gingold, Hermione. *How to Grow Old Disgracefully* (London: Gollancz, 1989).

Grossith, George. *"G.G."* (London: Hutchinson, 1933).

Harding, James. *Cochran* (London: Methuen, 1989).

Howard, Diana. *London Theatres and Music Halls 1850–1950* (London: The Library Association, 1970).

Hulbert, Jack. *The Little Woman's Always Right* (London: W. H. Allen, 1973).

Hyman, Alan. *The Gaiety Years* (London: Cassell, 1975).

Lawrence, Gertrude. *A Star Danced* (New York: Doubleday, 1945).

Lillie, Beatrice, with James Brough. *Every Other Inch a Lady* (London: W. H. Allen, 1973).

Mander, Raymond, and Joe Mitchenson. *The Lost Theatres of London* (London: New English Library, 1976).

_____, and _____. *Revue: A History in Pictures* (London: New English Library, 1971).

_____, and _____. *The Theatres of London* (London: New English Library, 1963).

Marshall, Michael. *Top Hat & Tails: The Story of Jack Buchanan* (London: Hamish Hamilton, 1978).

Marshall, Norman. *The Other Theatre* (London: John Lehmann, 1947).

Moore, James Ross. "Cole Porter in Britain," *New Theatre Quarterly* 30 May 1992, pp. 113–122.

Mordden, Ethan. *Broadway Babies: The People Who Made the Broadway Musical* (New York: Oxford University Press, 1983).

_____. *Make Believe: The Broadway Musical in the 1920's* (New York: Oxford University Press, 1997).

Morley, Sheridan. *A Bright Particular Star: A Biography of Gertrude Lawrence* (London: Pavilion Books, 1986).

Muir, Frank, and Simon Brett, eds. *The Book of Comedy Sketches* (London: Hamish Hamilton, 1982).

Nerman, Einar. *Darlings of the Gods: In Music Hall, Revue & Musical Comedy* (London: 1929).

Porter, Roy. *London: A Social History* (London: Hamish Hamilton, 1994).

Seeley, Robert, and Rex Bunnett. *London Musical Shows on Record 1889–1989* (Harrow: General Gramophone, 1989).

Weightmann, Gavin. *Bright Lights, Big City: London Entertained 1830–1950* (London: Collins & Brown, 1992).

White, James Dillon. *Born to Star: The Lupino Lane Story* (London: Heinemann, 1957).

Wilmut, Roger. *Kindly Leave the Stage! The Story of Variety 1919–1960* (London, Methuen, 1985).

Theatre Programs

"Kill That Fly!" Alhambra Leicester Square, October 14, 1912.

"Eightpence a Mile: The New Stop Press Revue," Alhambra Leicester Square, May 9, 1913.

"Not Likely," Alhambra Leicester Square, May 4, 1914.

"5064 Gerrard," Alhambra Leicester Square, March 19, 1915.

"Samples," The Playhouse, November 30, 1915.

"Some (More Samples)," Vaudeville Theatre, June 29, 1916.

"This and That," Comedy Theatre, September 15, 1916.

"Pierrot's Christmas" and "Poached Eggs and Pearls," Apollo Theatre, November 21, 1916.

"See Saw," Comedy Theatre, December 14, 1916.

"Three Cheers," Shaftesbury Theatre, December 22, 1916.

"Cheep!," Vaudeville Theatre, April 26, 1917.

"Bubbly," Comedy Theatre, May 5, 1917.

"Tabs," Vaudeville Theatre, May 15, 1918.

"Tails Up," Comedy Theatre, June 1, 1918.

"Buzz Buzz," Vaudeville Theatre, December 20, 1918.

"Bran Pie," Prince of Wales Theatre, August 23,1919.

"Just Fancy," Vaudeville Theatre, March 26, 1920.

"Jumble Sale," Vaudeville Theatre, December 16, 1920.

"Puss, Puss!," Vaudeville Theatre, May 14, 1921.

"The Co-Optimists," Royalty Theatre, June 29, 1921.

"Theatre de la Chauve-Souris: The Bat Theatre Moscow," London Pavillion, September 2, 1921.

"A to Z," Prince of Wales Theatre, October 11, 1921.

"The Midnight Folies," Metropole, Whitehall Rooms, December 4, 1922.

"London Calling," Duke of York Theatre, September 4, 1923.

"Carlot's Revue," Prince of Wales, September 23, 1924.

"Charlot's Revue as Played in America," Prince of Wales, March 30, 1925.

"How D'You Do?," Comedy Theatre, April 25, 1933.

"Hi Diddle Diddle," Comedy Theatre, October 30, 1934.

Radio Broadcasts from the (UK) National Sound Archives

The Impresarios: André Charlot
The Impresarios: Cockie! Charles Cochran
Close Up: Beatrice Lillie
The Time of My Life: Jessie Matthews

Radio Broadcasts from BBC Radio Archives

Buzz Buzz: The Lives of André Charlot, James Ross Moore, BBC Radio Two, October 19, 1993.

Revue: Richard Anthony Baker, BBC Radio Three, November 21 and 28, 1993.

Other Sources

Jeans, Ronald. Scrapbooks 1913–1955, press cuttings from publications in Liverpool, Manchester and London, Theatre Museum, London.

Wearing, J.F. *The London Stage: A Calendar of Plays and Players*, Volumes 1910–1916, 1917–1919, 1920–1924, 1915–1929.

Editions of The Play Pictorial: Volumes 157 *(5064 Gerrard),* 165 *(More),* 185 *(Bubbly)* and 190 *(Buzz Buzz).*

Index

Italicized numbers refer to pages with photographs or illustrations.